Brave Ship Brave Men

BRAVE SHIP
BRAVE MEN

LT. COMDR. ARNOLD S. LOTT
U.S. NAVY (Ret.)

NAVAL INSTITUTE PRESS
Annapolis, Maryland

Originally published in 1964 by The Bobbs-Merrill Company, Inc.

© 1964
by the United States Naval Institute
Annapolis, Maryland

First Bluejacket Books printing, 1994

Library of Congress Cataloging-in-Publication Data

Lott, Arnold S.
  Brave ship, brave men.

    1. World War, 1939–1945—Naval operations, American.
2. Aaron Ward (Ship)   3. World War, 1939–1945—Campaigns—
Japan—Okinawa Island.   I. Title.
D774.A2L6   1986   940.54'73   86-2372
ISBN 1-55750-523-3

Printed in the United States of American on acid-free paper ♾
04 03 02 01 00   9 8 7 6 5 4

Dedication

TO THE MEN ON THE PICKET STATIONS,
WHOSE BATTLES WERE TOO SELDOM RECORDED,
WHOSE DEEDS WERE NOT OFTEN ENOUGH REWARDED,
BUT WHOSE ACTIONS WERE ALWAYS VALOROUS.

Foreword

The Battle for Okinawa was the last major campaign of World War II. It was a bitter, hard fought contest in which for the first time during that war our landing operations met no surface opposition. The last serious surface effort of the Japanese Navy occurred on 7 April 1945, when the giant battleship *Yamoto* accompanied by the cruiser *Yahagi* and eight destroyers was intercepted and destroyed by Task Force 58 as they headed for Okinawa. Only four destroyers survived. Not once during the four-month-long struggle for Okinawa was there an engagement between the remnant Japanese Navy and the powerful U. S. Fifth Fleet, yet the losses suffered by the Navy at Okinawa were greater than in any major fleet action during the war—30 ships sunk, more than 300 damaged, and more than 9,000 men killed, missing, or wounded.

This destruction was wrought primarily by Japanese air attack, and in particular by suicide attacks. The greater part of it was inflicted on destroyers and smaller craft in individual engagements on the radar picket stations surrounding Okinawa. This was not a battle by vast opposing forces, but an unending series of small fights. Not one of them was important enough to become an epic in naval history, but each of them was highly important to the men who were involved. The Navy's defeat of this desperate, vicious attack was due in large part to the training, tradition, discipline, and devotion which made superb fighting teams out of what were, after all, rather ordinary ships and men, exactly like the ship and men whose story follows in these pages.

This ship was only one of hundreds of ships which took part in that long and determined struggle. If a book could be written about every deserving ship on the picket lines at Okinawa the shelves of naval history would indeed become crowded, for every ship there met the trial of battle with courage and bravery.

But Okinawa was twenty years ago. The logs have become dusty and our memories grow dim. This book may have to serve in place of many. The ship named here is the USS *Aaron Ward*, but the story might well be about any ship and every sailor who fought on the picket line. The title applies to them all.

C. W. NIMITZ
FLEET ADMIRAL, UNITED STATES NAVY

Treasure Island, California, 1964

Preface

This book had its beginning in 1956 when I was gathering material for a book on naval minewarfare operations in World War II and first talked with the "minecraft boss" for the invasion of Okinawa, Vice Admiral Alexander Sharp, U. S. Navy, retired. "Write something about the *Aaron Ward*," said the Admiral. "She was a great ship." *Aaron Ward* was only one of hundreds of ships under his command in that operation, but he had remembered her. He had boarded her the morning after the battle here described, to be impressed both by the destruction she had survived, and the superb morale of her crew. But in a book about hundreds of ships, there could be only one page for *Aaron Ward*. Her story had to wait.

Eventually, I located the *Aaron Ward's* skipper, and immediately began to understand why the ship and her crew so impressed the Admiral. Fifteen years after the battle the crew had spread to every corner of the United States and throughout the U. S. Navy, yet Captain William H. Sanders, Jr., U. S. Navy, knew where they all were. And the men, mostly civilians by then, still kept in touch with their skipper. The ship was gone, but the crew was an entity. They still called themselves *"Aaron Ward* sailors."

During the several years since then, I have "lived" with the USS *Aaron Ward* and her fighting crew. I have read the ship's logs, her war dairy, her action report, and all the Captain's own papers. I have had hundreds of letters from the crew, and read some of the letters they sent home from the battle zone to their families. I have traveled thousands of miles to talk with as many of them, and their wives, mothers, and sisters, as possible. And I discovered that the fighting spirit and morale "Bill" Sanders instilled in his crew in 1944 is still there. Twenty years after the one hour battle which was the ship's sole reason for being, the surviving crew members still think they had the best ship, the best officers, and the best crew, in the United States Navy. They are all men with whom I do not wish to argue.

Reference material for this book was provided by the Office of Naval History; the Bureau of Naval Personnel; the Naval Bureau of Ships; and the National Archives, in Washington, D. C. The "watches" heading each chapter are quoted from the official log of the USS *Aaron Ward*. Much valuable information on picket line operations off Okinawa came from those men who served in other ships during that campaign, but who still remembered the *Aaron Ward*. For all such help, my thanks.

I did not serve in this ship, nor did I ever see her. The book was really written by the officers and men of the USS *Aaron Ward*; my name appears here only because I have recorded what they did and said. And because, thirty years ago, I sailed in the first USS *Aaron Ward*.

ARNOLD S. LOTT

Annapolis, Maryland, 1964

Contents

(This book is written in "watches" to agree with the log of the USS *Aaron Ward* for 3 May 1945. The "additional remarks" section, a customary part of all naval logs, describes events subsequent to that day.)

Chapter One – Mid Watch, 0000-0400
ADMIRAL AARON WARD, HISTORY OF DESTROYER NO. 132 AND
DESTROYER NO. 483.
page 1

Chapter Two – Morning Watch, 0400-0800
THE CREW.
page 23

Chapter Three – Forenoon Watch, 0800-1200
THE OFFICERS.
page 53

Chapter Four – Afternoon Watch, 1200-1600
COMMISSIONING AND SHAKEDOWN, TRANSIT TO ULITHI.
page 88

Chapter Five – First Dog Watch, 1600-1800
INVASION OF OKINAWA.
page 132

Chapter Six – Second Dog Watch, 1800-2000
BATTLE.
page 159

Chapter Seven – Night Watch, 2000-2400
RESCUE AND TOW.
page 197

Chapter Eight – Additional Remarks
SALVAGE AND REPAIR. REPORTS TO NEXT OF KIN. "STATESIDE!"
VICTORY AND DECOMMISSIONING. A LAST TRIBUTE.
page 212

Conversations quoted in the text are based on interviews and letters. Commands and orders not attributed to an individual by name but which have been used in various instances have been set in capital letters. Italicized text presents thoughts expressed by or common to more than one person.

... In the early evening hours of May 3, four small groups of enemy aircraft attacked our shipping off the coast of Okinawa inflicting some damage on our forces and sinking two light units. Seventeen enemy aircraft were destroyed ...

—CincPoa Communique No. 351, 1945

United States naval vessels damaged, Okinawa area: Light mine-layer *Aaron Ward* (DM 34), by suicide plane, 26° 24′ N., 126° 15′ E.

—United States Naval Chronology, World War II. (May 3, 1945)

Brave Ship Brave Men

Chapter One

Mid Watch

00-04 Underway on Radar Picket Station 10 in area adjacent to Okinawa Shima, Ryukus Islands, Japan, in compliance with orders of CTG 51.5 and Commander Fifth Fleet Top Secret Operation Plan 1-45. Patrolling station on various courses at various speeds in company with USS *Little*, (DD 803), LSMR 195, LCS 83, LCS 14, OTC in this vessel. Boilers 1 and 3 on main steam line, boilers 2 and 4 standing by at 600 pounds pressure. Personnel condition III, material condition BAKER set, maintaining sound and radar search according to doctrine. Ship is darkened.

R. I. Biesmeyer, Lt., U. S. Navy

The way to the bridge was forward on the starboard main deck as far as the galley, then up a ladder to the superstructure deck, aft a couple of paces, up another ladder right alongside the hot stack to the gun platform, forward a couple of paces, then up another ladder to the bridge deck. In the midnight blackness, Biesmeyer made the trip with easy familiarity. He knew when to sidestep a swab rack, when to duck the life raft support, when to grab the ladder rail, how to avoid the gun crew around the 40mm mount.

In the past six months Biesmeyer had made the trip so many times, by day and by night, in rain and shine, calm and storm, that he could have done it with his eyes closed. Sometimes, when enemy planes had kept them at battle stations all night, he was so sleepy he might have done just that.

The ship moved with an easy rhythm, sliding her bow over the quiet sea and leaving just enough bow wave for him to judge she was making the usual twelve knots. By the time he reached the bridge deck his eyes could discern number two stack aft, the geometry of the mast and radar array making a slow sweep against a few dim stars, and the head and shoulders of the starboard sky lookout. A few feet forward he could see the 40mm gun director and just ahead of that, where the pelorus would be, the tall form of Tom Wallace, the Officer of the Deck on the 2000-2400 watch.

Using a shielded red flashlight, he checked the Captain's Night Order Book: Same as before. No change. While he read, he could hear voices around him in the night as the crew for the mid watch climbed up the ladders and went about relieving the men with the night watch. If the offgoing watch was lucky and no bogies appeared on the SC radar screen, they could sleep until five o'clock in the morning. The oncoming watch had been asleep since perhaps half-past eight or nine or ten o'clock, and that was all the sleep they would get this night, because by the time they were relieved at four in the morning and got into their bunks, someone would be roaming around the compartments calling the compartment master at arms who would then soon rouse out all hands for morning general quarters at five.

The night order book read and initialed, Ray checked the chart tacked to the table in the after starboard corner of the pilot house.

There was nothing there, of course, except the neat little circle marked "2000 posit," the ship's location as established by Wallace and the chief quartermaster at eight that evening. The nearest land, Kume Shima, was about twenty miles northeast, right where it had been for the last three days. The ship was merely steaming around in a circle, waiting, watching. There had been no enemy activity for three days.

Well, in a few minutes it would be Thursday, 3 May 1945. Another day, another dollar. May as well get the show on the road. He moved out to the open bridge, nudged Tom.

"Ready to relieve you, Sir."

Biesmeyer and Wallace went through the traditional routine of turning over the deck of a ship at sea, as they had for days now on this station, as they had in weeks past on other stations, as they had for months past on this ship, and as other officers had done on other ships clear back to the days of John Paul Jones. Except there were more details to remember now. Details these days could be important. The night seemed peaceful enough at that moment, but the next one could be another matter.

They might be sitting right in front of a Japanese submarine periscope; there might be a hot running Japanese torpedo pointed right at them; there might be a drifting mine just yards ahead; there might be a great big tough Japanese cruiser or battleship lurking out there five miles away with all guns trained on them; there might be some night flying suicide plane screaming down out of the sky to fry the pilot and half the crew in high octane. These were all possibilities to be coped with when they arose; meanwhile, the ship would go on, steaming as before.

Methodically Wallace and Biesmeyer went through the routine . . . . steaming as before . . . . patrolling on RPS 10 . . . . captain is in his stateroom . . . . ship is in condition III . . . . condition BAKER set . . . . both firerooms lit off, boilers 1 and 3 on the line, 2 and 4 standing by . . . . maintaining radar and sound search, radar reports no bogies on the screen, sound has no contacts . . . . the *Little* is on station, the small boys are patrolling about five miles to the south-

3

ward . . . . wind about twelve knots from the northwest, cloud ceiling about 10,000 feet, visibility about three miles, the sea is calm . . . . weather appears to be clearing.

Their voices were quiet. All around the bridge other men were passing information on to their reliefs in the same assured way; when everyone knew his job there was no need of shouting. Quartermaster, signalman, helmsman, annunciator man, messengers, phone talkers, lookouts, each gave "the word" and the appropriate badge of office—telephone, flashlight, or signal gun—to the next man, and went below to sleep.

"STEERING 270, NOTHING TO THE LEFT."

"GOTCHA!"

"BOTH ENGINES ARE AHEAD TWO THIRDS. NO CHANGE THIS WATCH. OOD'S OVER IN THE STARBOARD WING."

"OKAY . . . . I'LL TAKE 'ER."

"HERE'S THE PHONES. I JUST CHECKED 'EM OUT OKAY. CONTROL SAYS KNOCK OFF UNNECESSARY CHATTER ON THE CIRCUIT."

"OKAY, OKAY."

Elsewhere in the ship the same routine went on: forward engine room, after engine room, fire rooms, in CIC, the radio shack, radar room, sound room, in gunnery control, in the big 5-inch mounts, in the quad forties and the twin forties, all along topside on the little 20mm mounts. Men prepared to watch the one little world which was their responsibility, on which the safety of the ship might rest—the pointer on a steam pressure gauge, the glowing screen of a radar scope, the lubber line of a compass repeater, the dial of the engine telegraph, the bearing temperature on a turbine, the water level in a boiler gauge glass, one sector of a darkened horizon.

Throughout the ship, where one third of the crew was asleep, one third preparing to go to sleep, one third now on watch and hoping for the rapid passing of four hours so they could go back to sleep, men were reporting:

"FORWARD ENGINE ROOM. WATCH RELIEVED IN AFTER ENGINE ROOM."

"BRIDGE! AFTER STEERING RELIEVED."

"CONTROL! MOUNT 51 RELIEVED."

"BRIDGE! CIC RELIEVED."

On the bridge, Tom Wallace had completed briefing his relief. Biesmeyer had "the word." The two stood there for a moment, listening to the sea, looking into the night, smelling the darkness and what might be lurking in it. Then Wallace slipped the leather strap of the binoculars off his neck, handed them to Biesmeyer. They were the badge of office for the Officer of the Deck. The two saluted and Biesmeyer said: "I relieve you, Sir."

Wallace went off below to his bunk, while Biesmeyer moved around the bridge, checking. For the next four hours he was the Officer of the Deck of the USS *Aaron Ward,* the direct representative of the Commanding Officer. By Navy Regulations, he alone was responsible for the safe navigation of the ship, for the performance of duty by her watch, for enforcing and observing the orders of the Commanding Officer, for carrying out standard doctrine for a ship of the U. S. Navy in the battle zone as laid down by higher authority, and because the OTC on Radar Picket Station 10 was in *Aaron Ward,* for controlling the movements of that ship and others on the station until properly relieved of such responsibility.

More than the OOD's binoculars now hung around his neck; there was also the weight of responsibility for the safety of a ship which cost several million dollars, and for the lives of more than three hundred men—the invisible albatross of command which was his until another qualified officer removed it by saying "I relieve you, Sir," or he dropped dead, whichever came first. The watch, the binoculars, the ship, the vigilance of RPS 10, the whole damned albatross—they were all his.

One o'clock in the morning. The quartermaster checked the temperature and barometer reading, estimated the wind direction, made the routine entries in the log. The top of the page always read the same: U.S.S. Aaron Ward (DM 34), William H. Sanders, Jr., Commander, U.S. Navy, Commanding. The rest of the log would be pretty much the same, too. On the picket stations, it could be like that. In the engine room the engineers checked the shaft revolution counter—so many turns, so many knots steamed. They made entries in their log. There was only one way to stand a watch: carry out the routine. And when the planes came, shoot them down in a routine fashion. That was how to do business on a picket station.

"RADAR, BRIDGE. SCREEN CLEAR?"

"BRIDGE, RADAR. SCREEN IS CLEAR!"

"CIC, BRIDGE. HOW'S IT ON THE TBS? OTHER STATIONS REPORT ANY BOGIES?"

"BRIDGE, CIC. NO ACTIVITY TONIGHT."

It wasn't always like that. Ships had been around Okinawa since 18 March; the picket stations had been guarded since 26 March, and already over a hundred ships had been hit by Japanese air attack. At least a dozen destroyers and smaller craft had been sunk. This was the wildest, fiercest, longest, toughest battle the U. S. Navy had ever fought, and it seemed far from over.

Keep alert, you men. They smashed up the WADSWORTH *out here week before last. If they come up from Formosa this morning they'll hit Station 10 first. Keep alert.*

Radar Picket Station 10 was a spot way to hellangone out in the South China Sea, and with the exception of Station 8 some fifty miles southward, just about as far away from Okinawa as one could get and still expect to be a part of the fight. The picket stations, sixteen of them, ringed the island, all located by bearings and distances measured from a jutting point on its west coast with the Japanese name of Zanpa Misaki, but the American name of Point BOLO on invasion charts. RPS 10's exact address was 260.5 degrees true, distance 73.5 miles from Point BOLO—on a line which just ticked the southern tangent of Kume Shima.

On each radar picket station, CTF 51 had stationed destroyers or, when they ran out, minelayers or minesweepers converted from destroyer hulls, as was *Aaron Ward*. The larger ships were accompanied by some of the "small boys." These were the amphibious craft, so numerous they could not be graced by proper names, but went through the war in a welter of initials—LCSL, LCS, LCI, and LSMR—fighting just as bravely and hurting just as much when they were hit as if they had been named after the Navy's most immortal heroes. By 3 May, the little "amphibbers" had both fought and been hit. "Small boys" had an added practical value on the picket stations—when a destroyer was hit, they were at least close enough to report back what had happened.

So, a few miles away, the small boys—LSMR 195, LCS 14, and LCS 83—patrolled too. They were far enough off to keep out of the way if the big boys mixed it up with the kamikazes, but close enough to get in a few licks of their own if the fight got thick. In the darkness they were only three small blips on the SC radar screen, but they were friendly blips; the "picker uppers" when a bigger ship went down and left anybody to pick up . . . . *Hello there, small boys. Stick around and maybe later on we'll open up a keg of nails. And when the planes come, yell "bogie" loud and clear. Let the fleet know they're on the way.*

That was why the picket ships were out there; raiding planes aiming at the main forces in the transport areas had to get past them first. Their job was to spot the raid on radar, warn the ships at Okinawa, shoot down the raiders if they could, and try to stay afloat if the raiders hit them first. The planning for this operation was somewhat simpler than its execution. In CIC, where men tracked the incoming raids and the radio brought them the voices of men on other picket stations, the course of the invasion so far had been plotted in terse TBS transmissions. The voices were sometimes calm, sometimes tense, sometimes frantic, sometimes furious, as day by day they told the course of the war around Okinawa. The grim count had begun the first day the fleet started bombarding

Okinawa, on Sunday, 24 March, long before the amphibious landings:

DESTROYER KIMBERLEY HIT BY SUICIDE PLANE X FOUR DEAD X FIFTY SEVEN WOUNDED . . . . LIGHT MINELAYER ROBERT H SMITH DAMAGED BY SUICIDE PLANE . . . . HIGH SPEED TRANSPORT GILMER DAMAGED BY SUICIDER . . . . HIGH SPEED TRANSPORT KNUDSEN DAMAGED BY BOMBER

The next day, 26 March, planes had attacked the sweep unit where *Aaron Ward* was riding shotgun. *Adams* knocked one down. *Aaron Ward* didn't get a chance at them. But elsewhere around the island that day, the planes bored in, were knocked down, came flaming, and smashed up ships as they hit:

NEVADA DAMAGED . . . . BILOXI DAMAGED . . . . MURRAY HIT BY DIVE BOMBER . . . . PORTERFIELD HIT . . . . O'BRIEN, CALLAGHAN, FOREMAN HIT . . . . DORSEY HIT . . . . SKIRMISH HIT

The planes smashed at the transport areas when they could get in that close. But they had to cross the picket line first. There was almost always action out on the picket line where aerial dogfights rolled across the sky and the pickets kept their guns ready.

By day, a Combat Air Patrol of fighter planes from escort carriers orbited above each station, and when the picket ships spotted a raid coming in on their radar screens, the CAP was vectored out to intercept them. The CAP boys had splashed a lot of Japanese aircraft by 3 May, and the picket ships had knocked down their share, but duty on the picket stations had never been anything to write home about. So far, the Japanese had sent in more than 800 planes in four major air attacks, not counting all the small flea-bite raids.

At first the enemy raiders had tried to bore in for the fat, juicy targets—tankers, transports, and cargo ships—at Hagushi and Nakagusuku Wan, but with the element of surprise lost due to the vigilant radar pickets, they had been taking a consistent beating from CAP and the pickets. Now their tactics had changed and they tried desperately to knock out the pickets.

This was no longer the sort of air action the fleet had known back in the Solomons, where planes had made high altitude bombing runs or low level torpedo runs, and then gone home. At odd times during the operations in the Solomons injured Japanese aircraft had smashed into U. S. ships. As early as August, 1942, a suicide bomber had damaged the transport *Barnet* off Guadalcanal. But there had been no set pattern of deliberate intent until late in 1944 when the fleet hit Leyte in the Philippines, and suicide planes hit the fleet.

Now, with Okinawa the last piece of undefeated territory between the rampaging Fifth Fleet and the Empire, the Japanese concentrated on training suicide pilots. It was easy enough to qualify —all one had to do was get a plane off the ground and fly it somewhere. He didn't have to know how to get home or how to land when he got there. These pilots were not expected to come home.

The planes hitting the fleet at Okinawa were mostly on a one-way mission—some of them were actually incapable of making the round trip from base to Okinawa and back—and their pilots had said their prayers and sent home a lock of their hair before they started. Their purpose in life was to end it by smashing their planes into blazing destruction against one of the invading ships. Even when their planes were crippled, and on fire, they bored in. The only way to stop them was to knock the planes to bits before they got close enough for the pieces to hurt.

These were the Kamikazes—the Divine Wind—the fanatic, last-ditch supporters of a lost cause. With their gift for poetic nomenclature, the Japanese called such murderous massed attacks *Kikusui* —floating chrysanthemums. That was not what the U. S. Navy called them.

Two o'clock in the morning. The watch had gone for two hours, one hundred and twenty minutes. Keep things going. Keep alert.

Check the compass. Check the radar scope. Check the plot in CIC. Give control another growl, just as a matter of routine. Everyone on their toes. The minute one slacked off was the very minute they might come. You had maybe a minute to knock them down when they came.

"RADAR! BRIDGE. CLEAR SCREEN?"

"BRIDGE, RADAR, CLEAR SCREEN."

Keep it so.

There were days when they didn't come, and days when they did. The days when they came were easy to remember, if one listened to the TBS:

> 27 MARCH . . . . ADAMS DAMAGED BY SUICIDE PLANE
> . . . . 30 MARCH . . . . INDIANAPOLIS HIT BY SUICIDER
> . . . . 31 MARCH . . . . ADAMS HIT . . . . HINSDALE HIT
> . . . . LST 724 HIT . . . . LST 888 HIT

If you didn't hit 'em hard, they kept coming. On your toes, you gunners. You can't scare them to death with a near miss. Knock 'em down! . . . Aye, Aye, Sir. Knock 'em down it is!

Above Biesmeyer's head, the silent radar antenna whirled unceasingly in the night, its invisible electronic beam reaching miles out across the ocean, probing with delicate touch for any object big enough or solid enough to bounce an echo back to the ship. In the CIC room on the deck below, the radarmen peered into their glowing oscilloscope, watching the thin green line sweeping around in time with the antenna high above them, alert for the sudden bright point of light which meant an enemy was coming. The blip might possibly be a friend, but on the radar picket line ships regarded everyone as enemies. It was up to the friends to identify themselves before someone pulled a trigger.

There were no romantic ideals out on the picket line, no gallantry, no letting the other guy take the first poke. That kind of thing was a matter for determination by the top hat crowd in Washington and Tokyo. The big idea on the picket line was, get off the first shot. And even better was, get off the last shot too. So far the *Aaron Ward* had managed.

This might be a long watch. Better have a cup of coffee. . . .

There was coffee on the bridge, hot and fragrant. There was always coffee. Biesmeyer had smelled it when he came up to take the watch. The quartermasters kept a coffee pot perking continuously in a small locker over on the port side of the bridge. The Royal Navy sailed to fame on grog and rum, the Imperial Japanese Navy was headed to doom and destruction on tea and saki, but whichever way the U. S. Navy went, its sailors were going with mugs of hot joe, jamoke, mud, mocha, and sometimes even coffee in their hands. A man might be a long ways from home and mother, but he was never outside of sniffing distance of a coffee pot. He might not be on speaking terms with some of his shipmates, but that didn't prevent them sharing the same coffee pot. Officers and enlisted men did not pat each other on the back or loan money to one another, but there was nothing in Navy Regulations about not drinking coffee with each other.

Flinn, the quartermaster, had the coffee ready for the OOD. The watch which had just gone to bed had the coffee ready for Flinn. That was the unwritten rule on the bridge, the watch going off had coffee ready for the men coming on. There had been no provisions in the Bureau of Ships blueprints for coffee on the bridge, but somehow Flinn had talked some welders in San Pedro into doing a little extra work, and there was the coffee pot locker, as much a part of USS Aaron Ward as her starboard anchor. Flinn knew the importance of good coffee—he had been on a ship which had no coffee pot on the bridge, and she got sunk. He wasn't taking any more chances.

The coffee cups were emptied. Men throughout the ship made their routine reports. *Aaron Ward* and *Little* moved back and forth on their station. The hands on the bridge clock moved so slowly around the dial one would have suspected the hours were named January, February, March, rather than one, two, three o'clock. . . .

*Pass the time somehow, keep awake somehow . . . . say the names
of the states and their capitals . . . . try to remember all the Big Ten
winners since 1930 . . . . think of a girl's name for every letter of
the alphabet . . . . Joan, Kathleen, Laurel . . . . Laurel! . . . . better
try the states again . . . . lessee now, look at the clock again. . . . .
Half-past February! . . . that is, two thirty. Better check the calendar again. Still Thursday, too. Ought to be Saturday by now . . . .
Saturday, that would be 5 May. . . . . Wonder if the cooks would
turn out a birthday cake? Ought to, the ship would be a year old.
Happy birthday, dear* AARON WARD, *happy birthday to you.*

May fifth had been the first big day in the life of the ship, com-
parable to a person's birthday. It was marked on a brass plate
mounted on the bulkhead in the thwartships passageway on the
main deck, opposite the mine shack: Launched 5 May 1944. The
ship had been built by the Bethlehem Steel Company, in San Pedro,
California, as Destroyer Hull No. 773. When her sponsor, Mrs.
G. H. Ratcliff, smashed a bottle of champagne across her bow and
cried, "I christen thee *Aaron Ward*," it was the third time in twenty-
five years a ship of the U.S. Navy had worn the name. Old Admiral
Aaron Ward, who won his fame in the Spanish American War,
would have been proud of every one of them.

The year young Billy Sanders started to school in San Diego,
California, Admiral Aaron Ward retired in New York, at the age
of 62. Forty-two of those years he had spent in the U. S. Navy. He
had completed his education in Germany and France, entered the
Naval Academy at Annapolis the year after Admiral Farragut, the
hero of Mobile Bay, died. A remarkable linguist, the young officer
spoke French, Spanish, Italian, and Russian. This ability sent him
to Paris, Berlin, and St. Petersburg as Naval Attache, and to Japan
as naval aide at the funeral of the Emperor.

In July, 1898, Lieutenant Aaron Ward was Commanding Officer
of the converted yacht, USS *Wasp*, operating in company with the
USS *Leyden* off Port Nipe, Cuba, when the USS *Annapolis*, carrying
the senior officer present, ordered *Wasp* and *Leyden* to go in and

examine the bay. Pouring on the coal for about sixteen knots, the two craft steamed in and immediately spotted a Spanish cruiser, the *Don Jorge Juan*, at anchor there. The ensuing battle was described by Lieutenant Aaron Ward in a terse memorandum:

"1244 Enemy vessel opened fire. 1245 Opened fire on enemy vessel, 4,500 yards. 1247 Enemy fired again. 1250 Enemy fired again. 1256 Range 3,500 yards (too far). 1257 Range 3,000 yards (smoke interfering greatly) . . . . Range 2,500 yards . . . . Range 2,300 yards . . . . Range 1,600 yards . . . . 1:12 Enemy's colors down. 1:16 Made general signal, 'The enemy has surrendered.' . . . . 1:35 Spanish gunboat sinking."

"The conduct of the crew was fully up to the United States Navy Standard," Aaron Ward wrote. "They kept the guns hot, and expended 163 rounds of 6-pounder ammunition." For his part in helping the USS *Leyden* sink the *Don Jorge Juan*, Aaron Ward was commended for gallantry and advanced to the rank of Lieutenant Commander.

Retirement, years later, failed to slow down Admiral Aaron Ward. His home, Willowmere, on Long Island, became noted for its rose gardens. In 1914, the Admiral sailed in the steamship *Red Cross*, bound for Europe with a load of nurses, surgeons and medical supplies for the fighting nations; for his services in Europe he was decorated by the Emperor of Austria and made an officer of the Legion of Honor in France. When he died, on 5 July 1918, funeral services were held at Willowmere, where Aaron Ward was surrounded by his roses. Nine months after his death, the Navy launched a gleaming new flush-deck destroyer, DD 132, at the Bath Iron Works in Bath, Maine, and Mrs. W. L. Capps, a daughter of the admiral, christened the ship in honor of her father.

Three o'clock in the morning. Nothing had happened yet, the watch was on the downhill side. No sound contacts, no radar contacts. This night, at least, men would have a chance to get a few winks between watches. They would need them. Weather had been bad ever since they reported on station on Monday. That was the night the kamikazes got the destroyer *Bennion* and the minecraft flagship *Terror*. The Bushido boys had been grounded for three days now, but the weather was clearing and they would be coming in again. The last time, just a week before, they had milled overhead for hours. The crew stood at GQ all night, beat off ten attacks, shot down three planes. For the last three days not a ship at Okinawa, on the picket line or at Hagushi or in "the Retto," had been hit. No doubt about it, the kamikazes would be coming back soon.

"CONTROL, BRIDGE. ROUTINE CHECK. ON YOUR TOES UP THERE?"

"BRIDGE, CONTROL. ALWAYS ON OUR TOES."

"ALL GUNS, CONTROL. CIRCUIT CHECK."

"MOUNT 51, AYE . . . . MOUNT 52, AYE . . . . MOUNT 53, AYE . . . . MOUNT 40, AYE . . . ."

"CIC, BRIDGE . . . . HOW'S THE SCREEN?"

"BRIDGE, CIC . . . . SCREEN CLEAR. ALL CLEAR."

Only a couple of more hours to sunrise. Even at this moment they might be on their way.

Let' em come. AARON WARD *is ready.*

Aaron Ward had been designed and built as destroyer number 773, a fast ship, one intended to harry an enemy battle line with torpedoes. Before ever firing a shot, in practice or anger, she had been refitted as a minelayer, the DM 34. She still had to lay an offensive mine. The only enemy she had seen had been Japanese aircraft, flown by kamikazi pilots intent on cremating themselves in an American destroyer. So far she had sent nine of them to join their ancestors, without a scratch. But when they came, they came fast . . . . *You bridge lookouts, keep your eyes open now.*

What happened to the first *Aaron Ward,* probably no one on the ship knew for certain. But some of the old timers remembered her—destroyer 132, known among sailors in the old "four-piper" navy as the "Iron Duke." When their skipper had been a junior officer on the old *Broome,* he sailed in the same destroyer flotilla with *Aaron Ward,* in and out of San Diego. The old "Iron Duke" had served in the Navy longer than any man aboard DM 34, before she finally left.

On 9 September 1940, at Halifax, Nova Scotia, she was transferred to the Royal Navy and renamed HMS *Castleton.* Wearing the White Ensign, the ship put to sea again for Atlantic convoy duty, and within two months had rescued all the survivors of the torpedoed steamships *Daydawn* and *Victoria.* A year or so later her crew helped capture forty-one survivors of the German submarine *U-464* after they had boarded an Icelandic trawler. Less than two months prior to this day of 3 May, the proud old ship had finally dropped anchor for the last time; the Royal Navy put her into reserve at Grangemouth, Scotland.

Let's put this one in reserve too, when the war's over. All we have to do is to keep her floating and fighting until the last shot is fired. That first old AARON WARD *must have outlasted a dozen skippers in her time. Wonder if her first skipper was like this ship's first skipper?*

What no one on the third *Aaron Ward* knew was that the first skipper of the first *Aaron Ward* was still around—in fact, he was out there with them. He was now Admiral Raymond A. Spruance, Commander Fifth Fleet, with so many ships under his command—over 200 destroyer types alone—it took more officers than he had had in his first ship just to keep track of them.

Oddly enough, the first time the first *Aaron Ward* went to sea, her lookouts had been told to keep their eyes open for the very thing picket station lookouts watched for—aircraft. The ship had been commissioned on 21 April 1919 and less than a month later was out in the Atlantic, acting as a plane guard. On the night of 16-17 May, her crew heard the plane pass overhead. It was the NC-4, chugging down from Newfoundland to the Azores, and the first aircraft to fly across the Atlantic. If it had been low enough, they

15

could have knocked it down with a monkey wrench. Aircraft were things to cheer about in those days. No one expected them to grow up and start fighting destroyers.

But aircraft did more than fight destroyers at Okinawa; they wrecked them, burned them, killed their crews, and sank them. The score was getting longer every time they came in.

1 APRIL .... WEST VIRGINIA HIT .... SKIRMISH HIT ....
ACHERNAR, TYRRELL, ELMORE, ALPINE HIT
2 APRIL .... CHILTON HIT .... HENRICO HIT .... GOOD-
HUE HIT .... TELFAIR HIT
3 APRIL .... WAKE ISLAND HIT .... SPROSTON HIT ....
HAMBLETON HIT

Being on a ship assigned to a picket station was just about like playing Russian roulette. If you pointed the pistol at your head and pulled the trigger often enough, something was bound to happen .... *Keep a bright lookout, you men. We won't get any veteran's bonus unless we go home to collect it. Let's make it a round trip. We came out in the Aaron Ward; let's go home in the Aaron Ward.*

The first *Aaron Ward* had been a good ship, with a proud name. Less than a year after she left the U. S. Navy, her name was given to a second ship, destroyer number 483. Flinn knew about that one. He had sailed in her, for thirteen months, back in the rugged days when the Tokyo Express came smashing down the Slot at Guadalcanal. *Aaron Ward* No. 2 had been a fine new *Livermore*-class can, straight out of the Federal Shipbuilding and Dry Dock Company, at Kearny, New Jersey, and still with the smell of fresh paint in her when she sailed for the war zone.

Flinn remembered the brass plate on *Aaron Ward* No. 2, with her "history," such as it was, molded into it: destroyer No. 483; launched 22 November 1941, commissioned 4 March 1942. Miss Hilda Ward had sponsored that ship. It was a fine thing, the way the Navy hunted up the daughter of old Admiral Aaron Ward, so she could honor his name. The Admiral had retired in 1913, the year Flinn was born. But his daughter had walked the quarterdeck of Destroyer No. 483 just as she might once have walked the deck of another ship with her father, the old fighting admiral.

Duty on a ship named for a famous man was a little like being in the presence of ghosts, and yet inspiring too. When he saluted Captain Sanders on the quarter deck, he got back from the Skipper the same salute *he* had had twenty years earlier from some other skipper. That officer might well have had the salute from old Aaron Ward himself. One could almost imagine shadowy figures standing there on the quarterdeck in the night, ranked by seniority: Aaron Ward, Dewey, Farragut, Porter, John Paul Jones, and at the starboard end of the line, Nelson himself, straight from the quarter deck of HMS *Victory* at Trafalgar. They were all fast and furious fighting men, the kind of people who made history.

Life had been so fast and furious for *Aaron Ward* No. 2 that she had very little chance to make history. Back in the days of Trafalgar and Mobile there had been time for inspiring speeches when the shooting started, but down in the Solomons in 1942 no one had time for anything except shooting, and sometimes not quite enough for that. *Aaron Ward* No. 2 sailed from the West Coast for the Pacific on 20 May 1942, and less than six months later got clobbered by the Japanese during the Battle of Guadalcanal. That was enough to make any sailor superstitious, because it happened on Friday the 13th. During the same battle the Japanese sank the cruisers *Atlanta* and *Juneau*, and the destroyers *Cushing, Monssen, Laffey,* and *Barton.*

Aaron Ward took nine hits, had fifteen men killed and fifty-five wounded, was towed into Tulagi, later limped up to Pearl for a patching job. In February she was back with the fleet. On the last day of March, 1943, Flinn was transferred off the ship. This time luck was with him: he had been on board thirteen months, he was one of thirteen men transferred. Seven days later the Japanese got *Aaron Ward* for good; half a dozen planes jumped her and she went down, with twenty-seven men killed or missing and fifty-nine wounded . . . . *What they had done once they might well do again*

*. . . . Those radar gadgets might not always work. You men keep
your eyes peeled!*

For the first several days, after the invasion fleet reached Okinawa, the kamikazes hit in small groups, but on 6 April the Japanese
sent in a whole swarm of them. *Aaron Ward* had missed that fight,
because she was headed for Guam. In their first big massed raid,
the Japanese used over 350 aircraft. They came late in the afternoon,
but what happened around Okinawa then made for a long day:

BUSH SUNK . . . . COLHOUN SUNK . . . . EMMONS SUNK . . . . MOR-
RIS DAMAGED . . . . BENNETT DAMAGED . . . . HUTCHINS, LEUTZE,
MULLANY, HARRISON, NEWCOMB, HOWORTH, HAYNESWORTH, HY-
MAN, WITTER, FIEBERLING, RODMAN, FACILITY, RANSON, DE-
FENSE, DEVESTATOR, TAUSSIG, YMS 311, YMS 321, ALL DAMAGED.
The next day the planes hit again and increased the score of
wounded ships: HANCOCK . . . . MARYLAND . . . . LONGSHAW . . . .
WESSON . . . . YMS 81.

Aaron Ward's crew took slight consolation in being out of the
area at the time. They knew they would be going back to Okinawa.
And they knew the kamikazes would be back, too.

Kamikaze meant "Divine Wind," in Japanese. *What was that
old saying about an ill wind that blew nobody good? The only wind
we need is a twelve-knotter, courtesy of the engine room gang.*

In port, the ship wallowed at anchor, stewing in a miasma of the
various and assorted smells, odors and stinks arising from engine
rooms, fire rooms, stacks, exhaust fans, bunk rooms, galley, garbage
racks and a healthy crew. She sucked them all into her ventilating
system, amplified them, emphasized them, distilled them and
spewed them out again, hour by hour, day by day, until even the
seagulls left. But underway she made her own wind which scrubbed
her clean, leaving about the decks only a faint tang of fresh paint,
oil, and gunpowder—the mark of a fighting lady.

A man could feel the wind at sea. It flowed onto the forecastle in an invisible river, tumbled over the superstructure, smashed across the bridge, roared away aft, and leaped overboard from the fantail, carrying with it loose cigarette butts and now and then a white hat worn with too jaunty an air. The old timers could poke their heads out of a hatch, sniff the wind, and tell where they were without having to go bother the quartermaster for a look at the chart.

Off the West Coast, out to San Clemente and Catalina, the wind would be cold, dank, smelling of fog, fish, and seaweed. Farther west it grew clean and salty and sang in the signal halliards by day, keened around the gun tubs at night. As the ship moved down across the Tropic of Cancer the wind turned gentle and voluptuous, running warm fingers inside a sailors shirt and crooning in his ears and when they rounded Diamond Head, it skipped across the waves, carrying the scent of flowers and rain forests.

Across the Central Pacific the sun beat down, the decks of the ship shimmered in the blistering heat and the wind hot-footed off somewhere else. Not until they left Ulithi did it come back, herding a black squall ahead of it and slashing at the ship with sharp stinging bursts of rain and salt spray. Up to Okinawa the ship slugged against the wind while it beat and pounded on her, pushing her over on her beam ends, smashing dishes and furniture, ripping canvas, breaking pipes, flooding the decks, pinching men in heavy doors, drenching men in open hatches, shorting out electrical circuits. and slamming towering rollers down on her forecastle until her bows went under and the screws thrashed helplessly in the air as if the ship were drowning.

But that was a wind they could understand and fight against, and curse when it dumped them in the scuppers. Now, off Okinawa, the wind was something else again. Here it came at them out of the black night across the East China Sea, a wind they had never known before. This wind had filled the sails of junks and skirts of geisha girls before it came to them; it had tinkled wind bells in Kyoto and scurried across rice paddies in Kyushu; it had shaken peach blossoms into palace pools in Peiping, tossed dust in beggar's eyes in Tsingtao and teased paper dragons in Shanghai. This was a strange wind, filled with foreboding; as it shuffled out of the night toward them it might come with the swish of silken kimonos, or with the searing golden flame of exploding aircraft.

Any time. Any hour. Any minute.

Three-thirty in the morning. Two hundred and ten minutes in which nothing had happened. Already the bridge watch was bustling about, making certain things were in order for their reliefs. The sky was clearing and there were more stars. A few thousand yards distant, Biesmeyer could see the loom of USS *Little*, who shared the fate and fortune of RPS 10 with *Aaron Ward*. *Little* was a good friend to have around. She was one of the *Fletcher*-class destroyers, the same length and tonnage as *Aaron Ward*, but with two more 5-inch mounts which were very handy during kamikaze season.

Like the *Aaron Ward*, the *Little* had been named for an earlier ship of the same name. Like the first *Aaron Ward*, the first *Little* had also been a four-piper, a flush decker of World War I vintage. Launched in 1917 as DD 79, the *Little* was converted to a high speed transport in 1940 and moved into the Pacific with three other converted destroyer transports as a division. And like the second *Aaron Ward*, she had been sunk by the Japanese. *Little* ran into the Tokyo Express off Guadalcanal the night of 4 September 1942. Her puny 4-inch guns were no match for the hard hitting Japanese cruisers and she went down, taking half her crew with her.

Quarter to four. The mid watch was nearly over. If a man took the war just one watch at a time, he could make it. Just don't plan more than four hours ahead. The ship had been on Radar Picket Station 10 now since Monday when she came out to relieve USS *Brown*. The guns had not been fired since late Monday night, when they got a single-engine type plane for a probable kill. They were ready to try it again.

In the predawn light now, Biesmeyer could see the guns standing ready—the twin forties just aft of the bridge, the quad forties aft of number two stack, the big twin mount 5-inchers forward on the forecastle and the superstructure deck, another one aft on the fantail, the little 20mms scattered all over the bridge and superstructure, even on number two stack.

The barrels were elevated, each one sniffing in its own assigned sector. On the open mounts, helmeted men hunched their shoulders against the damp morning breeze but kept their eyes on the sky, searching for anything that moved. In the uncertain light of dawn and dusk, a man might not see a plane until it was within five miles of the ship. That gave them at most one minute to put up a curtain of fire, smash the plane, save the ship. They had done it nine times so far. They could do it again. When the planes came, there might not be time to get ready for them. A ship had to be always ready. This day, *Aaron Ward* was ready.

The day was coming now, wide and high. It circled out to the blue rim of the horizon, so far away the ship could never reach it; it towered up into the blue arch of space higher than man could imagine it. The ship swam always in the pinpoint middle of the gleaming sea; the horizon moved with the ship, always pushing away ahead, always drawing in astern. This was the day a man could see. But beneath it was another, a world of eternal silence, blinding darkness, and terrifying depths. Into that dismal day the skittering flying fishes vanished, out of it the frisky dolphins leaped, and somewhere in it the great gray whales cruised. Down there was a fearsome jungle where tiger sharks roamed and devilfish lurked. Down there might be a silent, stealthy submarine, waiting to blow an unsuspecting ship into pieces higher than her own masthead. Down there in the midnight blackness where mud lay centuries deep, was the dumping ground of the sea, the place where bones and buttons of dead men and their battered ships and planes settled into forgetfulness, into oblivion, into eternity.

"Ready to relieve you, Sir." That was Dave Rubel, the gun boss, on deck for the morning watch. Again they went through the procedure of relieving the watch. Throughout the ship, the first section watch relieved the third section watch. But while the men on the gun crews traded places, the guns still pointed at the sky. If this was to be the minute, *Aaron Ward* was still ready.

Finally Biesmeyer handed Dave the binoculars, and the albatross, and went below. There was just time to take his shoes off before morning GQ came and he had to put them on again. May third was now four hours old, and if the next twenty hours went that way, the war would be one day nearer over, the ship would be one day nearer home. Their fate was in the hands of the gods, and the Japanese air force. Either they came today or they didn't. All one could do was hope.

The morning was come of a mighty day. — THOMAS DE QUINCY

Chapter Two

Morning Watch

04-08 Steaming as before. 0515 sounded routine GQ. 0528 All
stations manned and ready, condition ABLE set. 0550 Secured from
General Quarters. Set personnel condition III, material condition
BAKER.

D. M. Rubel, Lt., U. S. Navy

Steaming as before. As the morning watch began, *Aaron Ward*
and *Little* still marched and countermarched across the particular bit
of ocean known as Radar Picket Station 10. Light welled up in the
east and the sky faded, the horizon became visible, a distant line
evenly dividing sea and sky. The sky was empty, only a few clouds
drifting across from the northwest. Except for the three smaller

craft, the two larger ones, the sea was also empty and looked peaceful. Rubel could see the small boys now, the 83, 14, and 15, keeping step with them a few miles to the south. They could have been a few miles off San Diego, except for one thing: the chart said they were on RPS 10 and beyond the horizon lay Kyushu and Formosa. Even at that moment the planes might be on their way. If the ship was to ever see San Diego again, that might be the very moment to keep alert. Dave could see his gunners, now, standing by their mounts from bow to stern. They were ready.

Section 1 was on deck. The morning watch was well underway. If a man has to go to sea, if he has to stand watches, the morning watch is the best of all. He has to get up for breakfast anyway, so he may as well be up a little early and see the world slowly turn beneath him, leaving the darkness behind, moving eastward into dawn, sunrise, and daylight. The ship was a world unto its own during the night, a floating fortress of steel pushing the sea aside, holding the darkness out, keeping its men safe and warm and dry. But as the sky fades and the horizon spreads wider, the ship grows smaller until finally in the vast infinity of a day as high as the sun it is no more than a small gray bug swimming in a flat world between sea and sky, never able to leave the sea, never able to touch the sky, never getting any farther away from one horizon, never reaching nearer to the other. Only the sun moves, only the hands of the clock tell how much it has moved, only the words in the log tell that time has passed, only the Plan of the Day tells the bug in the circle what it must do next.

There was a copy of the Plan of the Day clipped to the bridge chart desk. A one-page sheet, it detailed the schedule of events, insofar as Navy Regulations and the Executive Officer could predict them, for 3 May 1945, from reveille to taps. What went on between taps and reveille was covered by the Captain's Night Order Book. Dave Rubel, as Officer of the Deck, had checked both when he came on the bridge at four o'clock. It was his responsibility to see that the schedule, for meals, cleaning, drills, and other training, was carried out as ordered by the Executive Officer.

The Plan of the Day had been typed, mimeographed and distributed by Fowers, one of the yeomen in the Executive Officer's office, who flitted about the ship like a clerical owl, long after midnight, dropping the sheets in crew compartments, CPO quarters, wardroom mess, bridge, galley and sick bay. Fowers was the town crier for the ship; he spread the word after the Executive Officer decided what it would be.

Everyone went by the Plan of the Day except those who made it. The notes in the Plan of the Day about turning to on ship's work at 0800 and knocking off at 1500 were written by the Exec and typed by Fowers, but they didn't apply to them. The Executive Officer worked long hours, often until three in the morning, and the yeoman worked with him. All the headaching administrative details of a combatant ship were handled by the Executive Officer, Lieutenant Commander Karl Neupert. There were reports to be made; weekly, monthly, quarterly, and whenever someone in the chain of command wanted them. There were all the details of personnel administration; drill schedules, training sessions, training courses, examinations, recommendations for advancement in rating, fitness reports for the officers, and quarterly marks for the enlisted men. There were the matters of ship's organization to be kept current, the battle bill to be kept up to date, all the details of operation orders and invasion plans to study and know with absolute accuracy.

A perfect torrent of paper work flowed through the cramped little office. If the typewriter broke down or the mimeograph burned up, the repercussion would be felt all the way to Washington. Until that happened, Fowers spent the long night hours at his typewriter trying to keep up with the Executive Officer, who seemed to have some sort of computer inside his head. Fowers was confident that the Exec could answer absolutely any question about the ship, the equipment in her, and the officers and men assigned to her, except one. And that one was, "When do you plan on getting some sleep?"

Sleep seemed to be something the Exec saved for a time when there was nothing else to do, and so far that time had not arrived.

Plan of the Day, Thursday, 3 May 1945. It looked just the same as it had for days past, except for the date. The bridge watch could have gone on from there by memory. The first entry read:

0430 Call the ship's cooks with the day's duty.

That meant Castagnola, Bruna, Kinney. The boatswain's mate of the watch went below to rouse them out. In their hot little kingdom on the main deck, just forward of the fire room uptakes, the cooks sweated and swore and sliced salami when it was on the menu, and in some fashion or another fed three hundred men three times a day. If the weather was rough, the big pans slid across the cooking tops from one side of the galley to the other in blistering abandon. The huge steam kettles for soup and stew were big enough to cook a man, and would if the ship took a heavy roll.

Just above the galley was CIC; if a plane ever hit the bridge the scope peepers and their gear would come through and do the galley no good. And just below the galley was the forward fire room and two boilers panting with superheated steam; if that ever blew the crew had better hope it wasn't too far to the next hamburger shack, because it would be too far to where the galley went.

Sleepily, the cooks trudged in and got things moving. Come hell, or high water, or kamikazes, the crew had to be fed. The only thing afloat grouchier than a cook who had to get up and make breakfast before sunrise was the sailor who hadn't had a chance to eat it yet. And there had to be coffee, first—gallons and gallons of it. General quarters went every day, half an hour before sunrise, and a man couldn't tell friend from foe without his coffee, and probably didn't care at that point.

Fifteen minutes after he started awakening the cooks, the boatswain's mate of the watch again went through the ship, rousing out the section boatswain's mates, the master at arms, and the compartment master at arms. It would be their job to awaken the entire crew, have all hands turned out and on their feet when dawn general quarters sounded. This was standard wartime routine; attack was most liable at dawn and sunset, and all ships in the combat zone had guns manned at those times . . . . *Let 'em come. We're ready for 'em.* This morning, as always, *Aaron Ward* would be ready.

So began the fortieth morning since the U. S. Navy came to Okinawa. All around the island that morning, on the other fifteen picket stations, on the inner screen, in the transport areas, off Point BOLO, at Hagushi, and at Kerama Retto, even on the far side of the island in Nakagusuku Wan, other ships were sounding general quarters, other crews were manning their guns. Forty days and forty nights. Sometimes the Japanese didn't come, but when they came, they usually made up for lost time. Over a hundred ships had been hit so far; everything from battleships to spit kits. Ships hit by kamikazes could be classed in three categories. The ones which were only lightly damaged limped in to Kerama Retto, to be patched up and sent back to the picket line. Those badly smashed by what picket line sailors soon learned to call "a stateside hit" waited at Kerama Retto to be made ready for the long haul back across the Pacific to a mainland shipyard. Those in the third category were at the bottom of the sea.

Aaron Ward was one of twelve similar destroyer minelayers converted in 1944. The group began with USS *Robert H. Smith*, DM 23, and ran up through *Aaron Ward*, DM 34. So far the kamikazes had hit *Shannon*, DM 25; *Harry F. Bauer*, DM 26; *Adams*, DM 27; *Shea*, DM 30; and *Lindsay*, DM 32. No matter how one looked at it, they were coming right down the list.

"CIC, BRIDGE. HOW'S IT LOOK?"

"BRIDGE, CIC. SCREEN CLEAR, ALL CLEAR."

"CONTROL, BRIDGE. SUNRISE COMING UP. EVERYONE ON THEIR TOES."

"BRIDGE, CONTROL. EVERYONE ON THEIR TOES, AYE."

0500 Reveille. Relentlessly the boatswain's mates took up their chant.

"ALL RIGHT THERE, RISE AND SHINE!"
"DAYLIGHT IN THE SWAMPS, MEN. UP AND AT 'EM!"
"HIT THE DECK, SAILORS! LET'S LOOK ALIVE HERE."
"OUT OF THE SACK, YOU SACKRATS."

No matter how the boatswain's mates, master-at-arms, and compartment petty officers worded their invitation, a man hated to get up in the morning. Especially before sunrise. The boys who had left the farm to avoid such unpleasantness found that ships were even worse than mules in having to be taken care of early in the morning. And, in the war zone, no one went to bed with the chickens. This morning, section 1 was already on watch, so they didn't have to get up. The men in section 3 had come off watch around four o'clock, had had maybe half an hour of sack time. Section 2 had come off watch at midnight, so they had had what might politely be called all night in.

But the time to expect an enemy strike was in the uncertain light of dawn, or sunset. Those were the witching hours, when Tojo's bats came out.

Stir about, down there! Get the lead out. GQ goes in five minutes!

Be ready, men. Always ready.

0515 General Quarters. On the bridge Dave Rubel nodded to Holte, the first section quartermaster, who flipped the alarm switch. The strident, raucus uproar filled the ship. Sackrats who had managed to crawl back onto their bunk for one last wink scrambled out. Men pounded along the decks, hurried up ladders to the bridge, down escape trunks to the engine rooms and fire rooms, grabbed helmets, jerked on telephones, pulled switches, pushed buzzers, tested circuits. It was all routine, it happened every morning and every night. But no one could be certain that the Japanese didn't know this and planned to make a routine call.

Throughout the ship, the first section men who had taken over duties an hour earlier now turned them over to the GQ men and rushed off somewhere else to take their own GQ station. The guns had been only one-third manned in the condition watch; now they would be fully manned. At each gun, each station, as the last man slid into his position, a phone talker passed the word along to the next higher level in the battle organization:

"CONTROL! . . . . MOUNT 51 MANNED AND READY" . . . . "MOUNT 53 MANNED AND READY" . . . . "MOUNT 52 MANNED AND READY."

Those were the big ones, the twin 5-inch mounts, which required nearly two dozen men in magazine, handling room, and gun room to service them. When Castanian reported Mount 52 manned and ready, he meant really ready, for anything. In the magazine and handling room, four decks below, men stood silently by, ready to start projectiles and powder cases up the electric hoists. Down where they could never see the battle, never know who was shooting at who, were the magazine crew; Posey, McCoy, Peters, Rotter, Wise, Young; the outer handling room gang; Aves, Cain, Martinez, Marquoit; the inner handling room gang; Hammock, Reed, Clingenpeel, Stolz, Wilson; and in the mount itself; Castanian, Boles, Fletcher, Jones, Fenske, Von Paris, Thostenson, Hetrick and Thornberry; who would be too busy with the guns to see where the shots were going. There were just as many men in the two other twin mounts, all waiting, all ready.

The two twin forties and the two quad forties, with smaller crews, were unprotected, except for splinter shields. Everyone in the crews was out where he could see, and if action came, usually too busy to notice. Their ammunition came up from clipping rooms where again crews worked surrounded by steel, unable to know what was happening topside. The eight 20mm guns, with smaller crews, were completely unprotected; in fact, men on mounts 21 and 22 forward and 25 and 27 aft stood a good chance of having their helmets knocked off or being flattened by the muzzle blast of the big 5-inchers when they sometimes chased a plane all around their sectors.

"BRIDGE! ENGINEERING DEPARTMENT MANNED AND READY!"

Down there, tending the boilers, blowers, pumps, generators, power panels, turbines and other machinery that kept the ship moving and the guns shooting were nearly a hundred other men who, as far as the actual fighting was concerned, merely went along for the ride. Those who wore phones tied in to a bridge or control circuit knew to a degree what was going on and could pantomime or shout the word to others. In the forward engine room, where the Chief Engineer took his battle station, people at least knew on which side a plane was making an attack because Weyrauch, the phone talker, always moved to the opposite side of the ship, just in case. But there were no windows in the sides of the ship down below the waterline, no skylights in the deck overhead, and this enabled the engineers, when the shooting started, to concentrate on their engines and leave the Japanese to the gunnery department.

0528 All stations manned and ready.

Every man on the ship now was at his station. This was where they would be in battle, this was how the ship prepared for battle. Except for the medical personnel, who by terms of the Geneva Convention were considered non-combatants, every man on the ship was a part of a fighting group. If they were not prepared to fight the enemy directly, they were prepared to fight the damage he might inflict.

Amidships and aft, the repair and damage control gangs stood by, waiting. Shelley, the senior chief, headed up the gangs under Lieutenant Biesmeyer, who was First Lieutenant and Damage Control Officer. Two other old time chiefs, Ragan, the commissary steward and Offins, the mineman, helped the damage control people. The rest of them were firemen and seamen, and petty officers, trained and ready to put out fires, repair broken power lines, shore up damaged bulkheads, plug leaks, prevent flooding, and seal off damaged, burning, or flooded compartments.

They might hang around at GQ for days and weeks with nothing to do. Even when the ship went into action and shot down a plane, they had nothing to do. But if the plane got through the barrage of fire and dropped a bomb, fired a torpedo, or plowed into the ship, they would have plenty of work. They depended on the gunnery gang to keep the enemy from hitting the ship; they would have to clean up the mess if he did.

But this morning the Japanese didn't come. The radar probed the sky, the sonar pinged the depths, the guns lifted their muzzles and waited, and everywhere men searched the horizon and the empty space above it. This was not the time. At 0550 Bill Sanders nodded to the Officer of the Deck, and the speakers buzzed again:

"SECURE FROM GENERAL QUARTERS. SECURE FROM GENERAL QUARTERS. SET PERSONNEL CONDITION THREE, MATERIAL CONDITION BAKER."

Again men changed stations. Section 1 took over the condition watch while sections 2 and 3 went below to clean up, get ready for breakfast.

On the bridge, Rubel had the deck again. The ship still loped ahead at 12 knots, followed by the *Little*. Five miles out on the beam, the three small boys bobbed along. On all five ships now, men would be securing from general quarters, getting ready for the routine of 3 May 1945, whatever that might be. As wind eddied about the bridge superstructure, the smell of hot food came up from the galley. Breakfast! And about time, too. It had seemed like a long watch so far. And the day was far from over. Still only six in the morning. The bridge clock moved so slowly, one would suspect the hands were stuck.

Look at that clock again. You sure those hands aren't standing still? . . . . What difference does it make? We aren't going anywhere.

All around them, the horizon was a painted backdrop against which nothing moved. If one watched closely, he had an impression the sea was like a great flat wheel pivoted on the horizon, turning slowly past the ship. The ship itself was full of slowly turning wheels. Every time one went around the men changed watches on the bridge and guns. Every time another went around the cooks served out chow. When that wheel turned three times, the Exec's wheel went around once and he and Fowers got out the morning orders. When the morning order wheel went around seven times, the Commissary officer put out a new menu. And when the menu wheel went around twice, the crew got paid, if they were where there was any money.

But who needed money on a picket station? All one could spend there was time, and there was plenty of that. The idea was to hoard it, spend it carefully, make it last, save some to go home on. Use it up one hour at a time, keep those little wheels turning until that big one turned around and said "Home again." No one knew how long that wheel took to go around, or if it ever would. There was no way to tell, except wait it out. One hour at a time.

The next hour or so would be as happy a time as men could hope for on the picket line. Most men leaving their GQ stations made a rush for the crew's washrooms. There were about ten wash basins in each washroom, and over three hundred men to use them, so a man who would be clean of face must necessarily also be fleet of foot. Other conveniences in the washrooms were in the same limited supply as the wash basins. A man soon learned not to put off until tomorrow what had better be done today.

Day after day a man could come up from the crowded, warm, stuffy crew's compartment where only a connoisseur could have discerned the various odors of stale candy bars, dead socks, and dandruff remover among the overall atmosphere which filled the place solidly from deck to overhead—the smell of dozens of young sailors all busy sleeping, writing, itching, smoking, eating, reading, scratching, playing, arguing, goofing off, horsing around, sacking out, sweating, sneezing, dreaming, studying, hoping, and marking off days on a calendar. The days were always days since, never days to, because no one ever planned any farther ahead than the Plan of the Day and that was good only for twenty-four hours if the Exec and his yeomen got it out on time.

When a man left the crew's compartment to go on watch or for some more urgent reason, he reached the deck topside, blinked, sniffed, looked all around like a badger emerging from his den, and then sniffed again. Fresh air. If the ship was underway it flowed past him in a gentle stream or a battering torrent, depending on the speed. The wind was almost as good as a bath; it blew the taste out of his mouth, slapped his shirt against his ribs, shook the wrinkles out of his pants, pushed the hair out of his face, opened his eyes, and woke him up.

Then he could look out at the sea, rolling around him in a vast, flat circle, the same as yesterday and the day before and the day before that. No matter how fast the ship steamed, nor how long it was at sea, it never seemed to move across the ocean. The ship only moved the first few hours out, as it sailed away from land; one could see the shore dropping behind, growing dim, sinking into the horizon. But once the land disappeared the ship seemed not to move at all. Only the water rushed past alongside, but the ocean stood still, the ship steaming always in the exact center of the circling sea, until land lifted above the horizon. Then the ship would move again, leave the sea behind, and move up to the land.

In the distance, all around the ship, the sea lay still. Half a mile ahead, it crept slowly toward the ship, then moved, hurrying, leaping to meet her. The driving prow of the ship knifed into the long swells, split them into shining green walls of glass that lifted up on either side, hung motionless, curved down in a burst of brilliance, then rushed past in deep green rivers streaked with foam. The blinding white wake rolled out aft, spreading wider, moving slower, turning green again, fading away until half a mile astern it became a part of the vast circle again, blue, intense, motionless, the thin line between here and everywhere else. In the middle of it the ship sat, a little gray bug on a calendar. It never was able to crawl off the place marked "today."

The men came up from the stuffy crew's compartment, walked over to the rail, looked out at the horizon, up at the stacks, down at the waterline, then spit into the ocean. *So this is Thursday.*

A man marked time by such simple acts, repeated until they became a pattern, the pointers on the little dial which was his day, around which his shadow moved from act to act: eat breakfast, go on watch, go off watch, eat, go on watch, go off watch, eat, go on watch, go off watch, sleep. Seven times around that dial made a week . . . . Back home, somewhere which was now only a postmark on an envelope too seldom seen, someone else was going around her own little dial in the same way . . . . get up, feed the baby . . . . go to school, teach the class . . . . open the store, pay the bills . . . . milk the cows, feed the chickens . . . . go to bed . . . . Seven times around that dial also made a week. But the weeks were never the same. Each was in a different time, a different place, almost a different world.

Each spent the time, caught in a routine, a marionette in a never ending scene. The only memory a sailor had of home was a fleeting glimpse saved and remembered from a bus window five months before, a wave from the dock two months before, a letter read every night since it reached the ship three weeks before. All the woman had was a letter; "Here we are. I can't say where." Each played the same scene in the other's memory, time after time, until the mail came again, then the scene advanced quickly through two pages of a letter, through two weeks of time. And there it stopped, the little figure frozen in memory, waiting for another letter to give it the cue to move forward again. Sometimes, when the letters ceased, the last scene burned itself in *her* memory forever; the figure standing there, saying the last line over and over, slower and slower like a toy running down, farther and farther away across the years: "Here we are. I can't say where."

Radar Picket Station 10, that's where. Patrolling as before. Counting hours as before. Scanning the radar screen as before. Standing by the guns as before. Wishing there could be a letter from home as before. Arguing about whether flying fish fly or not as before. Sleepy as before. And hungry as before . . . . *Hey, you galley slaves! Didja throw that chow down the garbage chute? Let's eat!*

So now men prepared for breakfast, crowding against each other in the hot, wet intimacy of the wash room. Others made up their bunks in the sleeping compartments, three aft and two forward, where they slept in neat rows, stacked three deep like martyrs in

34

the catacombs, and with some slight chance of martyrdom themselves, because under the sleeping compartments were the magazines filled with high explosives. If a bomb or torpedo ever hit the magazines, the inhabitants of those compartments were certainly doomed to ascend, at least briefly, unto heaven, no matter what their past had been.

And elsewhere, a few men found time for silent, personal thoughts, time to project in their imaginations across the miles to home, wherever that might be; time to just stand on deck and gaze at the horizon, to consider the indisputable fact that once more they had lived through the night, somehow or other. The sky was the same, the water was the same, they were still in the middle of the same vast horizon, but the day was different; this was Thursday, 3 May according to the Plan of the Day on the crew's bulletin board, and wherever they were going they were one more day on the way.

One of these men was Fletcher, a tall, blonde, pleasant, quiet man, a seaman second in the U. S. Navy and a deacon in the Church of the Latter Day Saints. *Aaron Ward* was his first ship. Fletcher had worked with the ship's doctor and the hospital corpsmen, showing such proficiency that Doc had arranged some orders for him. The next time *Aaron Ward* fell in with a hospital ship, Fletcher was to be transferred on board for training as a hospital corpsman. Fletcher had more to look forward to than a crow on his arm. In the last mail, there had been a letter from his wife, Eva, in Salt Lake City telling him he was to become a father.

In contrast to Fletcher was Couie, a coxswain. Couie had been through a couple of years of combat in the South Pacific on other ships, without a scratch, yet of all the men on the ship, he was the most fatalistic. Couie knew he was going to be killed before the war was over, and the other men in the crew knew he knew it. Twice he had deliberately jumped ship, and one man or another had gone ashore, tracked him down, brought him back. He always came willingly, and bore no ill-will toward the Captain when he "busted" Couie from second class. Couie, a big, red-headed fellow, was no coward; he was as brave as anyone else in the crew. Some men were terribly afraid when the shooting started, but not Couie. He wasn't afraid of the enemy. He just knew that sooner or later they were going to get him. Most men didn't hold with this kind of thinking. Possibly a few of them believed it, just a little bit. Couie believed it all the way. He was probably a little surprised, each time morning came, that he had made it.

But here it was, 3 May. The Skipper was on the bridge, baseball cap on his head, pipe in his mouth, just like always. Mr. Ferguson, the junior assistant gunnery officer, was in the wardroom, making certain no one had sabotaged his collection of aircraft models, by which he hoped to teach the lookouts the difference between seaplanes and wild geese. Same as before. Mr. Rosengren, the Sound Officer, would soon be up in the sound room, listening to his ping jockeys and hoping that, with whales and Japanese submarines both loose in the same ocean, someone would not make an embarrassing mistake. Like always. Another day on Station 10 . . . . *We had one just like it yesterday, too. How'd that line in Shakespeare go? . . . . Tomorrow, and tomorrow, and tomorrow. Well, let's take them one at a time. Concentrate on Thursday for today.*

Thursday wasn't so bad, if you looked at it right. Somewhere back near the mineshack someone was singing "Oh, what a beautiful morning . . . ." That would be Joe Zaloga, the happy mineman. If anyone on the ship had a good reason for not being there, it was Joe. All his brothers had already died in this war; he was the last surviving male in the Zaloga family. There was a Navy Department order concerning such family tragedies; for "humanitarian reasons" a man in whose family others had died could ask for assignment to less hazardous duty.

"That applies to me, you know," Joe said every so often. "I can put in for safer duty."

"Well, why don't you?"

"I will, right after this campaign."

"This campaign," so far as Joe and the *Aaron Ward* were concerned, had gone on for three months now. He was still singing, still cutting hair, still friendly with men whose hair he cut. Joe was a better friend than he was a barber.

Joe was a member of another special group aboard ship, the minemen. The minemen were the people who gave *Aaron Ward* her designation—destroyer minelayer. She had been built as a destroyer, and she still looked like one. About the only way most people could tell she was a minelayer instead of a destroyer was by going aboard and falling over the mine tracks. This was comparatively easy to do, and almost everyone in the crew had done it. The mine tracks ran along both sides of the main deck, from the break of the superstructure all the way to the fantail. If she ever had to lay mines, *Aaron Ward* could carry about fifty of the deadly weapons on each track. She would steam into enemy waters at high speed and the minemen would unload them, rolling them aft on their little four wheeled "kiddy-cars," planting a long trail of destruction for any ship which came that way later.

The mines looked like big, black, ugly, dangerous eggs, and they were all of that. When a minelayer's egg hatched, it released a raging demon—the terrific force of hundreds of pounds of high explosive that would blast a ship completely out of the water. Most *Aaron Ward* sailors had only a dim idea of what a mine could really do until they saw the *Halligan* destroyed by a Japanese mine when they first reached Okinawa. After that they kept clear of the few sitting on the main deck mine tracks. Very few men knew that the mines were only dummies, filled with concrete, but even if they had they would have viewed them with deep suspicion. Mines were sneaky things.

The minemen, on the other hand, were a pleasant bunch of people, not at all the sort of men one would suppose were in the mass murder business. The Mine Control Officer, Gunner Siler, was an old-time regular Navy ex-enlisted, full of exotic knowledge about his dangerous weapons. The rest of the gang, Armand, Brown, Christofferson, Fields, Follett, Gross, Hitchcock, Mogensen, Offins (the chief), Weed, Wimer, and Zaloga, played checkers, sang songs, swapped sea stories, and helped on the guns and damage control parties. They had been trained to lay mines, but if there were no mines to lay, they'd do anything else that helped win the war: shoot down planes, help fight fires, carry provisions aboard, help eat them. Just get the war over and go home. But Armand, Zaloga and Follett were not going home.

0630 Breakfast for the crew. Watch 2 eat first. Long before the word was passed, happy chowhounds congregated in the port passageway outside the galley, where the ladder led down to the mess hall. The mess hall could seat only eighty-eight men at a time, so the crew ate cafeteria style. In that respect their superiors in the wardroom fared not much better; the officers sat down and had their food served to them, but those who were late for the first sitting had to stand outside and wait their turn. It was customary that the men about to go on watch ate first; this enabled them to hurry to their stations and take over so the offcoming watch could get in on the tail end of the line. This could lead to growls when a man going on watch moved ahead of a man off watch, and bruised knuckles when it was the other way around.

"Little Red" Little, the strongest man on the ship except for Moose Antel, had learned this when he tried to chisel in ahead of gunner's mate Larson, who was going on watch. Old enough to be "Pappy" for most of his crew, Larson took a swing at Little Red, who returned it with interest. Next morning they were both hauled before the Captain at Captain's Mast, where they were warned against such behaviour. Later Bill Sanders called them both to his cabin for a private word of advice: "There'll be plenty of fighting where we're going. Don't waste it on each other."

In the galley Frank Bruna stood over the duty cooks as they dished out the chow, growling a little. He probably felt they might not do a good job, otherwise. Frank didn't exactly trust the bridge crew either—he always wore his life jacket. Older than most, 32 years, Bruna sometimes didn't care for the lighthearted attitude of younger fellows, and was liable to be short with them. Yet a man could usually count on getting a small handout of chow at night if Frank was in the galley. The fates may have started him off wrong at the very beginning, for he was born on Valentine's Day, and grew up just in time to meet the 1929 depression head on.

During those hard times he had been out of work for six years straight. He had a saxophone, played a little in a band, finally took up beauty culture. But men were not popular in that field, and when he went to apply for a job he used to take his sister Blanche along to use as a demonstrator.

Bruna joined the Navy, he said, because he couldn't stand the Army. He wanted to be a machinist so the Navy made a cook out of him. Bruna didn't talk much, except to Kennedy, who could cure headaches but not homesickness; and when he went home on leave early in 1945 to visit his sister Blanche, he didn't talk much there either, except possibly to his old mutt dog Brownie who had missed him when he enlisted, and waited patiently on his bed for him to come home again. Dogs and sailors probably get along better together than any other people in the world. They all have troubles too deep to talk about.

But Frank had his good side, too. Hosking, one of the radarmen, knew which it was. Somehow or other, Hosking had come across several cases of canned cherries, languishing alone and temporarily unattended at a boat landing. As court martial language would put it, Hosking did then and there appropriate such government property to his own use, the United States then being in a state of war. Hosking figured he was in a state of war too, and every little bit helped. With the right kind of buttering up, Bruna could always be prevailed upon to turn out a hot cherry pie which gave the radarmen strength enough to watch their scopes on a long mid watch.

The radarmen were a tribe all their own. The rest of the crew understood in a general way what they did, but not many saw them do it. Radar was still a highly classified development at that time, and besides, they had no room for visitors.

The radar room, perhaps twelve feet square, was ordinarily filled with equipment. But at GQ the Radar Officer, the Assistant Radar Officer, and some twelve men had to pile in with it. Two men handled the Mk. XII and Mk. XXII radars—the surface and air search. A couple more worked the plotting board. Others manned phones, to the bridge, to control, and the TBS to the *Little*. Forward was the chart house, aft was the radio shack. On the deck underneath was the galley, and underneath that was number one fireroom. Directly above was the bridge. A man in the radar shack couldn't look out to see what was happening—in battle all he could do was watch pips on the radar screens and hope the gunners disposed of them before they got too close. Suicide planes had a habit of aiming at the bridge structure of a ship, and whether the plane hit the bridge and the fire came down or he lobbed a bomb into a fireroom and the boilers came up was really academic and something best not worried about.

Radar was one of the newest "weapons" the Navy had, and certainly one of the most technical. Only a few installations were in service when the war began, yet now it was the eyes of every ship. The glowing green oscilloscopes were miniature battlefields on which admirals watched the deployment of their ships, fighter director officers tracked approaching air raids and the "tallyho" of the fighter plane they sent out to attack them, and gunnery officers watched the "splash" of shells fired at unseen targets in the night. The existence of radar was one of the best kept secrets of the war. Radar was the one thing a radarman didn't talk about when he went ashore.

And the radar gang was, by rate, the lowest paid group on the ship. Other rating groups had their petty officers, and in the deck force, engineering departments, gunnery departments, there were chief petty officers. But the entire radar gang of twelve men, with an average age of twenty-nine, were low men on the totem pole, all seamen, not a petty officer among them. Even so, they took their work seriously. There was no reading in the radar room, no card playing, no gambling.

They were all first cruise men, but Woods and Hoskings were old married men, each with half a dozen or so children back home. Aylworth was probably the best traveled of the bunch—as a member of the Mormon church he had been sent to Europe several years earlier on a mission and had spent thirty months in France and Switzerland. He was also the only one of them with previous military service; he had been a private in the Army but resigned to join the Navy. A man didn't have to march everywhere he went in the Navy, the food was better and he could wear clean socks.

Cooks in the Navy seldom get decorated for bravery, although this is not because they do not deserve medals. The Navy figures any man who can dish out chow and insults to three hundred men three times a day and then walk among them unarmed doesn't need a medal. The crew knows he's a brave man; they know all cooks are brave men. Those who weren't probably jumped overboard after their first meal.

Laundrymen in the Navy never get decorated either, although they continually carry on in the face of the enemy; which in the case of the laundryman, is every sailor on board who is not a laundryman. *Aaron Ward*'s brave laundrymen were George Dart, Lester Spradlin, and Wesley Toye. They worked in a cramped, hot, noisy space, aft of the galley, battling a steaming, suffocating avalanche of dirty socks and underwear. The Navy believed that cleanliness was next to godliness, and while it didn't require a sailor to say his prayers at night, it expected him to turn out in clean clothes in the morning. With the assistance of Dart, Spradlin, and Toye, of course. In their private little bedlam, the laundrymen performed miracles. They were never credited with this; they were accused of it.

"Hey, looky this! I sent you clowns four sets of underwear. All I got back was eight shorts."

"That's funny. Ski did the same thing. All he got back was eight skivvy shirts."

"Doggone it! Last week you guys lost a pair of my dungaree pants. You think I'm going to run around the ship with just a shirt on?"

"Relax, chum, you don't have to. This week we lost the shirt too. Now you're even."

"What kind of a laundry is this? See these socks? They're for a dwarf!"

"Jeez! They are tiny, aren't they? Say, I didn't know you was a dwarf."

"I'm not a dwarf."

"Then what are you doing with those socks? Hand 'em back here!"

"Nossir. These are my socks."

"They aren't. We lost your socks."

"Aha! You admit you lost my socks. Where are they?"

"Right there in that big old bag."

"Then they ain't lost!"

"Yeah? There's about six hundred stray old socks in that bag. You wanna bet yours ain't lost?"

It was strange, how other people lost their shirts and socks. Laundrymen never lost their shirts and socks. Right there was the fine dividing line; if something got lost in the laundry, it obviously belonged to someone else.

The superstructure and main deck of the ship—Topside—belonged to the deck force. This was the domain of Chief Boatswain's Mate Shelley, who was variously addressed as Chief, "Boats," or "Crazy," according to who did the addressing. Shelley and his deck force had the biggest piece of territory on the ship, the 345 foot long main deck, the anchors, anchor windlass, boat, boat davits, gangway, and the heavy manila lines used when the ship tied up. Aside from two or three petty officers, all of Shelley's gang were seamen, and most of them were fresh caught recruits. These were Shelley's "kids." He bossed them, worked them, counseled them, taught them marlinspike seamanship, and put the fear of God and Navy Regulations in them when necessary.

Shelley was an old time chief, bronzed, salty, tough on the outside but gentle on the inside. He never lost his temper, never got excited, never lost control of the situation; he took complete charge of whatever he was given to do, did it efficiently and quietly. After his kids had sailed across a quarter of a million miles of salt water, helped half a dozen officers start up the long haul from junior division officer to captain, taught several hundred kids of their own to be snappy deck apes and hot shot boatswain's mates, had learned to spit to windward and rig a towing hawser on a dark night in a heaving sea, why, then, they could hope to be the same kind of man Shelley was. But this took time—more than there might be out on the picket stations.

Above the main deck the ship was all guns, below decks she was all engines. That was all a ship needed, actually; guns to use against the enemy, firecontrol apparatus and gun directors to aim the guns, electric hoists to bring ammunition to the guns, and engines to take the guns to the right place. *Aaron Ward*'s engines, high speed steam turbines in two engine rooms, were fed by four boilers in two fire rooms. Roaring oil fires under the boilers turned water into superheated steam at 850 degrees, 600 pounds pressure; a maze of pipes and valves fed it through the turbines which turned up a maximum of 60,000 horsepower at full speed. The engineers lived in a Rube Goldberg world of evaporators, condensers, feed pumps, generators, switchboards, distribution panels, blowers, service pumps, ventilation fans, booster pumps, boilers, fuel oil heaters, turbines, alarms, air ejectors, gauge panels, condensate pumps, phones, oil tanks, motors, pipes, wires, air lines, and more valves, dials, gauges, and meters than any one man could possibly understand.

After guns and engines were built into a hull, the designers and builders crammed the ship with fuel tanks, water tanks, ammunition storage, paint storage, chain lockers, gear lockers, fire fighting equipment, navigational gear, radar, sonar, radio and communication gear, damage control gear, spare parts for everything that moved, corroded or wore out, and a couple of tons of books on how to use it all.

Then, in what space was left, they jammed in the officers and crew. The only place a man could call absolutely his own was his bunk, where he had room to lie down but not sit up, and his locker, where he could either keep all his personal effects or perhaps a bust of John Paul Jones, but certainly not both. In all the times Sanders, Neupert, and the division officers inspected lockers on the *Aaron Ward*, they never did find a bust of John Paul Jones. That is, unless it was in the CPO quarters. The chiefs were the big shots aboard ship; they had everything else in their quarters, including a radio that picked up Tokyo Rose, so John Paul Jones would have been no surprise.

By the time they had gone through recruit training, joined the ship, and been thoroughly seasick a couple of times, most new men in the crew had at least heard of John Paul Jones. They knew he was famous for having said "We have not yet begun to fight," but some of them were probably a little fuzzy about when he said it. To a sixteen- or seventeen-year-old boy who thought that FDR had always been President, men like John Paul Jones went far back in history to a time when Daniel Boone, Moses, and Robinson Crusoe all lived together in happy confusion. Them, and those old chiefs down in the CPO quarters. They were all ancient; some of those old chiefs wore five hash marks.

At least half of the crew were non-rated men, seamen and firemen who had enlisted in 1944 or 1943, and most of them had gone to sea for the first time with *Aaron Ward*. Many more of the petty officers had also come into the service since the war began and were "slick arm" rates—no hash marks. A man had to have four years under his belt before he could wear a hash mark. But some of the chiefs wore five. They had entered the navy before most of the crew was born, had come in even before the Captain entered the Naval Academy. They looked, and acted, and talked like old salts, and they were. Even the younger chiefs had been around long enough so they did things with a certain air of experience that none of the ninety-day wonder officers in the wardroom could ever match, no matter how many semester credit hours went with their degree. When a chief said "Jump!" he didn't mean "If you please." He meant "Right now!" The way it looked to the men, the chiefs pretty much ran the ship. The Department Heads and Division Officers were in charge of things, but the non-rated men and petty officers seldom discussed business with their officers. When they had problems, or requests, they went to their chief. The chiefs ran things, and they kept to themselves even more than the junior officers did. One thing a man learned was, keep out of the CPO quarters unless he had been sent for. He saw his chief on deck, on his turn-to station.

Down in the engineering plant there was McCaughey and Mann in the engine room, Salisbury in the auxiliaries, and Smith and Panero in the fire rooms. Shelley ran the deck force, Ragan ran the galley, Hansell handled all of the ship's office work. Brusky was the senior radioman, Offins was the chief for the minemen, St. Clair was chief electrician's mate, Winston assisted the navigator, and Tedford headed up the hospital corpsmen. Sailors, in the comparative safety of their own compartment, sometimes called the chiefs "metal men," because they were known to have silver in their hair, gold on their arms, and alleged to have lead in their pants, but this last was not always easily proved.

Shelley and Offins could outwork any dozen men on the ship, and each of the chiefs probably knew more about his own department than all the other men in it put together. The junior officers were always reading books to find out how things worked and how to do things, but the chiefs spent their time playing hearts at a penny a point. They didn't have to read books. They knew. A sailor should live so long.

Somewhere between deck and engine rooms, between galley and bunk rooms, was the sick bay, the antiseptic sanctuary where Doctor Barbeiri and his crew of medics, Crider, Tedford, Kennedy, and Fletcher ministered to the aches and pains of mortal man and soothed mental bumps and bruises when they could. The sick bay was a convenient hangout for men with nowhere else particular to go, a social center where officers and men met on a slightly less than military basis ("Jeez, Doc, I'm all fouled up inside. That damn stuff ain't doing me no good." "Well, it isn't helping me either, and I'm the doctor. Here, take it!") and the place where, if one worked it right, a shot of medicinal brandy might be forthcoming.

The *Aaron Ward* sick bay offered one bit of entertainment positively not obtainable on any other ship in the fleet. All surgeons had nimble fingers but Doctor Barbeiri had nimble toes, and with his shoes and socks removed, could sometimes extract a pack of matches from a medical cabinet drawer, remove one match from the pack, and light it. Doc couldn't always do the trick, but the medics always encouraged him to try. They got a kick out of seeing him pull it off successfully, and they got an even bigger kick out of watching him blister his feet when he failed. They knew Doc would rather burn himself up trying than to admit defeat.

Doc's enlisted helpers encouraged their boss in other ways. They talked Doc into keeping the supply of penicillin in the wardroom refrigerator. It would be safer in there, where the Doctor could keep his eye on it. And to be doubly certain, they would check it every once in awhile. The medics checked the penicillin religiously. They always carried a small, official looking box with them. No one but the medics knew the box was always empty when they went to the refrigerator, and that it was usually loaded when they left. But not with penicillin. Kennedy and Crider knew that emergencies requiring penicillin for a patient were not nearly so numerous as those requiring midnight rations for the medics.

Doc was not a man to put all his pills in one place. His supplies were all over the ship, from the wardroom refrigerator to the first-aid locker in the fantail. Racked against the forward bulkhead of the crew's mess hall was the ice-cream machine. Destroyer minelayers didn't rate such luxuries, but the *Aaron Ward* was different. The ice-cream machine was different, too. Besides ice cream, it was loaded with blood plasma, thus proving that *Aaron Ward*'s doctor was also different. The usual allowance for such a ship was twenty-four units of plasma, but the Doc had stored, in the ice-cream machine and elsewhere about the ship, between 250 and 300 units.

Doc started collecting his medical surplus while the pre-commissioning detail was at Treasure Island, long before they saw the *Aaron Ward*. Being a Stanford man, he knew most of the medical people at the Treasure Island blood bank, he knew that blood donors would be given a comforting shot of whiskey if they needed it, and he knew that a good many men in the *Aaron Ward* detail needed, or at least thought they needed, comfort. So Doc lined the men up and marched them off to the blood bank by the tens and dozens, and for each unit of blood they left there he collected one unit of plasma. It was a good investment; many of them were to profit immeasurably by it at Okinawa.

Life could be quite pleasant in the sick bay. The medics cultivated all the right people. Gerry Simon, a storekeeper, had the keys to the big ice box and could be depended on to cement his friendship with offerings of fresh eggs, vegetables, or fruit. Larry Castagnola, who worked in the galley, kept the medics happy and healthy with fresh bread and rolls from the bakery.

A sailor could never tell when he might have to appeal to the medics for small favors, and while they had to take care of a sick man, there were subtle ways of making him realize it paid to be polite in the sick bay if one wanted to enjoy being sick. Several of the crew learned this when the ship visited Pearl Harbor. The medics rounded up those who had given them a bad time for one reason or another and invited them down to the sick bay for fungus treatment. Lots of people in the Pacific had fungus, and every medic had his pet treatment for it. The treatment, for these special cases, consisted of liberal applications of Gentian Violet. Aside from what the stuff did to fungus, it turned a man's hands bright purple, and a sailor on liberty in Honolulu, wearing spanking clean whites with purple hands hanging out of the jumper was enough to make timid souls move to the other side of Ala Wai Street. The fact that the medics had painted more than their hands purple was known only to the afflicted sailors, but it was a colorful secret and a mental hazard which considerably reduced their enjoyment of some of Honolulu's less publicized recreational facilities.

Aaron Ward's engine rooms and fire rooms were the special domain of the black gang, and topside ratings seldom ventured down there. An engineer had to walk across the main deck now and then, because it was the only way he could get off the ship, but he was probably happier down in his hot noisy world of pumps and motors, where the lights never went out and a man didn't have to worry about falling overboard on a dark night. The senior chief in the forward engine room was McCaughey, a Boston Irish type who was full of blarney and was naturally called "The Mick." Mick had been in the Navy for eight years, had served in one of the old four-stack destroyers, an attack transport and subchaser. Mick's equal in the after engine room was Mann, a much newer chief, one caught up in wartime emergency service. The other men in the black gang were typical of every black gang in the U. S. Navy and wore typical names like Ski, Wop, Mac, and Smitty. Each of them regarded his own assigned piece of machinery as more or less personal property and the most important in the ship, as indeed it was.

Down in the after engine room, Tony Macukas spent happy hours checking feed water pumps which were his particular charge. Tony loved fine machinery—back home he used to polish his old Hudson with a silk handkerchief—and he loved baseball, fishing, farming, ice skating, and people. First son of Lithuanian parents in Chicago, Tony had worked as a steel roller for Ingersoll Steel, turning out shell casings. Thirteen times he had been deferred, but finally quit the job so he could get into service. Tony was older than most of the men—twenty-eight—and bigger, too. He stood 6'3", weighed 210 pounds, and had once picked up two fresh punks in Chicago and rapped their heads together when they annoyed his sister Beatrice. Serene in the strength of his convictions, Tony got along with the somewhat frowsty black gang, carried a rosary, and read the Bible he kept in his locker. The only reason he was there was to help get the war over with so he could go home again.

In the engine room with Tony was Jim Parker, machinist mate second class, who manned the phones to the "front room," the forward engine room. Jim whiled away the hours with a tin whistle rendition of "Anchors Aweigh," "Beer Barrel Polka," "Yellow Rose of Texas," and all the old Stephen Foster favorites. The only problem was, he couldn't hear, in the noise of the engine room, exactly how he sounded—but when he tried to play in the crew's quarters where he could hear, so could other people. So he usually played it topside, sitting on the mine tracks and watching the water go by.

Jim had watched quite a bit of the ocean go by, both Atlantic and Pacific. He had come from the destroyer *Blakely*, had done convoy duty twice to Africa, been under German air attack in the Med, and had helped pick up survivors of those planes shot down. Jim was the one man, when the ship was commissioned, who didn't have to speculate about what kind of skipper they had—he knew. The skipper of Jim Parker's other ship, the *Blakely*, had also been Bill Sanders. Parker was pleased with his luck; not every sailor was fortunate enough to pick the same skipper twice, and a good one to boot.

In the unlikely event that Ragan and his galley slaves ever fell down on the job of providing adequate nourishment in the mess hall, the black gang down in the "front room" had taken private steps to forestall starvation. Weyrauch was their chief forager; if something edible was not locked up he felt that it belonged to whoever came along first, and that man was usually Herman Weyrauch. Besides the more or less official coffee, they pack-ratted away gallon cans of jam, and probably every bit of fruit cocktail aboard ship. In selected spots under the condenser where it would keep cool they stored chunks of cheese and luncheon meat to help while away the long watches. There was always fresh bread for sandwiches; all one had to do was pop up out of the hatch near the sick bay and into the bakery, where Andrade and Marston turned out fresh hot loaves every night . . . .The Captain liked his hot bread. . . . So did the crew.

Only once had Weyrauch bitten off more than he could chew. One night he managed to unpin the hinges to the ice-cream machine door and get away with five gallons of ice cream. They couldn't hide the stuff, or save it. They had to eat it. In such an emergency, they had to invite in friends who could be trusted to eat their share and keep quiet about it.

There were other ways of evading starvation, and boredom. In the forward emergency diesel room, the GQ station for Cezus and

Lunetta, it was possible to manage both at once. Cezus, the motion-picture operator, who was known sometimes as Cecil B. De Cezus and sometimes as"Jesus"Cezus, would rig the motion-picture projector down there and his friends, including, "Shaky," Kennedy, the hospital corpsman, would provide refreshments. As with "Bull" Weyrauch and the ice cream, they discovered this could be overdone. One night Steve Stefani walked in with a whole crate of eggs which had somehow got themselves lost between the refrigerator room and the galley.

This was manna from heaven—or at least, the makings of hot egg sandwiches. But after half a dozen eggs apiece, they began to taste more like scraps of derelict laundry soap. The second half-dozen apiece positively gagged on the way down. It would be difficult to explain eggs in the diesel room to the inspection party, since no hens had ever been quartered there, so the men silently got up, filled their dungaree pockets with eggs and tiptoed off to their bunks as carefully as if they were walking on egg shells, which they might well have done if the ship rolled. But a bunch of stowaway eggs in a locker presented other problems, chief of which was that as time went on they would grow strong enough to fight their way out into the compartment which already smelled bad enough without a few overripe eggs to add to the bouquet. So, finally, the eggs were carried topside in the dark and heaved overboard for the sharks which followed the ship. Steve and his friends figured for once the sharks got exactly what they had coming to them.

Just forward of CIC, and the radar room, on the starboard side, was the sonar room. That was what it was marked on the ships plans. But what BuShips called a room was only six feet long to start with, and the QCA apparatus filled the forward end of it. In what space was left, the sonarmen, the "ping jockeys," stood their watches. It was well that Chuck Storey, Niwinski, Jaroszewski and the rest of them were fairly friendly, because during general quarters at least four of them piled into the sonar room at once. They were nearly as comfortable as a trunk full of bulldogs, except that the ping jockeys had to go outside to scratch and couldn't even do that until they secured from general quarters.

Chuck Storey had worked as hard or harder than any man in the crew to get where he was this morning. When the news of Pearl Harbor blasted out of a dormitory radio at Yuba City Junior College, Chuck and fifteen of his classmates piled into an old 1926 Dodge and an equally decrepit Buick and went off to enlist in the Navy. The others made it, but Chuck was turned down because of a bad leg gained by playing football. "Can't get in with a leg like that," the doctor told him. "Maybe an operation would fix it up."

So Chuck quit school and went to work in the shipyards at Alameda. For five months he worked and saved his money to pay for an operation. Like the doctor said, the operation worked and his leg was fixed. And then Chuck got drafted into the Army. It looked like he was doomed to spend the war in a foxhole, but at the last moment, as the line moved slowly through the induction center to the ceremony which would make a private out of Chuck Storey, someone came in and announced that half a dozen volunteers were needed for the Navy. So Chuck volunteered out of the Army and a foxhole maybe six feet deep, and into the Navy and a sound room maybe six feet long. But the chow was better and the roof didn't leak. Every time GQ went, and the guns began hammering away at enemy planes, the sound room gang felt a little as if they were going to hell in a market basket. But they all agreed, that from the skipper up on the bridge down to Mr. Rosengren peering over their shoulders, they were going in mighty fine company.

By quarter to eight the morning watch was nearly over for the USS *Aaron Ward*. No planes had appeared in the western sky, no submarines had tried to slink beneath the sea where the five ships patrolled Picket Station 10. Breakfast was over; the last determined chowhound had finally roused the mess cook's eternal battle cry: "There ain't no more!" and had been evicted from the mess hall. Come hell or high water, kamikaze, typhoon, or pay day, the mess cooks had to get the place cleaned up before Doc came around to inspect. Doc Barbeiri was a real nice guy, but when he came around to inspect the mess hall it had better be clean. The way he went at it, one would think he planned on using it for an operating room.

By quarter to eight men had finally become fully awake, whether they had had any sleep the night before or not. There were still a few minutes for a line in a letter, time to open a locker door and sneak a peak at a photograph of a certain girl, time to read a page in a battered six months old copy of *Reader's Digest,* time to sit on the mine track and watch the ocean go rolling by at twelve knots.

By quarter to eight the sun was already high in the sky. Thursday was eight hours old, one third gone. The second section was getting ready to go on watch; when they came off at noon, they would have the day on a downhill pull. In another sixteen hours they could say goodbye to Thursday, 3 May, forever. That was how to handle the routine out on the picket station; you shot the planes down one at a time, you passed the hours one at a time, and you marked the days off one at a time.

The next day would be Friday.

Chapter Three

Forenoon Watch

08-12 Steaming as before. 0800 mustered crew on stations, no absentees. Made daily inspection of magazines and smokeless powder samples, conditions normal.

T. L. Wallace, Lt., U. S. Navy

The working day aboard ship commenced, officially, at 0800. All that had happened between midnight and eight in the morning might be explained away as minor irritations and annoyances due to exigencies of the service. But from eight in the morning to three in the afternoon, if one was not on watch, he was expected to turn to and earn a day's pay, thus being able to face the paymaster with an easy conscience.

But first, before a man could turn to, it was necessary to determine that he was actually on board and ready to turn to. This custom was probably initiated on the Ark, and the procedure has changed little since. The Navy counts its noses at eight in the morning, and so long as a man is present then, all is well. The misguided soul who has the misfortune to fall overboard at one o'clock might likely have seven hours in which to learn to swim before the eight o'clock muster reveals that he is not among those present.

So, at 0800 the PA system hummed into life. A boatswain's call peeped and trilled throughout the ship, and his voice followed it:

"NOW HEAR THIS. ALL DIVISIONS MUSTER ON STATIONS AND REPORT TO THE OFFICER OF THE DECK. TURN TO, TURN TO ON SHIPS WORK."

The day of 3 May was about to officially commence. From forecastle to fantail, petty officers hauled out their little black books and checked off the names of their men.

"Ahrens?"

"Yo!"

"Bahmiller?"

"Yup!"

"Bridgewater?"

"Roger!"

"Casaro?"

"Si!"

"Fitzpatrick?"

"Aye!"

"Marquoit?"

"Yowp!"

"Morgan?"

"Ho!"

No savvy sailor ever sang out with "Present" at a muster. The mustering PO might not have known what he meant. From bridge to bilge, names were checked off, bodies counted, presences accounted for.

"Where's Ski?"

"Still down in the head."

"Anyone see Smitty?"

"He's waiting to see the Doc."

"Where's Pete?"

"He's helping the Chief break out stores."

All present and accounted for. No one missing. Everyone some place. The section PO reported to his leading PO and he reported to the Chief. The chiefs reported to the Division Officers and they reported to the Department Heads. They reported to the OOD and when all reports were in, he sent the bridge messenger down to report to the Captain:

"Mr. Wallace reports all hands present and accounted for, Sir."

Let the day commence!

It commenced just like any other day. The ship's screws doodled a white trail across the face of the sea, and throughout the ship her crew doodled, as it were, another day off the calendar. In the ship's office the yeoman prepared to type more reports; in the galley the cooks prepared to brew more coffee, slice more beef, bake more bread; in the scullery mess cooks cleaned up more cups, trays, and tableware; in the post office the mail orderly cancelled more stamps and told more men he didn't know when the hell there would be more mail; in the radio shack the sparkies copied more pages of messages which might conceivably have been important to someone but certainly had no interest for *Aaron Ward*; in the laundry the button smashers washed some more skivvy shirts, and lost a few more socks; and in the sick bay Crider prepared to issue more sulfa pills to those who believed in such medical marvels.

"Okay, here are your pills. Now here's what I want you to do. I want you to take a different pill every two hours. Now repeat what I told you."

"I'll take a different pill every two hours."

If a man took enough of them that way, it counted for one more day.

Breakfast in the wardroom had long been over, but there was a fresh pot of coffee on tap and an officer could always talk Eddie Gaines out of a bit of hot toast to go with it.

"That was great, Eddie. Make it another coffee and toast, will you? And how's about a little jam with the toast this time?"

With such assistance from Eddie or one of the other mess boys, one could avoid starving to death before lunch time.

The *Aaron Ward* carried twenty-two officers. Twenty of them belonged to the ship. The two "Freddies," Danny Danford and Fred Koehl, had reported on board at Ulithi for temporary duty in Okinawa. They were the Fighter Director Officers; with their crew of enlisted experts they hung over the radar scopes and plot in CIC, handled the combat air patrol planes which orbited above the ship, and vectored them out to tallyho the bandits when they came. The Freddies and their gang were experts in a tough business and they were welcome boarders while the ship was on the picket line.

The incredibly complicated business of coordinating the combat air patrol on all the picket lines and meeting the raids as they came in was handled by the flagship *Eldorado* back in Kerama Retto. On the TBS, *Eldorado* was known as DELEGATE. For this operation, *Aaron Ward* was MONGOOSE. Ships out on the picket stations could always hear DELEGATE, although they might not be able to hear all the other ships on stations around the island, and the men in CIC soon learned to judge the course of battle by the terse words coming from the TBS:

"DELEGATE, THIS IS PAYDIRT. BOGIES BEARING THREE THREE ZERO DISTANCE ONE TEN MILES."

That would mean the raid was coming in over Picket Station 14, some seventy miles out northwest of Point BOLO and if the ships on Station 14 didn't get them, maybe those on 13 or 15 would. If PAYDIRT was lucky enough to have air cover at the time, the planes would be vectored out by PAYDIRT's Freddies, and hopefully the next message would be from a jubilant fighter pilot:

"PAYDIRT BASE THIS IS PAYDIRT THREE . . . . SPLASH ONE VAL."

But if PAYDIRT had no fighters handy, and the enemy got through the anti-aircraft barrage, the story could be very different:

"DELEGATE, THIS IS PAYDIRT. WE ARE ON FIRE AND FLOODING. ONE ENGINE OUT. HEAVY AIR ATTACK CONTINUING."

"PAYDIRT THIS IS DELEGATE. ROBINHOOD AND SPELLBINDER WILL COME TO YOUR ASSISTANCE."

Hold on, PAYDIRT. Keep the guns hot. Keep shooting and waiting. Hope you shoot straight enough, can wait long enough.

With the day safely underway, Bill Sanders could come down to the wardroom and relax for a few minutes. Tom Wallace, the Navigator, was on the bridge, but no matter who was OOD Sanders always made it a point to go below when he could. In so doing, he let the man on the bridge take complete responsibility for the ship, fleeting as such times might be. This was his way of letting the watch on the bridge, and the officers in the wardroom all know that he had complete trust and confidence in the OOD.

Tom Wallace was a tall, soft spoken man with a southern drawl and a degree in law. Tom had been at war ever since the United States was; he had enlisted on 8 December 1941, received his commission later when the Navy found out what they had caught. Even on the bridge, his legal training showed through his lieutenant's bars; he thought things out carefully before making a decision. Tom had spent most of his life in the deep south, in Harrison County, Mississippi, and when the war was over he would go back down south to practice law.

There were other men from the deep south on the *Aaron Ward*. Wallace's Chief Quartermaster, Winston, was from Louisiana; Cornett, Sanford, and Throneberry from Alabama; Sandow from Georgia and Padget from Florida. They were a valiant minority among a shipload of Yankees who insisted that black-eyed peas were really beans. There were still other southerners in the crew; Clark from Louisiana and Eddie Gaines from Arkansas.

Wallace had known many people like Clark and Gaines back home in Mississippi, for they were Negroes. They were messboys —steward's mates who waited on tables in the wardroom. Tom

Wallace had grown up with a natural prejudice toward Negroes, but some of it had rubbed off in the forty days since *Aaron Ward* reached Okinawa. Every man on the ship had a part in the fighting there, and Clark and Gaines did their share down in the stifling hot handling room under the forward 5-inch gun mount. Lieutenant Wallace had discovered that when his life depended on how fast a man could heave ammunition into a hoist, he didn't worry about the color of that man's skin.

0830. "NOW HEAR THIS. ALL GUN CREW MEMBERS NOT ON WATCH REPORT FOR LOADING DRILL." The men had drilled on guns before they ever saw the *Aaron Ward*; they had drilled on the *Aaron Ward*'s guns ever since they reported to the ship; but in Dave Rubel's gunnery department they kept on drilling. They had proved their skill by shooting down nine planes since they reached Okinawa, but skill was not enough. In the gunnery department they drilled.

The gun boss, Lieutenant Dave Rubel, was, like Sanders, Neupert, and Lavrakas, "Annapolis." He graduated from the Naval Academy in 1941, as an Ensign, made Lieutenant (junior grade) in 1942 while attached to the *Gridley,* and before that year was over made Lieutenant while attached to the *Hobby.* There was general agreement among the men in the gunnery department that Lieutenant Rubel was on his way up, and they knew how he was going to do it—drill Dave Rubel's gunnery department. The sailors in the gun crews belonged to the *Aaron Ward,* but the gun crews belonged to Dave Rubel. The men from Annapolis all went through the same school, but they still had different ways of handling men: an officer could set an example and let his men know he expected them to follow; he could ask them to follow; or he could demand that they follow. All three systems produced results. While *Aaron Ward's* gunners decided which system they liked best, they drilled.

The drills over, men went about their routine work again; cleaning guns, repairing telephones, chipping rust, painting—the hundred monotonous bits of work which would be done a thousand times over before they left the ship for some other of the Navy's ten thousand ships where they would do it all over again. There was probably nothing a man could do on a ship which needed doing only once, unless it was jumping overboard some dark night. So the men worked, in crews, in gangs, in pairs, sometimes in solitary concentration.

One man who worked by himself was the watertender, Cooper, who made frequent journeys throughout the ship with flashlight, dirty rag, steel tape measure and a clipboard.

Cooper could be seen, day or night, pursuing his mysterious rounds. He walked across freshly swabbed decks to the dismay of the compartment cleaners. He prowled around in odd corners, disturbing cat naps and crap games. He frequently removed little brass plates from the deck and fished through them with his steel tape measure. He was sometimes accused of leaving oily finger prints on clean bulkheads.

"What's that guy doing peeking down a pipe all the time?" a new man would ask after seeing Cooper make his rounds for a week or so.

"Him? He's the oil king."

A man needed a few days then, to work up to asking what an oil king did. By that time he had already been sent for striped paint, and looked for the mail buoy; he had learned there was no such thing as a bucketful of whistle steam or green oil for the starboard running light. He wasn't going to get caught again. But eventually he found out—the oil king was exactly that; he kept careful measurement of the oil in all the ship's tanks. On his figures the Chief Engineer based his inventory of the ship's fuel supply, and on those figures the Captain based his estimates of how fast the ship could steam for how far.

0900 The ship had steamed over a hundred miles since midnight, but was still right where she had been for three days. Whether she was, or was not, made little difference. The engineers, down in their electric-lighted compartments full of noisy machinery, lived in a timeless, motionless world; there was neither day nor night, nor winter nor summer, in the engine room. The engineers were not concerned about the time of day, the state of the weather, nor where the ship was going; their only job was to keep fires under the boilers, and steam in the turbines, and power on the guns when the gunners wanted it.

But though the deck force was seldom aware of the engineers force, toiling like grimy wizards in the caverns below decks, they could never have hoisted an anchor, taken a bath or perked a pot of coffee without them. The engineers powered the ship, made its water and generated its electricity, all through the magic of superheated, high pressure steam.

The steam was produced in the fire rooms, under the supervision of Lieutenant Clark, with Chief Smith in the forward fire room and Chief Panero in the after fire room making certain that their snipes and watertenders kept the fires hot and let no telltale smoke escape up the stacks. The head wizard, Chief Engineer Don Young, by custom stood his watch in the "front room," the forward engine room, while his assistant, Ensign Paine, rode along in the after engine room.

As befits all engineers, Lieutenant Young sought to be economical where oil, water and power was concerned, sometimes to the annoyance of less understanding folk. His first move, after the ship was commissioned, was to remove the shower heads which drenched a man with a glorious spray and replace them with bits of plugged pipe which emitted just about enough water to dampen a cat. There were no cats in the crew, and everyone else felt this to be an infringement of a valued personal right—singing in the shower. Who could vocalize in a trickle?

In the small room he shared with Doc Barbeiri, Don Young sometimes exercised his ingenuity by figuring out ways in which his engineers could change the fresh air vents and so halt the flow of fresh air to Doc's bunk while increasing it to their bosses bunk. But Doc could be ingenious too. When the air suddenly ceased flowing over Young's bunk, the engineer and his men spent several days in spirited discussion of this failure before they discovered that Doc Barbeiri had jammed a bunch of old socks into the engineer's own air vent.

Ingenuity could be exercised in other ways and the Chief Engineer knew them. The Captain was no great bridge player, but he enjoyed a fast game of cribbage. Every night at sea, when the ship secured from evening GQ, the same routine was performed.

"Feel like a game of cribbage, Don?" the Skipper would ask.

"I think I feel lucky tonight, Sir."

They always played three games. Don Young always let the Captain win the second game.

0930. Made daily inspection of magazines and smokeless powder samples, conditions normal.

Since the days of John Paul Jones, gunners and gunner's mates had been inspecting the Navy's magazines and powder samples and finding conditions normal. That was the only way they wanted to find conditions in the magazines. The *Aaron Ward*'s magazines, deep in the ship under the crew compartments, were filled with tons of high explosives, enough to blast her out of the water in pieces so small they would hardly splash when they came down. This was not an entirely remote possibility; less than six months earlier the *Mount Hood,* loaded with ammunition, had blown up in the Admiralty Islands—the ship and her crew had absolutely disappeared in one tremendous flash.

The powder cans lay in their racks in long neat rows, higher than a man's head, silent and inert, hundreds and hundreds of them, silent as mummies, yet each of them held a raging giant, waiting for the tiny spark which would arouse them instantly in tremendous frenzies of fiery destruction.

Entering the magazines was a matter of strict ritual governed by Navy Regulations, the Bureau of Ordnance Manual, and carefully posted Safety Precautions. It had been highlighted for the men by a warning from a tough old chief at gunnery school: "You men goof off in the magazines just once, by God, and it'll be the last time you ever do." That, and the Navy's favorite saying on the same subject: "A man who lights a match in the magazines can be put on report for leaving the ship without permission."

So, before entering the magazine where the god of fire lay sleeping, the gunner's mates cleansed themselves of any likelihood of offending him. They left their matches and lighters outside, were careful not to wear shoes with heel plates and carried nothing which might strike a spark. Their gods slept but lightly. Then, like nurses with a fevered patient, they recorded the temperature, maximum and minimum, of each magazine, and tiptoed out. The giants still slept, the heat had not yet disturbed their dreams. Conditions normal.

But powder made up only part of *Aaron Ward*'s punch. A charge of powder could be, and in the tumult and excitement of battle sometimes was, fired out of a gun with no projectile ahead of it. This was called "firing a bale of hay," and was just about as damaging to the enemy. Powder merely made fire and smoke. The message was carried by the projectile, hurled out of the gun at eight hundred miles an hour, to slam down like one of Jove's thunderbolts on an enemy miles across the ocean: *This one's from Thostensen, Hejhall, Rubel and me.*

Some of the projectiles fired by *Aaron Ward's* 5-inch guns were capable of a trick never dreamed of by either Jove or the Japanese. These were VT-fuzed, radio-proximity shells, a newer weapon than radar, and a secret known to far fewer people. Each VT shell carried a miniature radio set in its nose which was "lit off" when the gun spat it out. VT projectiles did not have to hit an enemy aircraft; if they came close enough to suit the little electronic wizard riding in their nose, the radio exploded the shell and one more kamikaze came flaming down.

The powder, the projectiles, the amunition hoists, the guns, gun mounts, and the gunner's mates and their training were the primary responsibility of Dave Rubel, the gun boss, and his assistants, Lefty Lavrakas, George Cathcart, and "Fergie" Ferguson. The mines, which *Aaron Ward* didn't carry, the Mine Control Officer, Gunner

Siler, and the minemen, whose job it was to lay the mines *Aaron Ward* didn't have, also belonged to the gunnery department. The captain might not see the inside of a gun mount or a magazine from one week to the next. But even as some gunner told John Paul Jones in *Bon Homme Richard,* so tradition demanded that some gunner tell Bill Sanders in the *Aaron Ward* the same thing. Whether the word came by McClure, Quimette, Gervais or the bridge messenger, it was always the same. The man pulled off his white cap, rapped on the door, stepped into cabin or wardroom and said "Gunnery Officer reports magazines and smokeless powder samples inspected, Sir. Conditions normal."

"Very well," Sanders replied.

That takes care of one more piece of Thursday. Another cup of coffee, anyone?

How many kamikazes had come down by that time around Okinawa, no one could say for certain, but the score must have run into the hundreds. *Aaron Ward* had not yet accounted for what the gunners considered to be their fair share, but of course, they had been out of the battle area for nearly three weeks when they went down to Guam and Saipan for repairs on the sound dome.

Two big raids had hit Okinawa in that time, and with the small nuisance raids which came almost every day, the kamikazes had racked up a sizable score of their own. The list of casualties had grown almost daily; Kerama Retto was always filled with shot up, burned out, torn-apart ships waiting for repairs.

9 APRIL . . . . GREGORY DAMAGED BY SUICIDE PLANE . . . . STERETT DAMAGED BY SUICIDE PLANE . . . .
11 APRIL . . . . ENTERPRISE HIT BY SUICIDE PLANE . . . .
ESSEX HIT BY DIVE BOMBER . . . . BULLARD, KIDD, SAMUEL S. MILES, ALL HIT BY SUICIDE PLANES . . . . HANK AND MANLOVE DAMAGED BY STRAFING.

Even when one wasn't in on the fight, the radio spread the news far and wide. The TBS ordinarily gave only sight line communications, but sometimes skip effect gave the transmissions unusual range. Aylworth had to smile to himself the night he heard DELEGATE trying to maintain circuit discipline during a raid.

"DELEGATE, THIS IS FROGMOUTH. OVER." came the urgent voice from the TBS.

But DELEGATE was busy then and refused to answer. So again FROGMOUTH went on the air:

"DELEGATE, I SAY AGAIN, THIS IS FROGMOUTH. OVER."

"FROGMOUTH, THIS IS DELEGATE! UNLESS YOU HAVE IMPORTANT TRANSMISSION, GET OFF THE AIR."

"DELEGATE, THIS IS FROGMOUTH. WE THINK IT IS IMPORTANT. WE JUST HAD A BOMB HIT ON OUR FANTAIL."

Such things didn't make headlines in stateside papers, but they were considered highly important by FROGMOUTH, JELLYBEAN, BALDERDASH and all the other ships around Okinawa who happened to be right where a bomb or a kamikaze came down. The point of view made a big difference, and the closer one was to point of impact, the bigger the difference.

The *Aaron Ward*'s wardroom was the only place on the ship big enough for more than three officers at the same time, except for the bridge and CIC, where they were expected to attend strictly to business. The tiny cubicles where they slept, usually three to a room, were politely called staterooms, but they would have induced claustrophobia in even a medium sized dog. Jammed as they were with clothing, helmets, life jackets, books, manuals, recreational gear, baskets of official correspondence marked "Pending," inventory lists, custody chits, foul weather gear, and pictures of wives and mothers or girls who were likely prospects, the staterooms more nearly resembled roomettes on the Santa Fe "Lark." Fortunately, one officer was always on watch, and with the second in his bunk, there was plenty of room for the third to turn around. The Navy planned on everything.

When Bob McKay brought his mother aboard after the ship was commissioned, she took one worried look into the oversize kennel he shared with two other officers, and decided he wouldn't like living in there. "You can learn to like anything—even hanging, if you hang long enough," said Bob.

The Skipper met his officers in the wardroom, for meals, and sometimes for a friendly cup of coffee or a bit of cribbage, but from the time the ship left port until she returned he would never see them all at once. Officers were always on watch, as were the men; in engine rooms, on the bridge, in CIC, in communications, and in gunnery control. It was possible to eat, sleep, work, and fight within a hundred feet of each other and yet not meet for a couple of days at a time. So the wardroom was dining room, club room, working space for inventory and court martial boards, social and information center, the place where they censored the crew's mail; the place to talk over results of last night's attack, and the place to check the progress of the war in Europe, and see what Tokyo Rose had said lately.

The one woman everyone on the ship knew by her voice, aside from Eleanor Roosevelt and perhaps Kate Smith, was Tokyo Rose. The ship had three broadcast receivers, shielded to prevent their regenerating a signal which might lead an enemy submarine to cut short their enjoyment of some Armed Forces Radio rebroadcast of the Hit Parade, and Tokyo Rose came in loud and clear on all of them. Everyone listened to Rose, in wardroom, CPO quarters, and crew mess.

Sometimes the music wasn't too bad. Even when she said "I will now play the American national anthem," and then gave them "Old Black Joe," no one minded too much. At least they knew the words and music to that. But her claims of damage done by the Imperial Japanese Navy often left the crew slightly hysterical with laughter. The Japanese Fleet was always sinking the U. S. Navy, according to Rose, but her skeptical Yankee listeners noted that each time the U. S. Navy got sunk it got sunk a little closer to Tokyo.

In explaining the loss of Iwo Jima, Rose said ". . . . even the enemy must have respect and admiration for those heroes who fought so bravely against such overwhelming odds and who finally succumbed to the lack of drinking water." But that wasn't the way *Aaron Ward* sailors heard it.

As the fleet began to pound Okinawa, Rose told her listeners of American "ships fleeing to the southward being pursued by a few Japanese fighters." But they must have come back, because she again warned this "little" bunch of ships to beware "for tomorrow they will be annihilated."

Rosie's bushido boys had got a few of the invasion fleet, that was a grim fact. But it was also a fact that in the 160 years the U. S. Navy had been sailing the seas, her people had managed, through shipwreck, fire, explosion, poor navigation and collision, to sink more ships of their own by accident than the Japanese had done on purpose.

It was considerably easier to sink a ship by accident than one might suppose. Even the *Aaron Ward* had come close, as Tom Wallace remembered. The first time he had the deck when the new ship was timidly feeling her way around San Pedro harbor, a tugboat which possibly used more steam in its whistle than in its engine ran afoul of the ship. Wallace had watched the tug bustle past on the starboard side and then, before he realized what was happening, had seen it turn hard left and cut directly under the ship's bow.

"All engines back full!" Tom ordered, but by that time the ship had hit the tug. And by that time Captain Sanders spoke quietly to Wallace.

"I relieve you, Sir." By these words he took the ship and all responsibility for what she might have done, out of Wallace's hands.

Then he turned to the quartermaster and said "Let the log show that the Captain had the conn."

Mr. Wallace knew that Captains always got credit when things went well. Here was one who stood ready to take the blame when they didn't. When Sanders assumed command of the ship, he took everything that went with command, whether it was for better or for worse.

The Commanding Officer of a ship is so ordered by the Navy Department. His authority to command is vested in him by Navy Regulations, and his title of Captain, no matter what his rank, carries the dignity of centuries of tradition. By Navy Regulations the captain commands the obedience of his crew. By the dignity of his office he insures their respect. But all the regulations and gold braid in the Pacific Fleet cannot enforce a sailor's devotion. This, each officer in command must earn on his own. The difference between obedience and devotion may be slight to a landlubber, but it is there, and a sailor can underline it subtly by emphasizing either the last or first words of "Aye, aye, Sir!"

There was never any question among *Aaron Ward* sailors as to what kind of captain they had. If they weren't smart enough to see for themselves, when they first met ship and captain back in Terminal Island, the CPOs got the word to them soon enough. In the Navy, the CPO's always have the word. A little bit grayer than they care to admit, a little bit more potbellied than they used to be, a little bit more tattooed than they really intended, the chiefs are top men on the enlisted totem pole. They left a lot of number ten tracks on the dress jumpers of other sailors while they were getting there. And by the same token, a lot of senior captains and admirals in the Navy climbed the frames of a lot of chiefs getting where they are. So the chiefs are well experienced, and when they met the new Skipper and found him a quiet, pleasant officer who didn't talk a whole lot they immediately classified him: "This new Captain, he ain't going to put out a lot of crap to you guys." But they also found out that he knew damn' near as much about their job—any of their jobs—as they did. The rest of the evaluation was: "And he ain't going to take none of it off'n you guys, either."

The Commanding Officer of the *Aaron Ward* had nearly as much salt water under him as any old chief. He was a destroyer officer—a "tin can sailor," from way back in the "four-piper Navy." In five destroyers, *Broome, Truxtun, Moffett, Corry, Blakely,* he had trained up from gunnery officer to commanding officer. A tour of duty in the old sub tender *Holland* didn't really count for much, among destroyer men; she used to swing around the buoy in San Diego so long that she was rumored to have gone aground on the potato peelings and beef bones the cooks threw overboard.

That the Skipper had put in his first sea duty on the "Prune Barge"—the old battle wagon *California*—was actually no disgrace because an ensign had to go to sea on something.

Chief McCaughey had a friend who had a friend who had known about Sanders over in the Atlantic, when he was Skipper of USS *Blakely* .... "Wild Bill, they called him!" The boys down in the black gang were not prone to repeat, if they had ever heard it, John Paul Jones's "Give me a fast ship, for I intend to go in harm's way," but they knew they had a fast ship and there was very little doubt in their minds that in harm's way was the only way they were going. The way to go, then, was with an old tin can sailor like "Wild Bill" at the conn .... *Gangway, Tojo, here we come.*

When the ship had returned to Okinawa from Guam nearly two weeks earlier, they had not felt quite so confident. The Japanese had sent in their second big raid, at the same time FDR died, and for two days the kamikazes gave the fleet a working over it remembered. The casualty list for 12 April made a small fleet in itself:

> BATTLESHIP IDAHO DAMAGED BY SUICIDE PLANE ....
> BATTLESHIP TENNESSEE DAMAGED BY SUICIDE PLANE
> .... DESTROYERS PURDY, ZELLARS, CASSIN YOUNG HIT
> BY SUICIDE PLANES .... DESTROYER ESCORTS RIDDLE,
> RALL, WALTER C. WANN, WHITEHURST HIT BY SUICIDE
> PLANES .... MINECRAFT LINDSEY, JEFFERS, GLADIATOR
> HIT BY SUICIDE PLANES .... DESTROYER STANLEY HIT
> BY PILOTED BOMB.

All during the hectic fall and winter of 1944, as the new *Aaron Ward* "shook down" along the Southern California coast, the crew was a little surprised to learn that their new Skipper, who wore plenty of gold braid, was also able to think like a "white hat." The explanation was simple; while most of them were still learning to tie their shoes, their skipper had been a white hat. There is no better training for reaching the top of the heap than to start at the bottom, and that was where William H. Sanders, Jr. started—Apprentice Seaman, U. S. Navy.

Bill Sanders was a little different in one other way, too. Most of the Navy's men come from inland; from the plains and prairies, corn fields and cotton fields, mills and mines, shops and shebangs, from Tacoma to Tampa. Their reasons are varied, perhaps not so much influenced by Melville, Masefield, and Conrad as by an older boy down the street back home who disappeared, only to return in a couple of years with interesting facts about Hawaii, Panama, or Hong Kong certainly not mentioned in any geography books they ever read. But Bill Sanders had grown up in San Diego, within sight of the ocean. He had heard the tin cans testing whistles and sirens every Monday morning—yeep—yeeeep—yeeeeeep—Boooo-oooo—as they got underway to disappear into the offshore haze beyond Point Loma, and knew how the tide of white hats surged up from the Fifth Street landing, the Sante Fe Dock, and Broadway Pier when the Fleet came back in. On the whole, sailors were not highly regarded as civic assets in San Diego in those days—and it must be admitted that on any given day, they were probably more numerous at Moosio's Bar than they were at the Fine Arts Museum. But, as the song went, everyone to his own liking. So went the sailors.

Young Bill Sanders graduated from San Diego High School in 1925 and went down town and signed an agreement with the U. S. Navy, whereby he obligated himself to work twenty-four hours a day or less if the situation permitted, and the Navy agreed to pay him twenty-one dollars a month and even more if he proved himself worth it. The next thing he knew he was a recruit, an apprentice seaman, at the Naval Training Center across the bay.

There is one slight advantage to being an apprentice seaman in the Navy. Advancement is open in all directions. In the Navy an apprentice seaman ranks with, but after, a swab. Almost anywhere a swab goes, an apprentice seaman is right behind it. In those days recruit training was not the sophisticated process it became in World War II, when men were classified as to their capabilities, interviewed as to their incentives, and questioned extensively as to their psychological processes. "Boots" in 1925 were oriented in their naval careers by salty old sixteen-year chiefs who would not have believed a recruit, or anyone else, had any of those things. They encouraged their young charges to keep their clothes clean, keep their rifles clean, and keep their noses clean. The chiefs were not well read, but they could use moving language, and heavy boots on those not sufficiently moved otherwise. The chiefs were not much on educational methods, but they certainly encouraged an apprentice seaman to become something else with great dispatch. One year later, Bill Sanders was on his way to the Naval Academy at Annapolis.

Being a plebe at Annapolis is probably only slightly less painful than being a boot in San Diego. There aren't so many tough old sixteen-year chiefs around, but it is surprising how tough an upper classman can be. After four years in the hallowed halls of Bancroft Hall a young man departs with the certain knowledge that textbooks and classrooms are not the only source of an education. And the bright ensign stripes do not necessarily mean he has finished his education. On the other hand, they are merely his badge of admission to the Fleet, and another twenty or thirty years of it.

As a shiny new one-striper, Sanders went back to his native California, and to duty with his state's cherished namesake, the "Prune Barge." In the battleship *California* he commenced learning the specialty which was to prove most worthwhile many years later at Okinawa—gunnery. On weekends he dusted down the highway from Long Beach to San Diego in his old Pierce Arrow—maintaining a sharp lookout for the traffic cop who was wont to hide behind a signboard in San Clemente—to visit his family and see his old home town. The old home town, of course, had changed, as home towns always do. To Ensign Sanders, USNA, class of 1930, the streets were not quite so wide, the buildings not quite so tall, as they had been to Bill Sanders, SDHS, class of 1925. And being a battleship sailor, the old four-stackers down in the bay didn't look so big as they used to, either. But the four-stackers had as much power as a battle wagon and could certainly outrun them. They were great for someone who liked a fast ship and who liked to go a-shooting. Two years later Sanders moved down to San Diego as Gunnery Officer of the USS *Broome*. She was a rootin', tootin', shootin' old four-piper and she taught Bill Sanders a lot of things he hadn't known. She was a pleasant change from riding around on the Prune Barge.

There were other pleasing changes in San Diego, for a bright-eyed young ensign. That girl, for instance, who lived half a block down the street from his family home. When Bill left for the Naval Academy, if he noticed her at all, she would probably have been all teeth. When he came home four years later as a new Ensign, that same girl—Betty Jones, her name was—had become all legs. But the next two years had considerably improved things, and Bill Sanders noted that now Miss Jones was all right. A short time later —29 October 1933, they became engaged. A methodical man, Bill Sanders finally found a use for the dashboard clock in his Pierce Arrow, which had lost all interest in the passing of time many months before. He set the hands permanently at 10:29 to commemorate the date. A few months later he brought the new Mrs. Sanders back from Yuma, to a furnished apartment for forty dollars a month on Olive Street. The wardroom officers of the USS *Broome* gave her a new name too—"Mrs. Guns."

Guns were grim, silent shapes to a girl visiting a destroyer in San Diego Bay in 1934, but they meant a career, and eventual command to her husband. Now, ten years later, on the picket line off Okinawa, they meant more than that to every man on the ship. They meant the difference between going home or not going home.

"Hey, gunner! You spend more time with that gun than you did with your old lady" .... "Bet your boots! I kept her from being an old maid, but only this gun will keep her from being a widow. That would be to my advantage, too, you know" . . . . "Yeah. You're right. The only guys who enjoy widows are other guys. Gunner, pat that gun for me too."

Lefteris Lavrakas, the assistant gun boss, was the fourth of the Annapolis men in the wardroom. Lefty had come to the *Aaron Ward* from the *Eberle,* in which he had seen action in the Med and North Africa, and like Rubel, he lived for his gunners and his guns. Lefty had practically hand-raised the gun crews; he had seen them selected in Norfolk, seen them training at Dam Neck, Virginia, and later at Point Montara in California, and had made certain they all spent a week at sea in the gunnery-training destroyer *Foote* before they ever touched an *Aaron Ward* gun.

Lefty was in the Navy only because he hadn't made the Army. He had tried hard enough to make West Point, but the entrance examination threw him. In Lefty's family, that just about wrote off college—the Ivy League was out of the grasp of the young son of a Greek immigrant. But then someone mentioned that Annapolis was also looking for officer material. Either way, West Point or Annapolis, the gods intended that Lavrakas would get into the fight at Okinawa, and here he was.

Fighting the Navy way was cleaner, more detached, much less personal in the final moments. In their big steel box of tricks the Navy called a Mark 37 Director, the director crew—Rubel, Lavrakas, and the fire controlmen Kroll, Despin, and Longlois—conjured with ranges and speeds, trajectories and target angles, to solve complex mathematical problems which sent the 5-inch projectiles crashing through the night to their targets.

Possibly the gods had other things in mind for this handsome young Greek in Navy khakis, once Okinawa was over. In his room Lefty had three letters from Billye Charleyville, a girl he had met in Long Beach just before the ship was commissioned. The letters, received some two weeks earlier in Guam, had led Lefty to devote considerable time to thoughts of Miss Charleyville. This, as the other young bachelors in the wardroom would have agreed, could be most pleasant, for they had all met the young lady. But Lefty had seen her first; and being a man of action, he acted.

Action had definitely been indicated that day Lavrakas rode an elevator down to the ground floor of a hotel in Long Beach. A real cute blonde got on at the sixth floor. On the way down Lavrakas introduced himself, learned that she was Billye Charleyville, mentioned that his ship was about to be commissioned in San Pedro, found out that she had never seen a ship commissioned, and gallantly offered to remedy this lack in her experience by inviting her to see his ship commissioned. On the ground floor Miss Charleyville said she'd love to.

The Navy needs men who can quickly analyze a situation, formulate a logical plan of operation, and implement its execution. Lieutenant Lefteris Lavrakas had qualified.

1030 All quiet on the bridge. The signalmen and quartermasters had swept and swabbed the decks where no dust ever came, tidied up the chart desk, lit off another pot of coffee. Winston, the Chief, had worked over the chart and marked another neat "0800 posit" to show where the little gray bug named *Aaron Ward* had been as the day officially began on that piece of ocean named RPS 10.

On the "remarks" page of the log book, Thorpe noted the progress the bug made crawling across the page for 3 May 1945. The gyro repeater clicked as the bow of the ship swung on a turn, and the signal halliards slapped as she rolled on the gentle swells. Above them the radar antenna whirled endlessly, peering far out across the horizon, watching, waiting. Everywhere on the ship, men waited; on the guns, in the engine rooms, on the main power panels, in CIC, in the sound room, in the director. They were busy, oiling breech block mechanisms; checking feed water temperatures; watching voltage fluctuations; studying every faint blip on the SC scope; listening to the monotonous "P-ING . . . . p-ing" of the sonar; testing out the automatic director control of the guns; but they were being busy to pass the time and help the clock around. What they were really doing was waiting, waiting for someone in CIC to sing out "BOGIES! BEARING 235, DISTANCE 45 MILES" and the almost automatic order from the bridge which would follow: "GENERAL QUARTERS! ALL HANDS GENERAL QUARTERS!"

But still the morning was quiet. Slowly the shadows on the deck grew shorter; slowly the ships wheeled around Picket Station 10; slowly the hands of the clock counted off the remaining minutes of Thursday. The ship and her men had come 7,000 miles from home, to claim one small piece of ocean as their own, and wait. If the enemy did not come, their waiting was still not in vain. If he did come, they were ready.

At Okinawa, the ships were always ready. And the enemy seldom failed to oblige by giving them something to shoot at. Ammunition was used up by the shipload; tracers filled the skies with thousands of angry red streaks for every flaming golden plane to come down. Somewhere around the picket line, off Hagushi, or in Kerama Retto, the guns bellowed almost every morning and every evening as the kamikazes bored in and the long list of damaged ships grew longer:

13 APRIL CONOLLY DAMAGED BY SUICIDE PLANE
14 APRIL NEW YORK, SIGSBEE, DASHIELL, HUNT DAMAGED BY SUICIDE PLANE
15 APRIL WILSON, LAFFY, TALUGA DAMAGED BY SUICIDE PLANE . . . . YMS 331 HIT BY SUICIDE BOAT
16 APRIL PRINGLE SUNK BY SUICIDE PLANE . . . . INTREPID DAMAGED, MISSOURI DAMAGED; BRYANT, BOWERS, HOBSON, HARDING DAMAGED BY SUICIDE PLANE . . . . MINESWEEPER CHAMPLIN HIT BY BOMBER
17 APRIL BENHAM HIT BY SUICIDE PLANE

Aaron Ward was rolling up from Guam, on 22 April, heading back into the battle zone, when the fleet took another pounding, and both sides lost.

SWALLOW SUNK BY SUICIDE PLANE . . . . HUDSON, WADSWORTH, ISHERWOOD, SHEA, RANSOM, GLADIATOR DAMAGED BY SUICIDE PLANES

There was no end to them. No matter how many were knocked down, more came the next time. It was like trying to swat hornets with a broom. The planes seemed no bigger than a hornet, even when they were within gun range; only in the last moments of their dive did they become big and fearsome. But their targets were a city block long and it was almost impossible for a determined pilot to miss. The ships had to knock them down when they were way out.

So, now, at 1100, men watched the radar screens as they had every minute since the day began, as they would every minute until the day ended, as they would so long as the battle went on. The idea was, get them first. *Mark the day on the calendar: today we got them first.*

Elsewhere on the ship, men marked the day in other ways. Up on Mount 42, the twin 40mm just aft of the port bridge wing, gunner's mate Larson fussed around his gleaming charge and remembered that he had been in the Navy exactly two years that day. Chuck Willand had the day marked on his own little private calendar because it was his mother's birthday. Chief Shelley had the date marked because, if he got through this one and one more, he would have reached the day on which he and Mary had been married exactly four months.

For many men the days had ceased to differ, one from another. They knew this was 3 May only because the Plan of the Day, posted on the crew's bulletin board, said it was. But aside from the date at the top, the Plan of the Day was like any other. It was only another day in which to stand another watch, play another game of pinochle, lose another buck at poker, read another book, sneak another half-hour in the sack, write another letter home. Tony Macukas took his letter up to Blunk's post office, dropped it in the slot. He started it the day before, to his sister Beatrice, who had scolded him for not writing to his mother more often "even though she can't understand it." Now Tony had scolded back, as nearly as he ever scolded anyone: "You wouldn't bawl me out for not writing if you knew what hell we're going through."

In his room he shared with Don Young, Doc Barbeiri relaxed after breakfast, confident that Crider would give the right pills to the right man, and read a bit more in *War and Peace*. Throughout the ship, men tidied up the results of wind and wave for the last two days, and watched the sky which had been filled with rain. The weather had been miserable.

But it was a nice day by now, a gentle wind moved out of the northeast at fourteen knots, there were a few scattered clouds at 10,000 feet, the sun was warm and the sea grew calm. For pessimists it was a bad day—clear skies meant Japanese air attack. For the optimists it was a good day—now they could see 'em coming. All around Okinawa, on sixteen different picket stations, radar probed beyond the horizon and anxious eyes scanned the sky. The Nippers hadn't bunged up anyone on the picket line since Monday. You could damn' well bet your boots they were coming.

Thursday, 3 May, was well along by now. For the optimists, it meant they were one day nearer home again. For the pessimists, it meant just one more day since they had left.

Back home that day, back where a man's heart and hope was, Thursday was quite a different matter. All that week the stateside papers rushed out one edition after another and headlines grew bigger and blacker as the war in Europe ground to a spectacular finish. HITLER DIES IN BERLIN said the *Rocky Mountain News* for Wednesday. CITY OF HAMBURG SURRENDERS said the *Sioux City Journal*. If there was a war going on in the Pacific that week, the wire services failed to mention it.

But there was other interesting news on the home front: The *Annapolis Evening Capitol* reported from Washington that golf balls would soon be produced for civilian use; the *Seattle Times* listed four cocker spaniels as missing; and in Sioux City, Iowa, a member of the police force was sued for eating seventy-five T-bone steaks at Mook's Cafe, and failing to pay for them. In Washington, a bill was introduced in Congress giving twenty dollars a week to veterans who served ninety days. There was no clause in it defining veterans as only those men who had spent the ninety days at Guadalcanal, Leyte, Anzio, or Okinawa.

76

The headlines ground out big and black at home, but by the time they had gone out on the Fleet broadcast circuits, been picked out of the air by Mr. Woodside's sparkies in the radio shack, whacked onto a stencil and run through the mimeograph machine by Harry Dolliver, they were not nearly so impressive. Nevertheless, the men read the press news avidly. They had no worry about the war in the Pacific. The Navy was there. Nimitz and Halsey and Spruance were there; Halsted and Tiwald and Kelly were there; and while the Japanese might be obstinate they were not invincible.

The war in Europe was more interesting than the one they were fighting in Okinawa, possibly because newspaper correspondents went along with the troops and filed reams of copy every time they captured another dairy barn full of Germans. There was a big chart on the wardroom bulkhead and the progress of the First, Second, and Third Armies was plotted as carefully as if the place were a command post and they expected Eisenhower to drop in. Hitler was dead, Mussolini was dead, Berlin was about to surrender. But where were the headlines about the war on the picket line? The corre-spondents usually got no nearer to Okinawa than Guam and what news they got from Okinawa usually concerned the Tenth Army. There were no press releases handed out on the picket lines.

"LOG ROOM, BRIDGE. WE HAVE A MESSAGE FROM THE LITTLE: DO YOU WISH TO TRADE MOVIES."

"BRIDGE, LOG ROOM. HOW'S TO TELL THOSE CHAR-ACTERS OVER THERE THE LAST MOVIES THEY SWAPPED TO US WE SAW THREE TIMES ALREADY."

Bridge and cribbage were the principal wardroom recreations. Karl Neupert, Don Young, Hal Halstead, Doc Barbeiri and Bob McKay were the high point bridge players. McKay was good at the game, but Karl Neupert was far better. It was Doc's firm conviction that no matter who played, or how they played, eventually Karl Neu-pert would win. The crew called him "The Brain" with good reason. Two weeks after the ship was in commission, he knew the name, rank, and home town of every man on board. Karl knew the ships organization and damage control bill better than Biesmeyer, the

First Lieutenant. He knew the myriad details of the voluminous operation order on the invasion of Okinawa. And to the continual dismay of the yeomen, he knew regulations, instructions, and directives better than they did, quoting page and paragraph numbers while they were trying to remember chapter numbers.

The crew could explain a part of this. They had heard that Lieutenant Commander Karl Neupert was top man in his class at Annapolis in 1933, and they knew a man needed plenty of savvy to top a class at Annapolis. Fowers, the Exec's yeoman, could tell them more. He knew that the Exec worked longer hours than any other officer or man on the ship, grinding through reports and paper work when other people slept at sea, when others were enjoying themselves ashore in port. A few of the more astute officers knew the rest of Neupert's secret: in his vocabulary there was only one way to express performance of duty and that was "outstanding." That a man did the best he could was not enough for Neupert; he had to strive to outdo himself.

The Executive Officer of a ship has the toughest job there is afloat. The Captain holds him responsible for the efficiency of the departments, the proficiency of the men, the battle readiness of the ship, the overall performance of the command, and anything that goes wrong up or down the line. The junior officers and the crew believe him to be responsible for inspections, too many watches, too little liberty, too much work and not enough time off, bad chow, late pay, and anything else that goes wrong up or down the line. A captain can afford to be friendly with the crew because he is the captain. An executive officer must avoid exactly that, if he is to be a successful executive officer. This is easy to do, if one is willing to be firm, impartial, and yet as considerate as regulations permit. The Exec could do this for twenty hours every day.

"Say, when we was in San Diego, did you hear what the Exec did, for Chris' sake? Joe put in a chit for leave 'cause his old lady died, and the Exec wouldn't let him go home. What a one way guy!"

The Exec had to make the decision Joe was not yet able to make for himself. Wartime travel was uncertain, Joe could not have crossed the country to get home in time for a funeral, his family urgently needed the money Joe would have spent in a frantic sentimental journey which could in no way alleviate the sorrow. So Joe stayed on board, bitter about the Exec, and the Exec stayed on board, saddled with the trials and tribulations of three hundred men who could not understand that Karl Neupert had problems of his own.

"You think that Exec's one way? Let me tell you about when we was in Pedro. Old Hank went to the Exec and asked if he could go home while his wife had a baby, and the Exec said no. Don't he have any feelin's?"

The Exec had feelings, but he kept them to himself. He denied old Hank only the same privilege he denied himself. Only Fowers, the yeoman, knew that the Exec's wife, Eleanor, was also about to have a baby, and that the Exec would not be able to go home to be with her. In fact, the Exec had purposely left his family up in Oregon, so that all the time the ship was going into commission and shaking down in California, he could devote full time to his job. A good Exec could work twenty-four hours a day, and Karl Neupert very nearly won that qualification.

So the men complained that the Exec was too rigid, bragged about his store of information, were impressed by his devotion to duty, and were amazed by his relentless drive. To them, he was an enigma. How could a number one man at Annapolis resign his commission after only nine months in the cruisers *Chester* and *Houston* and go civilian? Maybe Karl Neupert had done all right in business in Portland, Oregon. Sure, he had come in again when war threatened. For men who had to grind to make the petty officer exams, for those who had had to sweat through enough credits to win a degree, it was difficult to understand how one could give up what was obviously a head start on wearing admiral's stars.

They knew he already had orders for command, and would be sorry to see him go. The Navy always grabbed off the smart ones. In mess hall and wardroom, there was little doubt that Neupert was the most brilliant man in the Fleet, and that he could be Chief of Naval Operations if he stayed with it.

1115. Pipe Sweepers. Mess gear. The PA system hummed, the duty boatswain's mate stepped to the bridge mike, and his pipe shrilled throughout the ship:

"NOW HEAR THIS. SWEEPERS START YOUR BROOMS. CLEAN-SWEEP DOWN FORE AND AFT."

The deck force, under the direction of Lieutenant Biesmeyer and the personal supervision of Chief Shelley and his section POs, got out their brooms and made a clean sweep-down fore and aft. There wasn't any dirt to sweep up; the ship hadn't been near enough to land for days to collect even a bit of dust, but the decks were swept again anyhow. The deck forces' futile attempt to find dirt where there was none had a flavor about it of Alice in Wonderland.

" 'If seven maids with seven mops swept it for a half a year,

Do you suppose,' the Walrus said, 'that they could get it clear?'

'I doubt it,' said the Carpenter, and shed a bitter tear . . . .''

The deck force had been sweeping *Aaron Ward*'s decks for nearly half a year and the decks were always clean. But they kept on sweeping.

Technically, now, the day was half over. There still remained the formalities of winding the chronometers, taking the noon position, and eating dinner, but the traditional routine of the Navy would take care of all this in due order. The forenoon sweep-down had been made. The forenoon watch would soon be over. Lieutenant Biesmeyer and the men who had stood the mid watch would soon be going to their stations for the afternoon watch. The vast wheel of the day was slowly turning past, the lesser smaller wheels within the ship were turning in their own accepted time, the hours and minutes were passing. Tuesday and Wednesday on Picket Station 10 had been safely scratched off the calendar. Thursday was on the way. No strain.

Throughout the ship men still carried on the routine. In the radio shack, receivers chirped and peeped as men copied incoming traffic.

In the coding room, Mr. McKay, the Supply Officer, prepared to decode another radio message. The coding watch was not properly a duty of the Supply Officer, but Bob McKay had volunteered for it, and spent long hot hours in the tiny room when he might have been in his bunk in his own room. Bob McKay was willing, ambitious, friendly, helpful, and very often sick as a cat in a washing machine. Earlier that week Sanders had talked with McKay about his chronic seasickness and suggested that he would be glad to recommend him for shore duty.

"No, Sir, Captain," said Bob. "I'll stay here."

So here he was. Bob took the radio message, checked the external indicators, set up the ECM machine, and typed it out in English; a message which began with EWOID JUSWI BNPMK WEJSN might well read "Report amount dehydrated potatoes consumed . . . ." And if it did, Mr. McKay, as Supply Officer, would have to prepare the report.

Still young, still inexperienced, Bob McKay was probably the smartest man on the ship next to the Executive Officer. A highly popular man at USC, Bob had always been in the midst of campus activities and he had been President of Sigma Nu. Service in the Navy was purely and simply an interim affair for McKay; he was a fellow with vast potentials and when the war was over would be out and off and on his way up.

Unlike Dillon, who still carried Harvard into the wardroom with him, Bob tended to leave his college life behind him, except in one respect. He had finally written home and asked his mother to send his Phi Beta Kappa key to him. The only other officer in the wardroom who could wear a Phi Beta Kappa key was the Executive Officer, and he announced this fact to those to whom it meant something by displaying it on his dog tag chain. Ensign McKay's single gold stripe was considerably outranked by the Exec's two-and-a-half, but he had decided he could meet the Exec even up when it came to decorated dog tags.

1130. Dinner. Watch 3 eat first. As soon as the third section got through their meal, out of the chow hall, and off to their various stations to relieve the men on watch, the day would be exactly half over. So far nothing had happened. Perhaps this was the day nothing would, just another of those days the ships spent on the picket line, waiting.

There was a lot of waiting went on in the Navy. Men waited for meals, waited for mail, waited for pay day, waited for the movies. It was sometimes necessary to wait to get into the place which, back home in Arkansas, was just any old place that was handy. The essence of it was expressed by Ensign Paine, the Assistant Engineer, in putting another ensign in his place in the wardroom. Dillon, Ferguson, Halstead and Rosengren were called "ninety-day wonders" whether they really were or not, because, as reserve officers, they had won commissions by way of college educations and quick NROTC courses.

Paine, Kelley, Woodside, and Tiwald, by contrast, were "mustangs." They had enlisted in the Navy and worked their way up through the ranks, a process which could take considerably longer than going to college. Paine, especially, knew about waiting.

"Now, listen here, Junior. I've spent more time in this Navy waiting for boats than you have been in altogether."

And for meals, too, Chuck Paine. Don't forget meals. You haven't missed one since the first time Tommy served one.

The *Aaron Ward* carried more officers than there were seats in the wardroom so they had to eat in two shifts. Those who arrived too late for the first sitting stood outside and envied the early birds through the portholes. Even so, meals were worth waiting for. Many wardroom messes in wartime were fed by cooks who went to war, not because they wanted to, but because they were being **taken**. They gloomily assassinated cans of green peas for salads, considered cold canned peaches as dessert, and could make steak, ham, and chicken, all taste like liver. But *Aaron Ward* officers were lucky, as anyone in San Francisco could have told them.

In the city by the Golden Gate, true San Franciscans—those who left the "e" out when they pronounced Geary—knew the Golden Pheasant as one of the city's better restaurants. Ladies met at the St. Francis for lunch, but they were very likely to go across the street to the Golden Pheasant to have their lunch. The war changed all that. Ladies still lunched at the Golden Pheasant, but if the lobster Newberg didn't taste quite like it used to, it was because the Golden Pheasant's dapper little Filipino chef, Tommy Erice, was now an Officer's Cook in the U. S. Navy. The only place to get lobster Newberg the way Tommy Erice cooked it was in the wardroom of *Aaron Ward*, where Tommy Erice continued to cook, when he wasn't seasick, as he had in the Golden Pheasant. For gourmets like Bill Sanders and Doc Barbeiri, Tommy's curried lamb served up with ginger, raisins and chopped almonds was something to be enjoyed to the last crumb, despite the baleful glares of those who grew up in the tradition of man-sized midwest meals and suspicioned that Doc, as mess treasurer, was rigging the menu on them. The meat-and-potatoes men sometimes refused to speak to him until their palates had been reassured with more hamburger, roast beef or pork chops.

Bill Sanders, the Captain, always sat at the head of the table. Doc, as mess treasurer, sat at the foot of the table. Some captains ate on the bridge, wolfing down cold sandwiches, but Sanders made a point of coming down to the wardroom for his meals, even on the picket line, and letting the Officer of the Deck run the ship.

Doc, and Paine, the assistant engineering officer, were Tommy Erice's faithfuls; they never missed a meal. But riding a pitching destroyer was not like riding a cable car up California Street in San Francisco. Tommy Erice got seasick, green, miserable seasick.

This was a risk of the trade; so did Sanders, at times; so did Neupert; so did McKay, and Tiwald. When the Pacific got rough a man's stomach started doing nip-ups, whether he was captain or cook. At times like those, they were all in the same boat together.

Now, at the noon meal aboard *Aaron Ward* the officers were as much together as they ever were. In the next hour everyone passed through, to try Tommy's cooking, banter with friends, discuss small business with other department officers. If the two assistant first

83

lieutenants, Rainey and Cathcart, got in on the first serving, they would have a chance to talk with their boss, Biesmeyer, before he went up to take the afternoon bridge watch. If things worked out right, "Woody" Woodside might catch the signal officer, Tiwald, the radio Officer, Dillion, and the sound officer, Rosy Rosengren, all together for once. The gun boss, Rubel, was on the bridge, but there was a possibility his number two man, Lavrakas and one or both of the other assistants, Kelley and Ferguson, would arrive to represent the department. Of the two "Freddies," Danny Danford and Fred Koehl, one would be on watch, and the CIC officer, Hal Halstead, would be busy talking fighter director problems with one of them, either in CIC or the wardroom. The Exec would be in for lunch if it wasn't too rough and he remembered to stop working long enough.

Doc Barbeiri, as mess treasurer, held down his end of the table as usual. The Skipper, minus baseball cap and pipe for the while, would take his seat at the opposite end of the table. If there was to be ice cream, he would eat a bowl full of it before returning to the bridge. And if Ensign Dillon ate at the same time the Skipper did, Sanders might take another look at his beard. The wardroom was small; it was difficult to avoid Mr. Dillon's beard for long.

Possibly, the first morning, Mr. Dillon just didn't have time to shave between mid watch and morning GQ. Maybe, the second morning, he just skipped shaving because it felt so good to spend those extra few minutes in the sack. On the third, fourth, and fifth mornings, the fact became apparent to the entire wardroom that Dillon wasn't shaving. By the sixth morning the result was visible all the way down to the Captain's end of the table. Possibly Mr. Dillon hadn't learned this yet, but the Captain didn't like beards. On the whole, there were few things of which the Skipper did disapprove, but beards were definitely one of them. That night, as off watch officers relaxed a bit in the wardroom after evening GQ, the Skipper glanced up from his game of cribbage with Lefty, looked across the room at Dillon, and said "Sky, I'll give you thirty minutes to get rid of that beard." No one paid any particular attention to this, least of all Dillon. Until, half an hour later, the Skipper spoke again. If Dillon was to have a beard, let it be a good one.

"Dillon, your thirty minutes are up. You will wear that beard," he paused, and let that pronouncement sink in, "and *not trim it* so long as you are on this ship."

For a while, growing a beard was fun. Even the rest of the wardroom enjoyed it. But Mr. Dillon's beard turned into a big, bushy, wild, red thicket, the like of which might not have put to sea since the days of Leif Ericson. It grew. It spread. It was tremendous. And as the ship moved deeper into the war zone, farther west, closer to the tropics, the weather grew warm. In fact it grew hot, and then stinking hot. No one who has never tried to sleep in a small room on a destroyer, along with another man, sweaty khakis and dirty socks, can imagine how much sleep can be destroyed by a prickly, heat-collecting beard.

Finally, pride fell before comfort and Dillon asked the Captain if he could at least trim the beard. The answer was no. The weather grew hotter, the ship soaked up heat like a brick kiln. The beard thrived on heat and sweat. Mr. Dillon had to endure the beard along with the heat and sweat. Again he asked the Captain if he might trim the beard. Where beards were concerned, the Skipper was a man of few words, and all of them were no. Mr. Dillon still was able to sleep an extra couple of minutes by not shaving, and perhaps effected some small economy in razor blades. And among a couple of dozen other khaki-clad officers, even in the blackness of a mid watch on the bridge, he stood out. There was, undeniably, some pride of ownership in a beard certainly unmatched in the Navy, and the Marine Corps, and possibly only equalled by some SeaBee forgotten back at Tonga Tabu. But the damned beard was HOT. And Mr. Dillon was stuck with it so long as he stayed on board the *Aaron Ward*. This might be an exceedingly long war, before it ended. Those ancient mariners who stood OOD watches, Rubel, Wallace, and Biesmeyer, carried an invisible albatross, but for only four hours at a time. The one Dillon had was highly visible, and he carried it twenty-four hours a day.

Mr. Dillon carried more than a beard across the Pacific. There went with Mr. Dillon a certain regard for things having to do with the scenes of his childhood which, had he come from Eagle Grove, Iowa, might have been called provincialism. But in Boston such a word was only applied to people who came from somewhere else.

"Where are you from, Lefty?" Doc asked one day.

"Boston," said Lavrakas.

This satisfied Doc who, as a native Californian, knew in a general way that Boston was back there in the thirteen original colonies somewhere. But Schuyler Dillon who hailed from Roxbury and had worn a Crimson and Black necktie before the Navy limited him to simple black, would have none of this; Lavrakas came from across the Charles River and Dillon always pointed it out.

"Wa-ter-town," he would correct Lavrakas. "Wa-ter-town!"

Though Mr. Dillon was far removed from Peabody Square and Back Bay, his heart still belonged in the Hub of the Universe, and to keep his memories bright, he maintained in his room a copy of the Boston Social Register. Sometimes, before Doc and Bob made a sortie ashore, and while Mr. Dillon was occupied elsewhere, they would sneak into his room and pick a likely name out of the book. Then, at a meal the next day, Doc would casually mention their selection.

"Say, Sky! Bob and I met a fellow over on the landing yesterday who thinks he might know you. Harvard man. His name was—," Doc would pronounce every letter of it, "Pea-bod-y."

"P'biddy!" Sky would correct him. P'biddy!"

In a few minutes Sky would scurry back to his room to check the Boston Social Register, and discover what Doc and Bob already knew. There was a Harvard graduate named P'biddy and he had been in the University at the same time Dillon was.

What Sky could not fathom was the phenomonal luck Doc and

Bob had in finding Bostonians and Harvard men on any patch of coral in the Pacific, when he couldn't even manage to go ashore and find P'biddy.

1145 "NOW HEAR THIS. RELIEVE THE WATCH. ON DECK THE THIRD SECTION. RELIEVE THE WHEEL AND LOOKOUT."

Even in the wardroom the PA system kept its listeners informed of the progress of the ship's routine. There was nowhere to go on the ship where the metallic voice could not be heard. No one wanted to be where they could not hear it; the PA system never said much, but what it said could be highly important.

A few minutes later the bridge messenger appeared in the wardroom to make the usual report to the Captain:

"Navigator reports 1200, Sir. Chronometers wound."

"Very well."

With the oral report went a small slip of paper, the 1200 position report, as determined by Tom Wallace and Chief Winston: Latitude 26 degrees 15 minutes North, Longitude 126 degrees 28 minutes East of Greenwich. The figures had changed very little over the past three days. Topside, the neat circle on the bridge chart, marked "1200 posit" showed that the ship had moved only two miles from where she was at eight that morning.

There had been no sound contacts, no radar contacts, no alarms. The day was half over on Radar Picket Station 10, and it was going exactly as Karl Neupert had ordered it in the Plan of the Day. No pain, no strain.

Strictly routine.

He that outlives this day, and comes safe home . . . . — SHAKESPEARE

Chapter Four

Afternoon Watch

12-16 steaming as before. 1230 Assumed control of Four CAP. 1415 Four CAP planes left area to return to base. 1430 LCS 25 joined formation and commenced patrolling with smaller craft.

R. I. Biesmeyer, Lt., U. S. Navy

"12-16 Steaming as before." Once more Biesmeyer climbed the ladder to the superstructure deck, aft a couple of paces, up the ladder alongside the hot stack to the gun platform, forward and up another ladder to the bridge deck. As before. As he had done twelve hours earlier, when he went to take the mid watch. Tom Wallace was waiting to be relieved. As before. Again they went through the routine of turning over the deck. The situation was still as it had

been twelve hours earlier. Everything the same, *Aaron Ward* and *Little* on RPS 10, the small boys tagging along five miles on the beam, section three condition watch on deck, no enemy raids on the scope, the guns ready, the men standing alert, the big blue wheel of the day slowly turning toward afternoon and sunset now, the smaller wheels in the ship turning toward the next watch, toward supper, toward a bit of sleep, toward another day, toward Friday.

Keep alert, you men. Keep all the wheels turning. Let's take the ship back home when this is over, with the Rising Suns painted on the bridge, and show those stateside people what we did with her.

Back home. Stateside. California, for Biesmeyer and many of the crew; San Pedro for the ship. For having been born on the wrong side of the tracks, out among the fish canneries and tank farms, *Aaron Ward* had become a proud lady. She carried herself with an air no one could have suspected a year earlier, back in San Pedro.

During the early months of 1944, the ship had been created out of chaos, confusion, and hundreds of tons of steel which appeared to have been fabricated by madmen for assembly by maniacs. Ungainly cranes staggered around the building ways of the Bethlehem Steel Shipyard at Terminal Island, dropping beams, plates, castings and piping into odd places where grimy figures riveted, welded, and bolted the stuff together into what was intended to be a ship. Compressed air hoses crawled and hissed through the labyrinth of steel, riveting hammers beat out a devil's tattoo that drowned all conversation or sane thought, and welding torches filled the night with a hellish green glow. Yet out of the inferno the shape grew, long and slim and graceful, until on 5 May destroyer hull number 773 was ready to take the water.

The ceremony of transforming a hull into a ship was short and simple; a bit of colored bunting hung over the bow, a short speech, a prayer, and a christening. The christening was done by Mrs. G. H. Ratcliff, President of the Navy Wives Club of the United States, who smashed the traditional bottle of champagne across the bow of hull number 773 with the words "I christen thee *Aaron Ward*!" The band played, workmen cheered, and the big hull stirred, trembled, and started down the ways, slowly at first, then rushing as if eager to reach the water which would be its home. Hull number 773 was now a ship with the name of *Aaron Ward*, but it was not yet a ship of the U. S. Navy, nor was it alive; not until it was filled with the officers and men who, with the ship, would become the team the Navy would know as *Aaron Ward*.

The task of building the ship was only a little more complicated than assembling a crew for her. From a desk in the Navy Department in Washington, orders had gone out pulling experienced destroyermen into Receiving Stations to form a nucleus crew, sifting Training Centers for the many more needed to complete a crew, checking officer qualifications to find experienced senior officers and adaptable junior officers with which to build another combatant unit for the Navy. From a hundred different ships and stations the men had come, as the components of the ship had come from a thousand different manufacturing plants and subcontractors. Sanders had come from the *Blakely*, Neupert from the *Sampson*, Rainey from the *Warrington*, Lavrakas from the *Eberle*, Rubel from the *Hobby*, Young from the *Drayton*, Wallace from the PC 587, Biesmeyer from the *McFarland*, Tiwald from the *Cooper*, Halstead from the *Decker*, and Kelly from the *Dixie*. A new ship could ask nothing better than to go to sea with a bunch of officers and men from the destroyer fleet, and that was what she was getting—destroyermen.

The senior enlisted men came from everywhere: from the *Adario, Boggs, Cheleb, DuPont,* and right down the line. Chief Smith said he came from so many ships he couldn't remember them all.

The black gang, the engineering department, had its origin in the "Destroyer Pool" in Norfolk where the nucleus crew of the engineers was first assigned to the ship. There the experienced rated men, machinist's mates, watertenders and electricians were earmarked for destroyer 773. These included the old chiefs, Smith, McCaughy, Mann, and Salisbury, and petty officers, Gorcyzca, Anastasio, Antell, Coltra, Carroll, Haubrick, Forrey, St. Clair and Carpenter. After a couple of months of detailed training and instruction in Norfolk, the group split up—half of them went to San Pedro to be with the ship as the finishing touches were applied; the rest of them went to Treasure Island to help instruct the "boots" assembled there.

The gunnery officers, Rubel, Lavrakas, Tiwald, and Ferguson, also assembled at Norfolk, and went through a chain of schools even as did their men—Gunnery, Antisubmarine Warfare, Fire Fighting, Damage Control. Tiwald, who had first enlisted in the Army and been assigned to the 7th Cavalry, then went to Corregidor with the Coast Artillery. But some sailors, including his brother on the old four-stacker *Gilmer*, talked him into joining the Navy and there he was, right back with the guns again.

The majority of the *Aaron Ward* crew assembled at Treasure Island, in California. Most of them were raw recruits, straight from Training Centers in San Diego and Great Lakes, and no matter what the recruiters or draft boards had told them about the Navy, it wasn't enough. No one had explained to them what happened when a seventeen-year-old high school boy exchanged his individuality for a service number, a pay number, a few shots in the arm, a seabag full of clothes which were never clean enough to please everyone, and a bunk in what was not lightly termed "Bedbug Barracks."

No one had told them, either, about standing watches at night, standing inspections by day, drilling, going to fire fighting school, and moving things. Everyone in the Navy seemed to be always moving things, like ants at a picnic. Over on the Oakland side of the bay they could see ships with their booms rigged out, down at Hunter's Point they could see huge cranes able to lift a locomotive, and anywhere they went they saw the Navy's fork lifts, cherry pickers, crawler cranes, and other interesting gadgets for picking something up and putting it somewhere else. Yet it seemed that whenever the Navy needed something moved, the only cargo handling equipment handy just happened to be a bunch of sailors.

No one had told them about tough master-at-arms, senior petty officers with little black books, or officers. At Treasure Island the men met their Executive Officer, and while they were trying to remember that he was Lieutenant Commander Karl F. Neupert, U. S.

Navy, he found out and remembered everything worth remembering about every man in the crew. The first thing the *Aaron Ward* pre-commissioning detail learned was, "the Exec never forgets." He checked each service record when the men reported, and he filed the information away in his head for future reference.

"You're from Moorland, Iowa, I see. That's about ten miles from Fort Dodge, isn't it?"

"Yes, Sir."

"You can get a pretty good sundae at a little place across from the Post Office in Fort Dodge. Place called Constantine's."

That Exec never forgot anything.

"BRIDGE, RADIO SHACK. MESSAGE FROM CTF 51 IN ELDORADO. FOUR CAP ASSIGNED TO RPS 10 TO REPORT 1230."

"RADIO, BRIDGE AYE."

"CIC, BRIDGE. DELEGATE IS SENDING OUT FOUR CHICKENS FOR YOU FREDDIE BOYS TO PLAY WITH."

"BRIDGE, CIC. ROGER."

This was good news. Four fighter planes on their way, just in case the Japanese decided to come early. The bridge watch perked up. Airplanes were better to look at than nothing, especially friendly airplanes. In a few minutes the planes were in sight, and reported in by voice radio.

"MONGOOSE BASE THIS IS MONGOOSE LEADER OVER."

"MONGOOSE LEADER FROM MONGOOSE BASE. ORBIT AT ONE FIVE HUNDRED FEET."

For the next two hours, MONGOOSE 1, 2, 3, and 4 would be under the control of the Fighter Director crew down in CIC. If the enemy came, they would get first crack at him.

In the fall of 1944, as *Aaron Ward* neared completion in San Pedro, more orders went out from Washington and the crew began moving again. Some more of the East Coast detail went directly to San Pedro, to attend to the final details of putting the ship together.

Some of them were shipped out to Treasure Island, where they met the bigger part of the new crew. And eventually they all were hauled down to San Pedro. Most sailors had expected to start across the ocean as soon as they got into the Navy. They had not bargained for sightseeing trips across the country, first.

But even train travel could have its adventures, and adversities. On their safari from Norfolk to Long Beach, gunner's mate Quimette and three of his shipmates managed to get lost for a couple of days. Tiwald made out even better; he left Norfolk as a single man and arrived in Long Beach with a new wife. His girl, Venice, out in Omaha, had said "yes" several months earlier and this was the first time they'd had a chance to do something about it. Muirhead acquired a wart on the end of his nose, and with it the nickname "Hosenose" which would remain with him long after the wart had vanished.

Bob Winston crossed the continent with twenty-four men in a private car. Anticipating a long journey, they endeavored to fit their car with all the comforts of home, and a few "mom" might not have allowed. When the train stopped, Winston's charges had a habit of hopping out to investigate local conditions, and by the time he reached San Pedro there were more seabags on the car than there were men to carry them off, but the missing people all showed up within a few days, none the worse for being technically shipwrecked in Chicago, Omaha, and other places. For two days during the trip, the *Aaron Ward* car was coupled on to one carrying Spike Jones and a USO troupe. There was some question about who entertained who, but they all had a good time.

Another trans-continental journey made by Chief Giese and eight other men was also noted for its lack of dull routine. Their itinerary included Albuquerque, which was the home town of watertender second class Cooper. When the train stopped there, Cooper's family was waiting with a complete chicken dinner for all hands. Fortified by such treatment, and diverted by the happy discovery that the Santa Fe had added a carload of young ladies in new WAVE uniforms, Giese and his men were halfway to the Pacific Coast when they finally noticed that two of their company had been left behind in Albuquerque.

A man who gets himself lost out of a draft in the Navy has committed a serious offense, almost as bad, in fact, as that committed by the man who lets him get lost. Giese worried about this all the way to Treasure Island. Trying to explain anything in the Navy is seldom easy, and explaining to a strange and suspicious Chief Master-at-Arms is less easy, and attempting to do this at one o'clock in the morning is never easy at all.

"Draft for *Aaron Ward* reporting in from Norfolk Destroyer Pool. Seven men present, Holte and Rawlins missing and unaccounted for."

"Waddya mean, Holte and Rawlins unaccounted for? I got Holte and Rawlins present, and these guys Giese, Kennedy, Cooper and so on unaccounted for."

"No! That's not right. Giese and Kennedy—that's us—we're here. Holte and Rawlins are in Albuquerque, New Mexico."

"That's what you think. They've been here for five hours—right over there on that bench, asleep. Where you guys been?"

Yeah. Where had they been? Right there on the train, but the ones who got left beat them in after all.

Having missed the train, Giese's men hurried to the nearest Army base, talked themselves into a free airplane ride to San Francisco, and waited for their less speedy friends to arrive, proving that a determined sailor can beat the Santa Fe any day, and that confusion can easily be achieved in military affairs.

While the ship grew toward her completion date, the pre-commissioning detail in San Pedro crew continued to live ashore if they could. This was a break for McCaughey, who lived in nearby Santa Monica, and whose father let Mick have his 1941 Chevvy coupe to run back and forth with. Gasoline presented only a small problem; Mick needed ration stamps in order to buy the stuff, but there was a blonde in the ration office who fell for Mick's blarney often enough to keep him from walking.

Once the ship was commissioned though, and Mick ate and slept on board, he was no longer a member of the civilian community.

Sailors didn't need cars or gas rations. Blarney might have worked on the blonde, but not on the ration board, whose edict was "Give back those stamps."

This, Mick explained, was impossible, for any number of reasons, chief of which was, he'd spent them for gas.

Next, the ration board sent a directive to the Commanding Officer, USS *Aaron Ward*, concerning one McCaughey, C. R., CMM, U. S. Navy: Ration Stamps, return of. The whole affair was of some interest to Bill Sanders, who also was dependent on a 1941 Chevvy coupe for getting to and from his temporary home in Long Beach. Gas ration stamps were gas ration stamps, no matter where one got them. So Mick was called up to discuss ration stamps with the Captain.

"Look, Chief," said Sanders. "I'm not telling you you have to give the stamps back to the ration office. I just wonder how you worked the deal in the first place."

1300 Turn to. Ship's Work. The sun was moving westward now, through a nearly clear sky. The sea was smooth, just enough of a wind swell setting in from northwest to give the ship a comfortable motion. One could almost enjoy the afternoon watch, except for the constantly rotating radar aerial overhead looking for planes which might come at any moment, the elevated muzzles of the guns, ready to fire, waiting for the planes to come. The ships still marched and countermarched across the bit of sea marked on the charts as Radar Picket Station 10. Out of sight to the north and south of them, and both ways around a vast lopsided circle centered on Okinawa, other picket ships sailed and waited. The fleet had been out there on the picket lines for forty days now, and suicide planes had sunk or damaged ships on twenty-four of those days. There was only one thing to do—outmaneuver them, outguess them, and if they got close enough, shoot them down.

As the last days of October, 1944, fell off the calendar and the time drew near for the pre-commissioning detail to move down from Treasure Island to Terminal Island, a minor problem arose in the radar gang. Art Aylworth had invited the men in his watch out to the house for chow, or, rather, his wife Dayle, had proposed that he invite them. Such an invitation meant more than just "come out and have a bite with us." In offering a dinner to the men, Aylworth conferred on them a favor impossible to return; home and family was far away, for the others, and restaurant chow, no matter how good, never tasted like real home cooking. In taking the gang home for dinner Aylworth was also showing his pride in his wife Dayle, a sweet, lovely girl filled with quiet inner beauty. And underlying it all was the thought, no less real for being unspoken, that once the ship took these men to sea no one knew when again—if ever—they might hear grace at a table or take bread from a woman's soft hands.

So Dayle Aylworth saved and scraped on seaman's pay until she had enough to provide chicken for six hungry men. The big night was set. Woods, the only other man in the gang who had his wife in town, was of course one of the fortunate guests. Because a man could swap liberties with someone in another watch, and because there was also the chance that a man might be arbitrarily moved from watch to watch, there was considerable discussion in the radar gang as to exactly which men were going to be guests of the Aylworth's for the famous chicken dinner.

Finally, zero hour arrived. Dayle Aylworth fried up the chicken, whipped up hot biscuits, ladled out the honey. And when the doorbell rang and the door opened and the radarmen came in she nearly dropped dead. Mr. Neupert had heard about the chicken dinner for so long he finally ruled that all the radarmen could go, and there they were, twelve of them. Dayle Aylworth never saw fried chicken disappear so fast in all her young life.

By late October of 1944, the ship was nearly ready in San Pedro and the crew was ready in Treasure Island. The ship they thought was to be a destroyer had been redesignated a destroyer minelayer, but for the men who were wearing the uniform of the fighting U. S. Navy and had not yet gotten into the fight, going to sea in a destroyer minelayer was better than staying ashore in Bedbug Barracks. San Francisco had been a new experience for most of the men, but they wanted something different for a change.

And for once they got it. The overnight train ride down the California coast, in a train with no heat, very little food, and three hundred unhappy sailors, would probably never be mentioned in California history. Tom Wallace's endeavors in rounding up three hundred sailors, and his skirmishes with the Red Cross, Shore Patrol, and the Southern Pacific, were never recorded in naval history. It was as well. Those tales would have to wait for some fiction writers—no one would believe them otherwise.

In San Pedro, the men commenced to suspect why the Fleet fought so hard out in the Pacific. By the time a man had been through boot camp, schools, receiving stations, pre-commissioning detail and all the varied and assorted harassment that went with it, he was ready to fight anybody.

28 October 1944. The ship was ready now. The crew was aboard, provisions aboard, stores aboard, and spare parts aboard. Fires burned under the ship's boilers, and her intricate system of pipes and cables and wires pulsed with live steam, fresh water, salt water, compressed air, hydraulic fluid, refrigerating coolant, direct current, alternating current, diesel oil, and fuel oil. Fans whispered, blowers roared, generators whined, motors hummed, diesels rumbled, radio receivers chirped and peeped, typewriters clicked, pumps grunted and groaned, the master gyro sang in its cage, the spud peeler clattered away outside the galley, and coffee pots perked happily. The ship was ready.

In the late afternoon, the crew filed topside in their dress blues and clean white hats. Most of them wore watchmarks around their shoulders; white for seaman, red for firemen. The petty officers wore white eagles on their sleeves—"buzzards" to the initiated. A few of the second and first class POs wore service marks—"hashmarks" to those who wore buzzards. Most of the chief petty officers were loaded with hashmarks, each stripe signifying four years of service. These were the men Sanders would depend on to keep the nuts and bolts of the ship in order, to organize the divisions, indoctrinate the new kids, square away the wise ones, take a few corners off the tough ones if there were any, help the new ninety-day-wonder officers run their affairs while letting them think they did it themselves, and to be a salty, tattooed nucleus of forecastle horse sense and quarterdeck tradition around which he could build this new ship and new crew into a fighting unit of the fleet, a piece of the new Navy that would look and act like the old Navy.

The officers gathered on the superstructure deck, their gold stripes bright in the sun. Some of them were as new to the Navy as the ship was. Some of them had had previous shipboard service and combat duty. Some of them were ex-enlisted men, "mustangs" to those who wore hashmarks. They had worked their way from the forecastle to the quarterdeck without the educational trimmings of their companions who came in via the Ivy League, and were used to demanding performance, instant and complete, from the men and machines in their charge without entering into philosophical discussion as to the why or wherefore of their demands.

A Navy band took its position on the dock alongside the ship and the guests—wives, girl friends, acquaintances, and other interested persons gathered on the dock to watch. The ship was going to war; that was her only reason for existing, but war was not the martial affair it once was, and these sailors would go into battle without the stirring notes of trumpets and drums to inspire them. The band would play two tunes and then go back to their band room. If *Aaron Ward* wanted any music when the shooting started, someone on the ship would have to whistle "Dixie."

A few officials and dignitaries came on board, and the boatswain's pipes shrilled "Attention." At 1530 the commissioning officer made the usual introductory talk and read the Navy Department orders directing that the USS *Aaron Ward* be placed in commission. Then he turned to Commander William H. Sanders, Jr., U. S. Navy and said

"You may now assume command."

Sanders saluted, and ordered the band to sound off. The crew snapped to attention at the first note of the National Anthem; the ensign, the union jack, and the commissioning pennant broke out into the California sunshine. The same colors were flying in the

Med, and in Leyte Gulf. The men who remembered Guadalcanal, Casablanca, the Murmansk Run, Tassafaronga, Kolombangara, Midway, and Normandy, stood a little straighter. They were in the Navy now. The kids who were still not old enough to buy a drink squared their shoulders; this thing was a warship now, and when it went out where the war was, they were going along.

Sanders unfolded a sheet of paper and read a brief set of orders. They were filled with official naval terminology: "Commander William H. Sanders . . . . hereby detached . . . . proceed and report . . . . duty under instruction . . . . when directed detached proceed . . . . temporary duty in connection with fitting out USS *Aaron Ward* . . . . duty on board when commissioned as Commanding Officer . . . ." The original orders had been issued 13 May 1944, and they had collected thirty-three endorsements as Sanders had worked his way through various schools, training commands and headquarters on his way to this ceremony. They would receive yet one more endorsement, that afternoon, when he would sign his name under the simple statement: "Reported this date."

Finished reading, he handed the orders to his yeoman and said "I assume command of the USS *Aaron Ward*." He was now the Commanding Officer of the ship—the Captain, the Skipper, the "old man,"—solely responsible to the United States Navy for the safety of a multi-million dollar ship, the training and welfare of the 365 officers and men under his charge, and the performance of his command in all actions against the enemy.

"Set the watch!" he ordered Karl Neupert.

The PA system clicked on, and the boatswain's pipe shrilled the length of the ship.

"NOW HEAR THIS! SET THE WATCH. ON DECK, THE FIRST SECTION."

"The watch has been set, Sir," said Neupert.

Sanders nodded to the Chaplain, who delivered an Invocation while the crew stood with bowed heads. There would be bowed heads on the ship again, but never again the words of chaplain, minister, or priest. From that day on, those who needed more than

Navy Regulations to sustain them would have to draw on their own supply of inner faith. For the moment they were silent and serious. The voice of the chaplain reminded them that there was a very good chance they would become "those in peril of the deep."

She was the newest ship in the United States Navy, and they were her crew. She was clean and fresh, shining and bright. She still had to venture out of sight of the land which built her, still had to try her mighty engines against the fury of the sea, still had to swim alone across the top of the greatest ocean in the world where dark mystery lay beneath her keel, two miles deep. She was their ship and they were already in love with her. She was still a virgin, and when she went to consummate herself in battle they would go with her, all the way.

"Amen." said the Chaplain.

And then Captain Sanders, the first and only captain the *Aaron Ward* would ever have, spoke to the first and only crew the *Aaron Ward* would ever have, while riveting hammers racketed away on nearby ships, and the flag snapped in the breeze, and seagulls wheeled and cried in the bright blue sky.

"Those of you who have had previous experience will readily note that we have indeed been given the finest kind of ship and equipment to work with that it is humanly possible to build . . . . From my daily contact with some of you and by the service records of the others I have come to the conclusion that somewhere along the line, either by chance or careful selection, I have been assigned an excellent group of officers and men. For that you can be sure I am most grateful. Our job now is to learn how to get from this ship all the performance that was designed and built into it. We know that will take lots of hard work and long hours, but certainly we above all others are the ones who should realize the importance of it . . . . The key to success along that line is in the word 'cooperation' and you will notice that from the nature of the word, it is not a function of officers and petty officers alone, but of all hands. Please remember that. With the idea in mind that we will work together in training, fighting, and just plain living, the *Aaron Ward* will soon proudly bear the unofficial title of a 'happy ship' and then we will know we are ready when it is time to 'play for keeps.'

"The guests are now invited to come on board."

The band struck up "Anchors Aweigh," the Executive Officer ordered "carry on," and most of the men hurried off, met their friends, and introduced them to "my ship." But the ceremony had so impressed watertender second class Ballard that he had to go find a secluded corner and wipe the tears out of his eyes.

Out on Picket Station 10, the day was passing slowly by. *Aaron Ward* and *Little* plodded steadily back and forth across their post, the small boys bobbed along at a distance. Above them, the four carrier fighter planes wheeled in the sky like belligerant hawks. Twelve hours of the day gone. Thirteen. Everything quiet. No strain.

A small pip showed on the surface search radar, heading out toward them from Kerama Retto. Small boat, maybe eighteen miles away. In a few minutes the TBS sounded off.

"MONGOOSE, THIS IS DELEGATE. OVER."

"DELEGATE, THIS IS MONGOOSE."

"MONGOOSE THIS IS DELEGATE AT 1430 PARSNIP WILL REPORT TO YOU FOR DUTY OVER AND OUT."

Good old PARSNIP! That was the blip out there, heading for RPS 10—the LCS 25. Another small boy to join the crowd. The more the merrier; company always welcome out where the shooting went on. But better let the flyboys know. Keep everything under control.

"MONGOOSE LEADER FROM MONGOOSE BASE. SKUNK APPROACHING 090 RANGE SIXTEEN IS FRIEND-LY SMALL BOY."

"MONGOOSE BASE FROM MONGOOSE LEADER ROG-ER."

It had been a pleasant, peaceful afternoon like this, long months ago back in California, when *Aaron Ward* first joined the Navy.

The ceremony had been impressive, but short. Guests trooped through what parts of the ship were open to them, but the visit was hurried. Already she was in a hurry.

An hour later *Aaron Ward* sought her natural habitat. Although she had been in the water for many months, she had still been tied to the land by a maze of lines—fresh water lines, salt water lines, steam lines, compressed air lines, telephone lines, and the standard skein of heavy mooring lines. All but the mooring lines had disappeared before the commissioning ceremony. Only the brows connected her with land. Soon the air was filled with the high whine of blowers building up speed. In the firerooms the black gang peered through green ports into the inferno of the furnaces as the boilers worked up to steaming pressure. The engineers tested annunciators, turned over the turbines, adjusted valves, and hovered over pumps and gauges like surgeons feeling a pulse in a delivery room. In a few minutes *Aaron Ward* would come alive.

"NOW HEAR THIS. ALL GUESTS ARE REQUESTED TO LEAVE THE SHIP."

When a new ship slips into the great mystery of salt water, only her crew goes with her.

"NOW GO TO YOUR STATIONS ALL THE SPECIAL SEA DETAIL."

The old timers—all those with at least a couple of months sea duty in some other ship behind them—handled their jobs with studied ease. Those getting underway for the first time dropped lines, stumbled over bitts, tangled up phone cords, and gawked at the crowd on the dock.

Sanders leaned over the wing of the bridge, studied the situation with a practiced eye, and then turned to his phone talker, yeoman Wayne Fowers. Sanders had been getting ships underway for a dozen years. This was the first time for Fowers.

"Take one to the capstan and heave round" ordered Sanders.

This was exotic language to Fowers, who only four short months before had been pushing living room suites around in the University Avenue Furniture Store in San Diego. They didn't talk like that in the furniture business.

"Take one to the Captain and heave it around" Fowers said into his phones.

No matter what Fowers said, Biesmeyer and Shelley on the forecastle knew what to do, and they did it. The number one mooring line came in. The Captain said nothing, but Fowers could tell by the look in his eye that now was the time to learn the bridge-talker business.

"Cast off all lines."

Someone tugged the whistle cord and the *Aaron Ward* let out her first official cry, a long resonant steam powered bellow that scared the be-Jesus out of half the men on the ship.

"Port engine back one third."

A sigh seemed to run through the ship. She shuddered, trembled, and for one horrifying instant the new men in the crew had the impression the dock was slowly sliding away from them. Then the truth hit them: the ship was moving. They were on their way.

But not very far. Just around the waterfront to a drydock. Just long enough for the turbines to feel the first surge of power. Just long enough for the ship to feel herself swimming free. Just long enough for some men to suddenly realize the thing under their feet was alive, and that their stomachs did not like it.

Sooner or later, if she lasts long enough, a ship has to throw a ship's dance. A ship's dance solves many problems all at once. It offers the only accepted occasion for officers and men to mingle socially, other than in a court martial or at GQ aboard ship. It gives the wives and girl friends of all the white hats a chance to see that "the old man" does not possess fangs and a forked tail. It gives the wardroom wives a chance to see that their husbands are not going to sea with a gang of tattooed hellions, but rather a bunch of fellows that look like insurance salesmen, shop owners, school teachers, and boys who ought to be home singing in the choir, all poured into sailor suits and shoeshines. It gives the wardroom offi-cers a chance to see that some of their men can carry on with the lifted pinkie in the best tradition, and that sailors meet and marry dreamboats the same as everyone else. It gives the old man a chance to see more of his men together than he ever will again, and to prove to them that he can outdance or otherwise out perform anyone on board if he so pleases. And it gives everyone a chance to realize in a small way that so long as the ship floats and they are all attached to it, whether by regulation, or sentiment, they are all bound together in a common cause. A ship has to have a ship's dance: if she was to be commissioned on Monday and go down fighting on Wednesday, she would have to have the dance on Tuesday. There might even be a little fighting then, too.

The *Aaron Ward's* dance was held on 16 November 1944, at the Veteran's Memorial Building on West Broadway in Long Beach. It was an all hands affair, complete with wine, women and song in the best traditions of the Naval service. Mrs. Peggy Finley, the Military and Naval Recreational Director of the city of Long Beach, helped the ship's committee plan the affair and obtain what might be called logistic support from the community. For those who could provide none of their own, Mrs. William Loomis of the city of Long Beach shipped in a platoon of Victory Belles. The Naval Operating Base provided entertainment billed as "Gobs of Fun." In case anyone felt like singing, the Roosevelt Base Band was prepared. Dancing went on from eight in the evening until midnight, and refreshments were available while they lasted. Festivity was rife.

Everyone always has a good time at the ship's dance, except the duty section who has to stay aboard ship, and they hear all about it when the liberty party returns in the morning. And what happens after the dance is over should properly be a matter for delightful and private recollection. There is no need to relate the obvious.

But it was a pip of a dance. Doc Barbeiri remembered it for two reasons. It was his third date with a girl named Ginny, who he thought would make a fine doctor's wife. The name would be a natural—Ginny Barbeiri. He was right about that. And he had his first chance to work shoulder to shoulder with his new commanding officer. Before the dance was over there was a row in the head which grew with chain reaction into a joyful Donnybrook. Once started, no one seemed to know how to bring it to a halt. Finally Bill Sanders took the Doctor by the arm and said, "Surge, let's you and I have a crack at it." A few doors and windows were in bad disrepair when the two officers stepped in, and men were swinging punches all the way from their heels. And then the "old man" walked in. There was no fun in fighting with him watching. Peace was restored.

It was such a good party that Moose Antell was still happy after he and Bull Weyrauch had taken a couple of girls home, and started back to the ship. Moose found a potted palm in front of a hotel and decided it was just what the crew's quarters needed. It must have weighed twice as much as Moose, but he lugged it for a block before Bull was able to convince him that while the captain would put up with a lot of things, potted palms in the crew's quarters was not one of them.

On Picket Station 10 the afternoon droned on. The fighter planes wheeled across the sky, and the new small boy crawled slowly over the horizon and crept nearer and nearer, the galley crew started getting ready for supper, typewriters racketed in the offices, radio receivers chirped, officers worked on reports, the radar still searched the sky far across the horizon, and the engineers kept their fires bright and plenty of steam in the boilers. When you needed the stuff, you needed it in a hurry.

Again the TBS speakers woke out of their silence.

"MONGOOSE THIS IS PARSNIP REPORTING FOR DUTY. REQUEST INSTRUCTIONS."

"PARSNIP THIS IS MONGOOSE. TAKE POSITION ASTERN OF SMALL BOYS. FIVE MILES SOUTH OF STATION AND FOLLOW MOVEMENTS."

The LCS 25 obediently swung to port and trudged over to join the other "amphibbers."

A few minutes later the four fighter planes flew past the ship, waggled their wings, and headed eastward toward Okinawa. It was time for them to return to base; their fuel supply was getting low. *So long, fellows and hurry back if you want to be around when the fun starts. Sunset is coming, and that's when Tojo's bats come out. Let's be ready for them.*

1400. "NOW HEAR THIS. ALL GUN CREWS REPORT FOR LOADING DRILL."
For Cris' sake, Mr. Rubel! Again?

The gun crews had been loading those guns, or other guns exactly like them, for months now—in Norfolk, at Point Montara, at Pacific Beach, in the school ship *Foote,* and finally in the *Aaron Ward,* their own ship. They could load with their eyes closed, in the dark, and they might well have to do exactly that very soon. But meanwhile, it was a nice sunny afternoon and there was nothing else to do . . . . *All right sailors, put some life into it now. Snap to it* . . . . Larson especially, a gun captain on the port twin forty, drilled his men unceasingly, relentlessly, until the first loaders, Woodward and Rader, were nearly as much a part of the gun as the controls for the trainer and pointer, until Blunck and Merrington, the pointer and trainer, could keep the gun on target despite hell and high water. Before the day was over, Pappy Larson and the shooting sailors on Mount 42 would save the ship.

Sailors could endure drills, starvation, typhoon, shipwreck and no letters from home if only the Navy would knock off Saturday inspections. Inspection aboard ship is the perfect example of Murphy's Law—if something can go wrong, it will. A sailor can work from five in the morning until nine, getting himself and the cleaning station into absolutely spotless condition for inspection, but the captain will find something wrong . . . . that's one reason he is captain. Let the engine room be gleaming with white paint and shiny brass, and the captain will find a dirty coffee cup lurking behind a switchboard. Let the spotless galley be filled with hot ham sandwiches and fresh pie, and without fail one drunken cockroach will stagger out and fall at the captain's feet. Let the yeoman's office be in such perfect order that even the paper clips all point the same way, and the captain will merely touch the pencil sharpener and it will fall apart to spill shavings all over the waxed deck. Let the bridge be dazzling in its efficient array of charts, stadimeters, and binoculars, and while the quartermaster wipes one lone finger print from the binnacle stand a passing seagull will leave his calling card right where the captain's foot first touches the deck.

As *Aaron Ward* went through her shakedown period, her crew put up with, endured, and suffered through the usual sequence of inspections. One Saturday, late in November of 1944, the inspection party had wound its way through the scrubbed and polished ranks, with the yeoman's notebook recording the names of those whose tonsorial elegance was a whit less than perfection. Then it had sailed around the ship like a brassy comet, first the Captain, then the Executive Officer, the Chief Master at Arms, the yeoman with his little black book, the Department Head through whose dominion they passed, the Division Officer, among whose men they stalked, and the petty officer or seaman personally responsible for whatever untidy swabs, dangling phone cords, or smeared paint work they might discover. When the party reached Mount 52, Boles was ready for them. The twin breeches of the 5-inch guns were so shiny and clean one could almost have enjoyed being shot at by them. Check-off lists were posted, switches marked, even the test case, a dummy powder can used in training, had been polished.

Boles remembered the test case at the same instant the Captain's eyes lit on it and he ordered,

"Hand me the test case."

The reason Boles suddenly remembered the test case was that, for some strange reason, the night before, he had found himself safely returned from liberty with a bottle of Schenley Black Label inside his jumper. No sane sailor would stash contraband away in his locker —Captains always looked in lockers—so he put it where no one would ever think of looking, in the test case . . . . *Exit, to the brig, one*

107

Lloyd Boles, ex-gunner's mate second class, shot down by Murphy's Law.

As the Skipper spoke, McClure, the Chief, reached up for the case, flipped it over with a hand on each end, and felt something slide against his palm. McClure was an old time chief, and could recognize a bottle with his eyes shut.

"She's clean as a whistle, Captain," he sang out, and slapped the test case back in its rack.

Boles swore off for a week.

Next to inspection, a sailor's greatest worry was the affair the Navy calls a working party. Working parties were the Navy's answer to automation. Everything the Navy ate, used, or shot at the enemy came in packages small enough for a sailor to lift. The stuff progressed from supply depot to receiving sheds to dockside to storerooms, moved by sailors who knew that the emphasis was always on the "working," never on the "party." Absolutely the only thing that ever came aboard in quantities so small sailors were not needed to carry it was money. And when a sailor still had a bit of lettuce in his jumper pocket and knew a couple of cute bunnies who would help him spend it, a working party could be a definite threat to the pursuit of life, liberty, and happiness. Especially in San Pedro, where the pursuit was ever hot. This afternoon, while a working party straggled out to heave ammo cans aboard, Pete Peterson, Pappy Anderson and Moose Antell pussyfooted off to the after diesel room where they sought to conserve their energy for another kind of party ashore later on. The Exec, as is the habit of all good executive officers, then set out to do a bit of pussyfooting of his own, which eventually led him to the after diesel room. Mr. Neupert knew why the men were there, and the men knew why he was there, so no explanations were needed on either side.

"Go put yourself on report," he said, and left.

Next day, having checked the list of offenders against good order and discipline and noting not quite as many names as he remembered bodies, Mr. Neupert called Weyrauch in for an explanation.

"Well, Sir," said Bull, "it was this way. After you told me to put myself on report, I got to considering my previously good record and decided to give myself another chance."

As happens so frequently in the Navy when opinions differ, the Exec's opinion held more weight than that of a sailor. Weyrauch got another chance—several of them, in fact—at further working parties. The Exec made certain that liberty did not interfere.

When the ship was in port, back in the good old "stateside days," the crew knocked off work for the day at 1600. The poor unfortunates in the duty section had to stay aboard, with nothing to do but take a hot shower, eat chow, write letters, go to the movie, eat some more chow, perhaps stand a watch or so, and spend the rest of the night in their bunk. The lucky ones, those in the liberty section, provided they had clean uniforms, shined shoes, and some money, were free to invade San Pedro, Long Beach, or the less distant provinces of Los Angeles in a search for whatever it was their buddies in the western Pacific were supposed to be fighting for. Endeavor along this line was met with varying degrees of success, depending on how thorough a man was in his search.

A man with a raging thirst needed go no farther than the "Blue and Gold" bar in Pedro. This was a favorite hangout for sailors, especially as Ben, the genial owner, was always willing to subsidize some suds until pay day. There was no lack of other pleasant places to spend an hour or a sawbuck, and the *Aaron Ward* crew investigated them all—The Clipper Club, the Bamboo Inn, the Pango Pango, the Blue Star Inn, the Gay Inn, Melody Lane, and the China Seas. Depending on his mood, a man could feast, frolic or fight—and if all this palled, there were girls; girls in all shapes, sizes, and degrees of pigmentation, an infinite variety of them among which even the most fastidious was certain to find just the right one.

There was a great deal of success along this line, too—the vital statistics of the crew changed considerably between the time they all arrived in California and the time they left. Perhaps an all time record was set by George Coward, who came all the way from Norfolk to meet Mary Bodlovich, a girl who had been right there in San

Pedro waiting for him. After one look at Mary, George bid adieu to the boys at the Blue and Gold.

In the next three weeks, he made twenty-one liberties and spent twenty of them with Mary Bodlovich, after which they made a trip to the Normandy Wedding Chapel in Long Beach. Even under the best of circumstances, a fellow couldn't acquire a new wife absolutely free, and at that point money was one thing George had little of. But there were always shipmates. Shipmate Jim Parker loaned him enough money to make the plunge. The honeymoon lasted four days. Three days later the new Mrs. Coward, not yet used to a ring on her finger, said "Goodbye" to George. The ship sailed for Hawaii and Mary commenced saying Novena's for his safe return.

If one ventured as far as Figueroa Street in the City of the Angels, there was an especially exotic place featuring three dancers—the Rose Girl, the Gardenia Girl and the Orchid Girl, each of whom wore three of her favorite blossoms in a fetching triangular array. There, Pete Peterson, Moose Antell, and assorted friends sought shelter one rainy night. Finally Moose decided he wanted to go somewhere else, but couldn't find his raincoat. A sailor has better sense than to go out in the rain without his raincoat.

Moose came by his nickname honestly—he qualified as to size, disposition, and voice, and he now commenced demonstrating all three.

"I want my raincoat."

"I won't go until I get my raincoat."

"I'm going to get my raincoat if I have to tear this place apart, board by board."

With Moose, this was not so much a threat as a statement of fact, and the master of ceremonies hastened to forestall disaster. Moose demanded his raincoat. Then The Rose Girl stepped in and tried to soothe him. This was better, but Moose still wanted his raincoat. The Orchid Girl and The Gardenia Girl joined them. Pete and his friends drank up every minute of this—a sailor didn't often meet roses, orchids, gardenias, and other wonders of nature at such close range. When the master of ceremonies made the mistake of stepping between Moose and one of the girls, he hoisted him aloft in one hand while he continued roaring for his raincoat. Moose generally talked with his hands, and suddenly discovering an impediment in his speech, he looked at the afflicted hand and found the master of ceremonies, still waving aloft.

"I think I'll just bash you on the floor until I get my raincoat," he announced.

A moment later, Moose and his friends were on their way out. They all had raincoats, but no invitation to return, which was unfortunate in view of their suddenly aroused interest in botany.

In the crowded, three-dimensional community known as the crews compartment, men had neighbors on all sides of them, fore and aft, both sides, "upstairs" and "downstairs." A man could borrow a smoke without getting out of bed, provided one of his neighbors within reaching distance had some under his pillow. A man in the top bunk who dropped his socks could get them back from the deck below if everyone "downstairs" was home and in an agreeable mood. The compartments were what roadsigns in New England called "thickly populated" and a man unfortunate enough to live where the inhabitants went in and out might as well have tried to sleep in Grand Central Station.

One of these luckless inhabitants was Greenoe, who had the top bunk in the big after crew compartment, right where everyone came down the ladder from topside and, if the ship rolled a little bit—or they did—probably fell into the bunk with him. As a result, Greenoe knew everyone in the place, coming and going. His situation was especially noticeable when the ship was in port and Greenoe was in the duty section. Then, as the liberty hounds returned, each one of them stumbled, slid, or fell down the ladder as was his custom, bumped into Greenoe, woke him up, and told him of his adventures ashore. As soon as Greenoe got to sleep another celebrant would flop up against his bunk and go through the routine again. In this fashion Greenoe could vicariously enjoy drinking his way through several bars, stowing away half a dozen steaks, making various kinds of time with assorted blondes, brunettes, and indefinites, getting into three or four fights, seeing two movies, and having a taxi ride all the way back to the ship. These gay evenings in bed never cost him a cent, but left him so tired he could hardly fall out of the top bunk in the morning.

After the ship was built, launched, and commissioned; after she had tried out her engines and her guns; after she had got the feel of the sea into her frame; then it was time for the Captain to learn a few things about her: her characteristics—how fast she went, what her advance and transfer were on a turn, how soon she would stop. One morning off San Diego when the sea was calm and smooth, Sanders decided it was time to find out. He spoke to Michaels, quartermaster third class, and sent him down to the chart room for a stop watch.

"Now, Mike, here's the procedure. You straddle the bridge rail out here where you can see the water alongside. I'm going to ring up flank speed, and when the ship is making turns for flank speed ahead I'm going to back her down full speed astern. You start the watch when I reverse her, and you stop it the instant you see she isn't moving in the water."

This ought to be fun. Mike rode the rail while the ship built up speed. The wind whipped past his ears. The ship leaped ahead, lifting herself across the long flat swells like a hound coursing a field. The wake stretched out astern, half a mile, a mile, as the turbines hummed and the screws rumbled at 340 turns a minute and the wind sang in the rigging. She must have been doing forty knots when Sanders barked "Mark!" and swung the annunciator handles all the way back for a panic stop. Mike punched the stop watch; for a few seconds the ship still flung herself ahead and then all hell broke loose. The engineers poured steam to the reversing turbines and the screws, with 60,000 horses behind them, began smashing astern while the ship, all 2500 tons of her, still slugged ahead. She trembled, rattled, bucked, and shook like a shivering dog as the old battle between inertia and power was fought out again. Dishes in wardroom and mess hall went smashing to the deck. Loose gear everywhere flew forward into solid bulkheads. So did a few loose sailors, and the same bulkheads gave them bloody noses and skinned knuckles. The ship groaned, complained, shuddered, heaved and panted, but she finally stopped, and when the boiling water along-side no longer moved aft, Mike punched the stop watch again.

Sanders strode over to the bridge railing and said "Well, Mike, what does she say?"

Mike looked at the stop watch, and felt as if he had swallowed a seabag full of dirty socks. All the hands still pointed straight up. He had forgotten to wind the damned thing! He was considering whether to jump overboard feet first or head first when the Skipper spoke again.

"What does she say, Mike?"

Mike thought of all the busted dishes, bloody noses, and bent and broken gear on the *Aaron Ward,* and wondered what would happen to him.

"Sir, I forgot to wind the watch."

The Skipper bit down on his pipe, and Mike watched a red flush spread up the back of his neck. Finally he spoke.

"Well, Mike, let's not make this mistake again."

As the underway training period drew to an end, a group of officers came aboard in San Diego to check into what might be called the ship's "last request" before she left for the distant Pacific.

"You have your priority list ready, I assume," said the senior officer.

"Right here, Sir," replied Saunders.

The art of preparing a successful request list in the Navy is like that of playing winning poker. One has to bluff; know how far to go, when to stop. Sometimes an overwhelming bluff will wilt the opposition completely. The first item on the *Aaron Ward's* request list stopped the inspection party cold.

"An ice cream machine! What would you do with an ice cream machine?"

"Make ice cream."

"But this ship isn't big enough for an ice cream machine. Besides, you don't rate it."

"But we need it."

"You don't have room for an ice cream machine."

"We'll make room. Take off a 5-inch gun if you have to, but I want an ice cream machine."

The inspection party left. Who ever heard of an ice cream machine for a destroyer? No one, possibly, because the one *Aaron Ward* got was big enough for a cruiser. The ship had ice cream to eat, give away, and trade. Bill Sanders loved ice cream as much as he liked fresh hot bread, and after that, when the galley gang hauled the hot bread out of the ovens about ten at night, the Captain would be on hand for a helping of both.

Soon after the ice cream machine went into production, "Woody" Woodside brought his wife Martha to the wardroom for dinner one night. Eddie Gaines, the duty mess boy, was pleased to have a lady at the table, and took good care of her. Dinner was fine, until the dessert arrived. Eddie proudly served the ice cream to Mrs. Woodside exactly the way the Captain liked it served—a great big heaping soup bowl full of the stuff. He couldn't know that Martha Woodside really didn't like the stuff.

The night before *Aaron Ward* sailed from the West Coast, Steve Stefani reported on board two days late in returning from leave. In the press of preparing the ship for sea the next morning, there was still time for Captain's Mast. Offenders against good order and discipline in the Navy must be brought to justice swiftly, and punished in accordance with their offense.

The yeoman read the notation in the Mast record book: "Steve Stefani, fireman first class, United States Navy, over leave for a period of forty-eight hours."

"What do you have to say for yourself, Stefani?" said the Captain.

Steve explained his predicament. He had obtained leave to go back home, to Cleveland, so as to get in the coal for his wife, Rose, for the winter. But the coal dealer was three days late in delivering it, and he had to haul it all, in a wheelbarrow, from the street around back of the house and into the basement. This took another couple of days. And the best he could do, traveling from Cleveland back to California, was another two days. Steve knew the difference between a reason for being late, and an excuse for being late, and he knew his reason would not qualify as an excuse. The Skipper was pleasant, but he could be tough . . . . *What was that old saying he'd heard sailors use? "Lock him in the brig and throw away the keys." So long, Stefani!*

"You have committed the offense of being over leave, Stefani," said the Captain, "and I have no choice but to punish you." He turned to the yeoman and said "Record the punishment: loss of all liberty for a period of ten days. Mast dismissed!"

Steve went off about his work that morning with a vastly increased respect and admiration for his commanding officer. Loss of all liberty for ten days! Steve knew, and the Captain knew, and everyone else on the ship knew, the *Aaron Ward* would be leaving the United States that day and no one—Steve, the Captain, or anyone else—would be getting any liberty at all for the next ten days.

Plan of the Day for Friday, 9 February 1945. 1630 Underway.
"NOW GO TO YOUR STATIONS ALL THE SPECIAL SEA DETAIL. ALL DEPARTMENTS MAKE PREPARATIONS FOR GETTING UNDERWAY AND REPORT TO THE BRIDGE."

The routine was old hat now. But this time it was different. There was a certain finality about this operation. A man couldn't help sneaking a last sad peek at the Long Beach skyline and wondering when he would see it again. Those who had spent Thursday evening at home with wives and families tried not to think too hard about when the next evening would come. This was the moment they had trained for, planned for, looked forward to, or perhaps feared a little bit, for the past months. For the past months they had been attached to a combatant ship and wearing the uniforms of fighting men, but they had been steaming around in sight of the lights of San Diego, Oceanside, and Long Beach.

Now they were heading out where the fighting was, to places like Torpedo Junction, Iron Bottom Bay, and Coffin Corner. From here on their fate was in the hands of the gods, and for the next six days those of Commander Western Sea Frontier, whose confidential serial 5153 of 8 February directed the ship to sail to Pearl Harbor.

The anchor chain clanked in, dragging black mud from the bottom of Berth 228 DOG across the clean forecastle deck. Finally, Shelley, hanging over the bow of the ship, sang out "Anchor's aweigh!" Ray Biesmeyer picked it up. "Anchor's aweigh," and the phone talker passed it to the bridge, "Anchor's aweigh." The forecastle gang hosed the mud away, almost with regret. That was the last bit of U. S. soil they would see for a long time.

An hour later the ship had worked her way out of the anchorage, through the channel, and stood offshore. A quartermaster made the note in the log: "1731 With Los Angeles light bearing 141 true distance 4.8 miles, took departure for Pearl Harbor, Territory of Hawaii."

"Steer 270" said the Captain.

"Steer 270, Aye, Aye, Sir" replied the helmsman.

West!

Aaron Ward settled down to a steady sixteen knots and headed west. For the next six days the boys who believed that old gag about joining the Navy to see the world would find out that the song had it exactly right—all they would see would be the sea. And for the timid soul who lay in his rolling bunk at night, listening to the thunder of waves smashing at the thin hull, there was the sobering thought that no matter how wide the sea was, there was still lots more underneath.

By midnight, the U. S. was a hundred miles astern. Wherever they were going, they were on their way. Home was now only a memory, to be called up at odd moments like a happy genie if one was able to find time to rub the lamp of recollection. Home was far away, lost in the purple dusk astern. Even the seagulls which had swooped and screamed in the sunset wake turned about and headed home.

For those men who had never gone to sea before, now was to come the first realization of how big the Pacific could be. For those who had sailed the Pacific before, there was the dull thought that maybe they hadn't seen anything yet. Alone, untried, yet filled with determination, *Aaron Ward* and her crew sailed westward through the night.

For the first time in her career the ship sailed out of sight of land, all alone. For the first time in their lives most of the crew found themselves in a limitless black waste of wind and wave, as strange, as unknown, as it had been to Magellan. For the first time they could put their hands in front of their faces and literally feel the night.

Night can be an impressive thing when a man first goes to sea. It comes down, close and solid, like nothing ever known before. Back home in Indiana, the night is wide and filled with friendly sights and sounds—the rustle of a corn field, the glow of headlights moving along U. S. 20, faint music from a roller rink on the edge of town, the slowly moving beacons of planes heading east from Chicago. But at sea when the last flush of color fades from the sky, the horizon disappears, the limitless reach of lonesome ocean turns from cobalt to ultramarine to mysterious black. Then the night creeps out of the sea, floods upwards to the zenith, thick, intense, pressing in on one's eyes until they throb with the futility of trying to see anything where surely nothing can be.

And then there are the stars. Not until land has been left far astern does one ever see the stars in their ageless procession across the night. The few faint points of light one knew back home in Salt Lake City or Waukegan turn into flashing jewels, glowing with color as they hang above the dark sea. Canopus, Capella, Vega, Sirius—all the mighty lighthouses of navigators for ages past come out first. As the night grows deeper, lesser stars, without names, beyond all numbering, swarm across the sky, through the luminous dust of forgotten constellations, a sea of splendor, of infinite wonder, of perpetual silence.

There is a first time for ships to go to sea, a first time for men to go to sea. There is a first time for them to shed a tear on leaving home, a first time to be sick, a first time to be cold and wet and sleepy. And there is a first time for them to look above the masthead at the nighttime sky and know that above all sailors the stars will shed their everlasting glory.

There they are, the same stars that shone on Sidon and Tyre when the first sailors steered from Phoenicia down to Egyptland, the same stars seen by Copernicus and Galileo, the same stars which guided Magellan across the Pacific and Marco Polo home from Cipango. There is an infinite fitness about the scheme of things, that the navigator steering his ship by the light of Vega always finds the star in the same place—right ascension eighteen degrees and thirty-four minutes, declination thirty-eight degrees and forty-four minutes north—whether he comes from Hamburg, Houston, or Hiroshima.

Six days later, on the morning watch, the dim blue shape of Molokai lifted above the horizon. Old timers thought happily of Wo Fat's and the Black Cat Cafe, the malihini's among the crew strained their eyeballs looking for palm trees and hula girls. As the ship rounded Diamond Head and crossed in front of Waikiki and the Royal Hawaiian, Smitty, the chief water tender, climbed out of his boilerroom to take a look. Just like old times, almost—except no meatballs in the air. Of all the men on the ship, Smitty had been at war with the Japanese Navy longer than anyone else. He had been right in that same piece of ocean, thirty-eight months earlier, on a ship with almost the same name—USS *Ward,* when she sank a Japanese submarine trying to sneak into Pearl Harbor, and had watched the raiding planes come in and lay their eggs on battleship row.

Now the *Aaron Ward* nosed her way into the crowded base and her sailors were amazed. All those ships! Here was the U. S. Navy at last. Here, for the first time, was evidence of war—the twisted hulk of the *Arizona,* rusting in the mud since 7 December 1941, and along

Ten Ten Dock and in West Loch, cruisers and destroyers fresh in from the combat area with smashed superstructures and burned out turrets. Men who remembered loading ammo in Long Beach— 16,000 rounds for the 5-inch guns, 45,000 rounds for the twenties, 14,000 rounds for the forties—no longer wondered why.

1500 "NOW HEAR THIS. PIPE SWEEPERS. KNOCK OFF SHIP'S WORK." There wasn't a lot of time before chow—forty-five minutes—but Chuck Willand made the most of it. He took a shower and combed his hair. Chuck had had a short crew cut in Hawaii, and the hair took a long time to grow out. This was the first time he'd been able to comb it in weeks.

A few men scrunched themselves into corners to write letters. A sailor could write all the letters he wanted, but while his output might be voluminous, it was hardly literary. In the first place, there was really very little for a sailor to write home about. One day aboard a ship was very much like any other, and having been told once when a man gets up, when he goes to bed, and how often he washes his socks, very few correspondents waited breathlessly to hear the same routine a second time. But a man had to keep on writing, if he wanted to get any letters.

Next to the paymaster and the cooks, the most popular man on the ship was the mail orderly—so long as he returned from the Fleet Post Office with a bag full of letters. Money was, after all, only money, to be sent home or spent quickly before something dreadful happened to it, such as being borrowed by a shipmate. A man had to eat some food, but the stuff was not really good once one got to thinking of home, and besides, the portions were so small. But one could read a letter again and again, each time finding some small juicy tidbit overlooked earlier, some delicious implication hidden in prosaic words. A real flamer of a letter from the right girl was like good cheese; the older it grew the greater its tang and zip. Life for Blunck, the mail orderly, would have been happier if the crew would just have been content with cheese; he could always get that at the Safeway or steal a piece on some store ship. But if a girl didn't write a letter, Blunck couldn't deliver it. In such situations, unhappy sailors grew disenchanted with their girl friends, and almost suspicious of Blunck.

"Ya got a letter for me today, Blunck, old kid?"

"Sorry, no letter today."

"Whaddoya mean, no letter! I didn't get no letter yesterday either."

"Maybe she didn't write you no letter."

"Yeah . . . . Say, how'd you know she didn't write me no letter?"

"Well, you didn't get one, did you?"

"That's right! Two days now no letter. Wonder why she didn't write me a letter?"

"Maybe she did. You just didn't get it."

"I know I didn't get it. How come I didn't get it?"

"Search me."

"I got a good mind to do that. You and that fouled up Post Office. I know she wrote me a letter!"

"Then how come you didn't get it?"

"Now listen here, Blunck. That's your job. You better get me a letter tomorrow, see?"

Fortunately for Blunck, both the U. S. Navy and the Post Office Department frown on shooting anyone having to do with the U. S. Mail.

Once the ship left the United States, communications grew even more difficult. There were no post offices at sea, so no matter how much a man wrote it just stacked up in Blunck's little office until they reached the next port. And no letter left the ship until it had gained that stamp "Passed by Censor." A man who could write his girl the best letters in the world suddenly lost a good deal of his magic touch with the censor looking over his shoulder; the fact that someone up there in the wardroom had to read his stuff was enough to shoot holes in a man's best efforts.

And if a man strayed too far from the cut and dried "I am fine, how are you" routine, the censor might actually shoot a hole in his letter with a sharp knife—cut out anything which could possibly be of interest or aid to the enemy.

Thus, Rae Good's first letter to his mother after the ship reached Hawaii contained this fascinating passage: "I sure got a surprise yesterday when we went into a barber shop. Most of the barbers are (CENSORED). They give good hair cuts too." If Violet Good wasn't acquainted with Hawaiian customs, she must have puzzled for a long while about where Rae was, and what kind of barbers they had there: three-legged, cannibals, drunkards, or maybe trained chimpanzees? That hole in the letter wouldn't have fooled the Japanese for a moment; the only place in the Pacific with barbers worth writing home about was Hawaii, where they were women.

Wartime Hawaii was not quite the Pacific Paradise one used to read about in the Matson Steamship ads before the war started. The place was so full of sailors and soldiers that every time a shipload of them came in from the States another shipload had to leave for the Western Pacific. The crew went to see Waikiki Beach—covered with sailors; they visited Kapiolani Palace—full of sailors; they ate chop suey at Lau Yi Ki's—with other sailors; and went back to Pearl Harbor, which was filled with sailors. After a couple of weeks of that, mixed in with more training, more drills, and more loading of ammunition and provisions, going to sea again might be a pleasure. At least, there weren't so many sailors. And there was no doubt they were going to sea. The place was full of ships, the tempo was increasing. Something was up, and *Aaron Ward* would be in on it this time.

Just before the ship left Hawaii, Brooks, a shipfitter, was transferred, and with him went one of the more intriguing mysteries of the after crew's compartments—that girl in his locker. Almost everyone had a picture or pictures in his locker—pin up girls, Petty girls, girl friends, sweethearts, fiancees, wives—and many pleasant moments could be whiled away comparing the various and delightful feminine statistics thus represented. This was a recreation in which Brooks never participated. Through devious questioning it was learned that he had been on duty in Hawaii before the war started. It was further deduced that Brooks had a girl friend in Hawaii. Among those few men who had not spent all their time at the Sub Base PX or the Bishop Museum, there was conjecture that the girl was an Oriental . . . .

"You know those Chinese babes. Wow!"

"Yeah? Well, I ain't never been to Hong Kong, but I still don't believe all you Asiatic sailors."

But Brooks kept the girl's picture safely in a large envelope, and no one got to see it.

"Aw, come on, Brooksy, lessee the dame."

"No, dammit all. If I show you, you might laugh, and if you laugh I'll be mad."

So Brooks and his girl's picture left the *Aaron Ward,* with Brooks still not mad at anyone. Whether he had reason for this or not, no one ever knew.

As Brooks left, a few more men joined the crew: Warrant Gunner Siler, the new Mine Control Officer; Robert Follett, a second class mineman, and Wayne Schaefer, metalsmith first class. Schaefer took a long look at the wreck of the *Arizona* as they stood down the channel. His first cruise in the Navy had been spent on that ship. Now he was an experienced destroyerman. He quickly settled down into the routine, found that "Doc" Crider, and storekeeper Richard were pretty good pinochle players, and learned to enjoy coffee breaks on the bridge with the quartermasters, Holte and Flinn. As the ship steamed westward, Schaefer spent his spare time with Flinn in a way most unusual for sailors—reading Shakespeare.

Sunday night in Hawaii. There was probably a song that told what it was like at Waikiki, but that was not what it was like in the crew's quarters of the USS *Aaron Ward*. The atmosphere was a little more tense than it had been previously. That evening, Lieutenant Rubel told his gunnery gang that they were getting under way in the morning, to join Admiral Spruance's Fifth Fleet. Anyone, whether American or Japanese, who had ever heard of the Fifth Fleet, knew that where the Fifth Fleet went there was going to be trouble. Only a few of them, and some of the chiefs, had been west of Pearl. They didn't need to be told what to expect. The others got the word from Dave Rubel—"the going will be tough, and casualties are expected."

Casualties, eh? . . . . Well, hell. Casualties are what happen to someone else.

Monday morning, 5 March 1945, *Aaron Ward* singled up all lines, cast off at 0700, stood down the channel where hundreds of other ships had gone to sea in the past three years and three months. Off Pearl Harbor the crew took a last look at the pink and white hotels at Waikiki, shining against Diamond Head. They weren't going that way. The ship swung her bow to starboard, rounded Barber's Point, and headed west. She joined up with three destroyers, *Purdy, Metcalf,* and *Hart,* the escort carrier *Sangamon,* and the old battlewagon *Maryland.*

For fireman Eddie Strine, this was like meeting an old friend. It had been a long time since he'd seen that ship—not since he was ten years old and his Sunday School teacher back in Baltimore took the kids down to the waterfront to see the ship named after their state. As much as he remembered the huge battleship, Eddie also remembered some other ships, black hulled fellows flying flags with big red balls on them. Eddie's teacher said they were Japanese ships. What Eddie wondered was why were they hauling all that old junk and scrap iron back to Japan.

The ships of Task Unit 12.5.4 headed west, and the last faint trace of Oahu dropped behind the horizon before chow time. The only thing between them and Tokyo now was the Pacific Ocean—and whatever was left of the Japanese Navy. The men who thought there was a lot of water between San Pedro and Hawaii hadn't seen anything yet. And the men who hadn't met up with the Japanese Navy hadn't seen anything yet either.

That evening the PA system buzzed into life and men pricked up their ears.

"This is the Captain speaking. We are underway now to join the fleet. We are headed for the Carolina Islands, for a fleet base at Ulithi. Where we go after that even I don't know. But I can tell you one thing. We are going to see action. When the time comes, I know I can depend on all of you to know your jobs, to know what to do."

There were a few baffled looks down in the crew's quarters when the speakers clicked off. They had argued among themselves about where the ship was headed: China, the Philippines (. . . . MacArthur said "I shall return," didn't he? Okay, let's take him . . . .), India. But Ulithi, who the hell ever heard of that?

If anything, the men got to GQ a little bit quicker that night than they ever had before.

As Hawaii and the niceties of civilization dropped farther over the horizon, the crew assumed an increasingly shaggy look. Despite her load of modern equipment, despite her movie machine, radio receiver, and ice cream plant, the *Aaron Ward* lacked one thing—a barber. Finally Shelley took action. From somewhere he produced a pair of clippers and some scissors, rounded up four or five likely looking candidates, and ordered them to turn to and give each other a haircut. The results resembled coconut plantations which had undergone an invasion by Task Force 58.

"Who did this one?" Shelly asked, pointing to the least gruesome of the lot.

"I did," said Joe Zaloga.

So Joe Zaloga became the ship's barber. He had not joined the Navy to become a barber, but there was a war on and besides, no one argued with the Chief Boatswain's Mate. As for the rest of the crew, they had not joined the Navy to be trimmed by Joe Zaloga, either, but the reasons they had for letting Joe cut their hair were just as good as the reasons Joe had for cutting it.

Halfway between Kwajalein and Ulithi, the heat was unbearable, and the ship wallowed and rolled incessantly across the brassy sea. It was enough to make a Chaplain swear. As Fowers left the Captain's cabin after putting the log on his desk, he slipped, dented himself on the bulkhead, and commented strongly on the situation as he had heard the chiefs do. Fowers was a big boy now, he thought—if he lived one more year from this day he would be twenty-one years old —and the language he used was full of salt.

The door to the Captain's cabin flew open and the Skipper poked his head out.

"Fowers! Come back in here!" he ordered.

Fowers crept back to the cabin. "Yes, Sir?"

"What would your mother say if she heard you talking that way?"

A man could get in trouble enough in the Navy without the Skipper calling on his mother. Fowers decided he'd better wait to talk like a chief until he was one.

"Dear Mom: If any one ever tells me flying fish don't fly, I will tell them to their face they are liars. Today we saw some go as far as forty or fifty yards . . . . "

The first time a man saw them break the surface of the sea and flash off like blue darts, he could not believe his eyes. Wings shining in the sun, they skittered over the waves and disappeared before one had time to do more than shout. Then they flashed out again, and again, sometimes dozens of them at once. There was no doubt about it, they were fish. But there all certainty ended and the arguments began.

"Look at 'em fly"

"They don't fly, all they do is glide."

"They do fly, damitall! Howja think they got up in the air? They don't glide there!"

"Sure they do; they just get up lots of speed before they take off."

"No they don't—they keep going faster. That's flying!"

"No! That's gliding. If they flew they'd flap their wings. And fish ain't got wings!"

"Baloney! That gooney bird back there ain't flapping his wings, but he's flying."

"Okay, you watch him! All he's doing is gliding."

"Sure, with fins like a fish, maybe?"

"Hey, you two down there! Knock off that chatter and get busy!"

"But Chief, he's trying to tell me flying fish fly."

"Well, if they don't fly whyinhell do you call them flying fish?"

In quiet moments, as the ship plowed toward Ulithi and what uncertain fate lay beyond, Flinn drilled Schaefer in his favorite speech from "As You Like It":

All the world's a stage
And all the men and women merely players;
They have their exits and their entrances;
And one man in his time plays many parts . . . .

Huddled in the wing of the bridge under the stars, with mugs of hot coffee in their hands, the two men worked over the Bard's lines on a stage such as he had never dreamed of, a sleek gray ship, pushing her way through a vast sea, while around them were men strangely like the soldier described by Jaques:

Full of strange oaths, and bearded like the pard,
Jealous in honour, sudden and quick in quarrel,
Seeking the bubble reputation
Even in the cannon's mouth . . . .

It was difficult to conceive that sixty days after they left Pearl Harbor, some of them would have indeed made their exits into

. . . . mere oblivion,
Sans teeth, sans eyes, sans taste, sans everything.

Two days before *Aaron Ward* reached Ulithi, the dull monotony was broken.

"BRIDGE, CIC. WE HAVE A SURFACE TARGET, RANGE FIVE MILES."

Surface target! There were no other U. S. ships ahead of them on the track to Ulithi. Could it be a Japanese submarine this far from the Empire? Every eye on the bridge searched the sea. The gunners perked up considerably.

This might be something! Finally a bright-eyed lookout spotted an object ahead, studied it carefully through his binoculars.

"Small boat, Sir. Looks like a lifeboat."

In a few moments it could be plainly seen, riding low and sluggishly on the swells. No sign of life aboard. What could it mean? Small boats didn't go sailing around the Pacific by themselves. Men eyed the derelict fearfully. Could it be a trap? Was there a submarine lying doggo underneath it, waiting for some Samaritan to come along and be blasted out of the water for his trouble? Maybe the boat was booby-trapped with a depth charge. The *Aaron Ward* circled the thing warily, like a suspicious dog. Bill Sanders kept his distance, kept the ship moving, studying what looked like a Navy motor whaleboat but might be something else. Still underway, *Aaron Ward* dropped her own motor whaleboat and sent a searching party to investigate.

The boat crew moved up cautiously, circled the boat, circled it again. Shelley stood in the bow, eyeing the other boat. It was a U. S. Navy boat, no doubt about that, undamaged but nearly filled with water.

"Go alongside!" he ordered.

The two boats touched, and he jumped aboard the derelict. No bodies. No bullet holes. She looked all right. Tentatively, he punched the starter button; the engine growled once and burst into life. The boat moved ahead under its own power. Triumphantly Shelley sailed her back to the ship. The boat was Navy property so they took it along to Ulithi with them.

The mystery finally turned out to be no mystery at all. The boat belonged to the minesweeper *Recruit* at Ulithi, had slipped its mooring and drifted out to sea with the wind. If there was any explaining to be done, some unlucky sailor on *Recruit* did it.

Two days later, *Aaron Ward* steamed into Ulithi. Sightseers hung over the rails, after breakfast, waiting for their first glimpse of green palms and white surf ringing a coral atoll. What they saw, no one could believe, but there it was lifting above the rim of the sea just after quarters—a forest of gaunt black tree trunks. The whole horizon looked like timber land in Oregon after a forest fire. Tree trunks, out here in the ocean? Then they knew—what they saw was the masts of ships, hundreds and hundreds and hundreds of ships, filling the great lagoon with the most magnificent fleet the world had ever known. As the ship moved nearer, rounded

Azor Island, entered Mugai Channel, her crew stared in amazement. Men who had once sailed with the fleet and all those who thought they had seen the fleet back in Pearl, grew silent in awe.

Here, at last, was the U. S. Navy! Flat tops and battle wagons by the dozens, cruisers **and destroyers** by squadrons, and beyond them all, ringing the horizon with a wall of guns, fighting tops, radar antenna, cargo booms and king posts, were tankers, transports, cargo ships, amphibious craft, reefers, beef boats, ammunition ships, hospital ships, repair ships and tenders.

Somewhere around was Ulithi atoll, and the famous Pacific paradise for sailors, the little island of Mog Mog which was rumored to be paved solid with flattened beer cans. It was apparent to all hands, beer-bellied chiefs and fuzzy-cheeked seamen alike, that the stupendous armada of ships was not waiting for a crack at Mog Mog. The entire anchorage crawled with boats, each trailing an urgent white wake, as they shuttled from ship to ship, and the radio circuits were absolute bedlam, with every ship in the anchorage, seemingly, talking at once. No one had to read the Captain's mail to learn that something big was in the air. Almost before they knew it, the ship had received her mail, topped off on provisions and taken on oil. And almost before they knew it, they were at general quarters. Suddenly over the air from OTC came the urgent: "ALL STATIONS THIS CIRCUIT FLASH RED CONDITION YELLOW." That was the real McCoy—it meant "air attack imminent fire on any plane in sight."

The general alarm broke into its strident gong-gong-gong and men made tracks to their guns. Truk was only eighty miles away. Here they come! But the raid was repulsed, miles away, by fighter aircraft, and the gunners relaxed. Not yet.

Back home, the day was St. Patrick's Day, but in Ulithi there was no time for jigs and reels. All day and night the radio circuits blared with urgency, flag hoists whipped in the air across the lagoon, and in the midst of it all a group of serious men climbed on board and more or less disappeared into the CIC room. Their names went in the log. These were Lieutenant Danford, Lieutenant (jg) Koehl, and four radarmen, Reichard, Neumann, Wenta and Reed. *Aaron Ward* had been redesigned to lay mines, was a minelayer, but these fellows didn't look like minelayers.

"What do you suppose they're going to do?"

"Chief says they're fighter directors."

"We're no aircraft carrier! Destroyers don't have fighters."

"Chief says we're gonna have fighters."

That night men avoided the sweltering compartments as long as possible, clustering topside to look at the multitude of ships, wonder if they had a friend on any of them, try to guess how many ships there were, and most of all, speculate on where they were all going.

The next day they would find out.

On Picket Station 10 the afternoon watch for 3 May was nearly over. Again the PA system announced one more event in the routine of the day:

"NOW HEAR THIS. RELIEVE THE WATCH. ON DECK THE FIRST SECTION."

The time was now 1600—four in the afternoon.

The men who had helped the ship through the first four hours of Thursday had now stood their second watch for the day. They would eat supper, have the first and second dog watch—from four to six and from six to eight—off, except for evening GQ. Then they would stand the night watch, the last watch of the day, and Thursday would be over. If nothing happened. In another eight hours it would be Friday—that is, if nothing happened.

"Dear Folks: Here it is, four in the afternoon. I wonder what you are doing? We have been here for four days now, and . . . ."

Nearly 7,000 miles east of Picket Station 10, as the heart flies, was California—San Anselmo, Santa Maria, Merced Falls, Dinuba, Bellflower, Palo Alto, Hollywood, Los Angeles, San Francisco; home, to many men in the *Aaron Ward.*

By this time, night had already come down out of the mountains of California, to fill the sleepy valleys with purple shadows, and turn on the beacon lights at Point Fermin and Point Loma in case a ship was heading that way, coming back from Empire waters, coming back home. Where windows faced the sea, one could always take a last look, just before sunset, hoping. Whether a ship was there in the golden light or not, one could always hope. For someone nearly seven thousand miles out across the Pacific, it took a lot of hope.

By this time, lights were on at home. Perhaps someone there was reading the last letter with that "Passed by Censor" stamp on it, trying hard to find among the words some privacy, trying to forget the censor peering over a shoulder. Perhaps someone there was writing another letter, filled with the same trivial words, the same unspoken wishes. The letters followed one another off westward across the Pacific, like white doves, like the sad "La Paloma" always on the air from some radio station in Tia Juana, and if they weren't blown up or shot down or eaten by cockroaches, perhaps they would finally get to where they were supposed to go. Perhaps. It was such a big ocean, and out there somewhere was one small ship. Perhaps . . . . perhaps.

The lights were on at 3542 Herbert Street, in San Diego, the small white frame bungalow which had been home to Betty and Bill Sanders for several years. Bill had ranged across two oceans since their marriage eleven years earlier, but home was still only two blocks from where both of them had grown up.

Home for the Sanders now included ten-year-old Bill and seven-year-old Nancy. Hopes had gone out from that house, too, to wherever the *Aaron Ward* might be, for everyone in the house was intimately connected with the ship. With Betty Sanders were three other *Aaron Ward* wives—Gen Biesmeyer, Shirley Rubel, and Margaret Kelley. Margaret and Gen were houseguests, Shirley lived with her parents elsewhere in San Diego.

The wives had tried to make a festive evening out of it. They had crowded into a car and gone to Old Town for a Mexican dinner, at Ramona's. But no matter how good the enchiladas were, one could always remember how much better they had tasted when there had been fewer wives but more husbands at the table. On the drive home they went along the Embarcadero to take a look at ships in the bay. No one really expected "their" ship to suddenly show up there, but one could always hope. Back home again, Shirley Rubel made fudge, and they talked about the progress of the war, and the ship, trying carefully to steer the conversation between the Scylla of fear and the Charybdis of rumor.

None of them really knew much about what the ship was doing, but they were big girls now and had their suspicions. In letters, Bill Sanders had inferred to Betty that the ship was merely a training craft, a seagoing school carrying out its peaceful routine far away from possible enemy action. Betty tried hard to believe this, but deep down inside she knew it could not be. Besides, they hadn't had any letters in a long time. If the *Aaron Ward* was a school ship, why didn't their husbands skip a class and write home?

The evening almost over, Betty and Margaret walked the children two blocks down the street to the home of Bill's parents, where they were to sleep. The night was quiet and peaceful; the moon had lifted above the black peaks of the San Jacinto's, had climbed above the palm trees and was riding across the sky toward Point Loma and the distant Pacific. Somewhere out there was their ship.

"The moon is so bright tonight," Margaret said. "It could make a ship easy for a submarine to find." Again their hopes went winging westward, followed by the moon. By the time the moon looked down on *Aaron Ward* that night, hope was about all the crew would have left.

Chapter Five

First Dog Watch

16-18 Steaming as before.

D. M. Rubel, Lt., U. S. Navy

The 16-18 watch, the first dog watch, could be the social event of the day on a ship at sea. Ship's work had been knocked off an hour earlier for the day and men found time for a few quick winks, a tepid shower, a fast game of cards, a letter home, a bit of reading, or friendly arguments. The evening meal would be piped in fifteen minutes; the crew ate early at sea, so supper would be over before sunset general quarters.

Boles, whose section went on watch next, had time to get out his little black note book, check over the names of men in his gun crew, and bring his diary up to date. In the back of his book, in happy disregard of the strict order prohibiting such records, Boles kept a terse diary. It would have been of no comfort to the enemy, but it helped him remember what day it was. The weather had been so rough the past two days he had written nothing at all, but now he scribbled.

"*3 May. The weather has been extremely bad and rainy the last two days, hence no air attack.*"

There, that took care of Thursday.

The little journal was a model of brevity. Boles had written off the vast fleet concentration at Ulithi, the staging for the invasion of Okinawa, the launching of Operation ICEBERG, with less words than he needed to tell a girl goodnight back home.

"*16 March*" he had written when the ship completed its passage from Hawaii, "*arrived Ulithi. The most tremendous spectacle of concentrated naval power that I have ever witnessed.*"

No one could have said more. Ulithi had been the ultimate. It was so big no one could have seen it all. There were so many ships in the huge Fleet no one could count them all. There was such a rush of last minute preparation for the next big battle no one could comprehend it all. Ulithi marked the culmination of a three-year drive across the Pacific, the final push against Japan, the beginning of the end. *Aaron Ward*'s crew hung over the railings for the better part of two days, when they were not handling stores, provision, or fuel lines, marveling at the greatest fighting armada the Pacific had ever seen. That was Task Force Fifty One, spread out from horizon to horizon, and they were a part of it. They were still looking when the speaker system blared into life:

"NOW GO TO YOUR STATIONS ALL THE SPECIAL SEA DETAIL."

The entire atoll had been a seething stew of ships and activity for days. Now it had reached the boiling point. Vice Admiral Kelly Turner was about to lift the lid.

"ON THE FORECASTLE THERE! HEAVE 'ROUND. TAKE THE ANCHOR RIGHT IN."

"SECOND DIVISION. SECURE THE WHALE BOAT FOR SEA."

"ENGINE ROOM. STAND BY TO TEST MAIN ENGINES."

"ALL DEPARTMENTS, REPORT READY FOR GETTING UNDER WAY."

In the anchorage around them, dozens of other ships were getting under way. In the midst of the preparation, a tropical storm crossed the atoll, and as *Aaron Ward* sailed out the channel in a stream of ships, driving, blinding rain cut visibility to a hundred yards. No one could see where they were going. It didn't matter. Very few of them knew.

That night Boles made another entry in his journal. *"19 March. Under way for the big show"* .... Back home in California, 19 March always made newspaper headlines, because it was St. Joseph's Day, the day the swallows came back to Capistrano. If the *Aaron Ward* crew had known where they were going, they would have considered themselves lucky to know that they would just get back to Ulithi.

As *Aaron Ward* steamed out of Ulithi, the Captain and all his off watch officers met in the wardroom. There on the table in front of him was THE WORD. The package he unwrapped contained a big black book with silver colored letters:

"TOP SECRET. Commander Task Force Fifty One, Commander Amphibious Forces, U. S. Pacific Fleet, Operation Plan No. 1A-45. CAUTION. *Every precaution must be taken to prevent this plan from falling into enemy hands. If capture or loss of ship is imminent this plan must be destroyed in its entirety."*

Then, in case one missed the security classification the first time, there it was again across the bottom of the cover: "TOP SECRET."

Well, where are we going? Open 'er up and let's see.

The inside cover page was as innocuous as a PTA program. The essence of it was; Some of this plan is here, some of it is not. The plan shall be downgraded to CONFIDENTIAL as of 1 August 1945 .... *August! Well, we'd better have the war over by then, I guess* .... Signed, R. K. Turner.

But whereinhell are we going? Turn the page!

There it was: General Instructions for the Amphibious Phase of the Operation for the Capture of Okinawa and nearby islands . . . .

"Okinawa, eh? Okinawa! Surge, go get the Atlas."

Okinawa was not so famous then as it was to become in the next few weeks. If one read farther in the operation order, he would learn that Okinawa was in the Ryukus Islands. If one hunted around through the Atlas long enough, he learned that the Ryukus were also called the Luchu Islands. Nobody had been there since Perry sailed across the Pacific in 1854 to open the door to Japan and let out the young dragon which had ravaged the Pacific for over three years.

On the second day out, Bill Sanders spoke to his crew over the PA system. "You all wonder where we are going. Our destination is Okinawa. It is an island, about ten miles wide by sixty miles long, only a very short distance from the Japanese homeland. There are supposed to be half a million people on this island. We expect they will put up a hard, bitter resistance. We will be operating within range of aircraft from Japan. Not much is known about Okinawa. The last time Americans landed there was when Commodore Perry sailed across the Pacific in 1854 to open the door to Japan. I can assure you we are going to see action. I have assured myself that all of you will do everything in your power to help the ship give a good account of herself."

Okinawa, eh?

Stand by, Tojo. We're coming to open the door again!

That night the ship steamed through stormy seas toward the big green island no man among them had ever seen. Whatever the veterans among them knew of battle—and Shelley alone had been in thirteen major engagements, including the Coral Sea, Santa Cruz, and Tarawa, and had seen *Yorktown* and *Hornet* sink—they had yet to learn that Okinawa would be a battle such as none of them had ever known. There was a sentence, buried a couple of hundred

135

pages deep in the top secret operation plan that held grim promise " . . . *strong and persistent attacks by Japanese aircraft based in the Empire, Formosa and Nanshei Shoto must be expected, with intensification of recent employment of suicide tactics.*"

Whoever opened the door this time had best be prepared. More than dragons were coming out.

From Ulithi up to Okinawa, for the next five days, *Aaron Ward* and hundreds of other ships slogged along in rough seas. Neupert and Tiwald missed lots of meals. Tommy Erice didn't mind, he was too sick to cook then. In CIC Vermie and Beadel divided their time between the radar screen and a handy bucket. As they neared Okinawa, two floating mines appeared and the ships shot them up. Don Young finally had to shut down the port engine due to a leaky valve. That valve worried more than the engineer—the ship could keep up with the formation on one engine, but she wouldn't be able to maneuver to avoid an attack. Sure enough, that night enemy planes circled the formation at sunset, but several ships opened fire, and drove them off before an attack developed. No strain so far.

On 24 March the mine flotillas were in their assigned areas off Okinawa, sweeping for mines. *Aaron Ward's* business was laying mines, not sweeping them. There were no mines to be laid, so she "rode shotgun" for the sweepers—trailed along astern to shoot up any mines cut loose by the sweepers. There was little to see, not much to do except ride around, and men began to think maybe Okinawa had been overrated. By that time they had heard that Okinawa was a fortress, with everyone in it armed to the teeth— there were 16-inch guns in the hills, there were 3,000 airplanes hiding in tunnels and ready to pounce out, the Japanese would fight to the last man. But no one had seen any guns, planes or Japanese so far.

Next day, things got more interesting. The ship sighted Kerama Retto, a cluster of green little islands fifteen or twenty miles west of the southern end of Okinawa. As the sweepers moved in, they could see the place under intense attack by carrier planes, but still there was little opposition. Just some light anti-aircraft fire. On the beaches, in little coves, one could see fishing villages, and on the steep green slopes of the islands, tiny terraced fields and simple little peasant shacks. It seemed almost improper: no one on the *Aaron Ward* was really at war with a bunch of poor Japanese farmers who could only fight back with hoes.

But all the Japanese weren't fighting with hoes. Suddenly there was a mine ahead, lifted by the sweepers, and *Aaron Ward* cut loose on it with the port quad forty. The guns barked and empty brass clattered out on deck and the projectiles stitched patterns across the sea until they found the mine. There was a deafening explosion, a dirty column of smoke and water lifted a hundred feet in the air, and bits of shrapnel screamed overhead. After that sobering demonstration of what the Japanese could do purely by accident, no one wanted to question what they might do on purpose. And after that everyone remembered to wear their helmets. The war might start any minute after all.

An hour or so later, they thought it had. One of the lookouts shouted the alarm:

"BRIDGE! PLANE ON THE PORT QUARTER, HEADING IN!"

All in the same instant, the OOD snapped "Sound General Quarters—all engines ahead full!" The quartermaster's hand hit the alarm switch, the annunciator to the engine room clanked and the black gang poured a full head of steam to the turbines, the guns whined to life and began sniffing off the port quarter like hungry hounds. In the wardroom the Skipper nearly turned the table over on Doc as he catapulted himself out; by the time they both had pounded up two flights of ladders to the bridge, the plane was low above the water, heading on a course parallel to them, maybe a mile out. It was a big fat F6F. Friendly!

"CONTROL TO ALL GUNS! PLANE IS FRIENDLY, RE-PEAT FRIENDLY. HOLD FIRE. PLANE IS FRIENDLY."

The gun crews relaxed slightly. After running all the way to

GQ, a man itched to get in a few shots at something. But the plane was friendly, no doubt about that now, and he was also harmless—his engine was dead, the prop slowly windmilling as he came down. Two more planes circled the wounded craft, guiding the ship to the rescue.

From his vantage point on the bridge, Doc Barbeiri noted that Chief Shelley was already on the forecastle. Doc smiled. He knew that even if the pilot climbed aboard by himself, "Crazy" Shelley would jump overboard to rescue him anyhow, thus entitling himself to two ounces of medicinal brandy for his exposure to the elements.

The ship raced along, bow slicing the waves and heaving up bursts of sparkling spray. Half a mile ahead the plane skimmed just above the waves for a moment, nosed up, bellied in, and disappeared in a great white splash. Then they could see it, wallowing like a winged duck, and all hands cheered as the pilot climbed out of the cockpit and onto one wing. The other planes circled the downed craft, zooming over the spot, and one dropped a dye marker. The plane was slowly sinking and the pilot stood there on the wing, going down with his ship as it were, until *Aaron Ward* slid alongside with a great rumble and swish of screws backing full astern and Sanders stopped her with the bow neatly in position near the plane, now awash. A line snaked out from the forecastle, and the pilot knotted it about himself.

Splash. "There goes Shelley!" someone cheered. Doc knew it —"Crazy" was going to cinch that shot of brandy.

In another minute the pilot was on the bridge, soaked but unharmed to report to Sanders.

"I'm Lieutenant Dalton, from the *Bennington*," he introduced himself in a Texas drawl. "Man, was I glad to see this old dee-stroyer!"

His engine had lost its oil supply and froze up he explained, so he picked the nearest ship and dunked in the approved fashion.

"Come down to the sick bay," invited Doc. "I'll check you over to make certain you're all right . . . . Shelley! You'd better come along. You might also need medical attention."

Lieutenant Dalton remained on board the ship for the next four days, and it seemed to the wardroom that during every hour of those days he was beseeching someone to get him off that dee-stroyer and back to his big, safe old carrier. It just wasn't healthy out in those little boats, so far as Lieutenant Dalton was concerned. They might get shot at.

The day after Dalton came aboard, *Aaron Ward* worked with a sweep unit clearing mines in the area between Kerama Retto and the southern end of Okinawa. Enemy planes attacked the unit, but only briefly, and the only plane that got near enough to cause trouble was splashed by *Adams* before he had a chance to do any damage. Hosking, one of the radarmen, saw the plane start to smoke, turn into a ball of fire, and come spiraling down into the sea. Back home in South Dakota he had dreaded bloodshed, had hated to have to kill a chicken, but he felt no pity even though he knew a human being had burned to death before his eyes. Now it was a case of the hunter and the hunted and he thrilled as if seeing the first duck fall in open season.

This war was still no pain, the crew felt. But by sundown most of them had changed their minds.

The off watch was lined up for chow, waiting in the port passageway. Eddie Strine was looking right at the USS *Halligan* steaming along a couple of miles away, when a column of black suddenly towered two hundred feet above her like an evil genie and the ship broke in two. In a few seconds the dull *whoomph* of the explosion hit their ears, and they watched a PC and some little amphibious craft hurry in to the rescue. There was not a lot of chatter in the chow hall during supper. While they had watched, the Japanese had sunk the first ship in the Okinawan campaign without firing a shot, and one hundred and fifty-three men had died in front of their eyes.

"Well, boys," said Sanders when he entered the wardroom later. "You realize now you're in a war. Everyone had better be on the lookout."

From that moment on, everyone was on the lookout. The dread that a mine might at any instant be under the ship, ready to blow her sky high, made one take terrific interest in the work of the sweepers and keep both eyes peeled for any mines they might miss. Two days later the radiomen picked up the word on the TBS—mines got the *Skylark* over near Hagushi. The sneaky, unseen, stealthy things made a man want to tread lightly on deck.

Riding around down there on the water where one could get blown up by mines or torpedoes was not for Lieutenant Dalton. He finally got off that dee-stroyer and went back to his carrier. The next thing *Aaron Ward* heard, he had been given another airplane, and that one had been splashed too. Lieutenant Dalton wasn't lucky that time.

Aircraft pilots needed all the luck there was at Okinawa. The only enemy the surface ships had there were aircraft, and sometimes an excited gunner shot at the wrong one. This happened on 28 March during sunrise general quarters.

"BOGIE! BOGIE CLOSING FAST!"

They could see the plane then, heading for them. Ahead of *Aaron Ward,* the *Robinson* opened up first, made a solid hit. The plane started down, smoking, and only then did they identify it. Friendly!

It was a Corsair, a U. S. Navy carrier plane. In CIC, the men listened in sad silence as a voice on a carrier somewhere beyond the horizon began calling the missing plane over the CAP circuit:

"JIG FOUR THIS IS JIG BASE."

"JIG FOUR THIS IS JIG BASE. COME IN PLEASE."

"JIG FOUR THIS IS JIG BASE. DO YOU READ ME?"

Why the Corsair had flown toward the ships, no one would ever know. The rule for ships was, shoot any unidentified planes within 12,000 yards. At Okinawa any plane headed directly toward a ship had to be considered hostile. If a hostile plane got close enough to be shot down, that was the only thing to do. A couple of seconds wasted in speculating that a plane might be friendly could mean the loss of a ship if he turned out hostile. The men in CIC listened to JIG BASE calling JIG FOUR, over and over, until somewhere men finally realized that JIG FOUR was not coming in.

The battle flamed and swirled about Okinawa, and the TBS chanted the roll of ships hit, burned, and sunk. Eventually everyone knew that the big day would be 1 April. That was D Day—the day the troops hit the beach. On Saturday night Boles scribbled in his hip pocket diary: *"Tomorrow is the day of the big push. Also is Easter Sunday. A shame, so many of our boys have to die on that day."* Boles was still the eternal optimist; if something happened, it would happen to someone else.

On deck, that night, sailors watched the sun go down as a huge red ball of fire. Yet when Hosking came topside, he saw the stars, serene as they had been back home. There was Regulas overhead, Denebola a litle to the east, Sirius and Procyon in the west. It was difficult to remember that out of the quiet night a plane might hurtle at any moment, loaded with death.

There was a little rhyme the kids used to say back home, on summer evenings .... Star bright, star light, first star I see tonight .... Then they wished for something. What could a sailor possibly wish for, in that strange sea, that he had any hope of getting? To see the same star again tomorrow night. That would be all anyone could possibly want, off Okinawa.

1630 Supper. Watch three eat first and relieve the watch for chow.

For the eighty-third time since leaving the states, the men lined up in the port passageway opposite the galley and traded taunts with the galley crew while they waited for the chow line to start past the steam serving tables. Section three was first in line; they had just come off watch at 1600, had just about time for the sailors traditional beauty treatment—shower, shampoo, shave, and shine, before going on watch while section one ate. Then section one would go back on watch and section three could goof off a little until time for evening general quarters.

The conversation in the chow line generally hinged on consumer-producer relations. A sailor could always open such a discussion by shouting at the cook: "Bellyrobber!" The proper reply to this was always "Pelican." The rest of the conversation was as cut and dried as the menu.

"What's for chow?"

"Liver."

"Just what I'd ordered if I went ashore."

"Hey, back there! If you guys don't like liver, supper is practically over."

"Chowdown! Grab it and growl!"

Supper eventually was over. The men who liked liver ate it as if it was the last supper they would ever have. The men who didn't like liver growled, but they ate it anyway. For some of them it was the last supper they would ever have.

By 1700 supper was over and the men had time to consider again the tedium of going to sea. The sea was always the same, the days always the same. Supper had been the same as always—the same faces, the same chow in the same chow hall, the same waiting and pushing through the chow line, the same chatter while eating and the same rush to get it over with and topside where the air, if not cooler, was at least moving. Now they settled down to do the same things they had always done at this time.

In the same private little corner where he always wrote his letters, behind the ready ammo box for a 40 millimeter gun, Seaman Rader began a letter to his wife, Lucille, back home in San Pedro. In the same bunk where he always could be found, Hosenose Muirhead settled down for another little nap. Throughout the ship men on watch went about the same dull routine again and again, now repeated for a hundred times, a thousand times, ten thousand times: log the sea water temperature, check the feed valve to the luboil pump, sound the peak tank, break out another crate of spuds for the galley, check all firing circuits, type the provisions inventory, test the phones, make a report, report, report, report. Throughout the ship they kept their eyes and hands and mind on the job at hand, while their hearts hurried off to Lancaster, Pennsylvania; or Salem, Nebraska; or Dinuba, California—to any place called home.

. . . . Let's see now. What will Marie be doing right this minute? Five o'clock in the afternoon; she's been out to look in the mail box for a letter from me—fat chance!—and the baby is waking up and

she's heating a bottle. But hell, it wouldn't be five in the afternoon back there, would it? More likely five in the morning . . . . Yeah, but what morning? It's Thursday on this side of the Date Line, must be Friday on that side . . . . or is it yesterday on that side and tomorrow on this side? Can't be tomorrow here, has to be today. Then maybe it's tomorrow already where Marie is. Hells fire! If I died right now she'd never know it because she's already past Thursday. I'd better play it safe, and last until tomorrow, then I'll be back in the same day she is. Or will I? Hell of a way to run a war, this is . . . .

"Control! You call me? . . . . Who's doping off? I'm right here, right here with these phones on my ear, man . . . . You bet I'm keeping on my toes. On 'em all day yesterday, been on 'em all day today, prolly on 'em all day tomorrow, too. If there is any tomorrow . . . . Okay, bud, you wanna bet?"

In the after crew's quarters Rae Good got out his box of stationery and his book of six cent airmail stamps and addressed an envelope to his mother, back in Bellflower, California. This was an important date in the Good family, and Rae remembered it. While his bunkmates frisked about in their skivvies, Rae started his letter. One of them, Harry Abercrombie, was from his same town, went to the same school, and had had Rae's mother for a teacher.

"USS Aaron Ward
Thursday 3
May, 1945
Dear Mom,

"Happy birthday, Mom. Of course this won't reach you until after your birthday, but I can't tell you in person so have to write what I am thinking.

"You and Pop are probably going out to dinner tonight. Sure wish I was home to go with you.

"We had liver for chow tonight. It would have been pretty fair except for the dryness. All our meat is usually quite dry. Either that or it is mutton. Both are bad . . . . "

All around him men were changing clothes, swabbing themselves off after clattering down from the shower on the deck above. Someone chased Rae off his locker top so he moved his letter to another. Someone else chased him off that locker to yet another. It took a man quite a while to scribble a few pages in such crowded conditions, but Rae finally made it, and ended with the hope of all sailors at sea—mail.

". . . . What about Glen—is he still around? In a couple of days we should be getting some of our mail from the earlier part of April. The latest letter was April fifth, I believe.

"Almost time for sunset GQ so will close.

Love
Rae"

Rae tucked the letter in the stationery box and shoved it under his bunk. Mail it in the morning. He would never know that his brother Glen, a Marine, was less than a hundred miles away on the island of Okinawa.

During the first days of the invasion of Okinawa, *Aaron Ward* was plagued by the same trouble she had brought up from Ulithi with her—a leaky valve which kept one engine shut down a good deal of the time. The ship could make eighteen knots on one engine, but out on the picket lines a ship needed two engines and twenty-eight knots. Besides, while maneuvering in Kerama Retto's shallow waters, she had bunged up the sound dome, and this limited her underwater search ability. So, on 4 April CTF 51 ordered the ship back to Saipan for a six day trip for urgent repairs. With her went an assortment of minecraft—*Salem, Keokuk, Dorsey,* and *Ardent.* For a couple of weeks *Aaron Ward*'s crew could breathe a little easier, yet they left Okinawa with reluctance; the fight there was far from over and they felt they had not yet done their part.

On 10 April they steamed into Saipan, to learn that repairs could not be made there. On to Guam.

As *Aaron Ward* herded her charges into the quiet harbor at

Guam, some of the crew licked their chops in happy anticipation of a run on the beach. Down in one of the holds, safely stashed away for use at the proper time, were 400 cases of Pabst Blue Ribbon beer. Since the ship was certain to have a couple of fellows who didn't drink beer, there appeared every chance in the world that a couple of other fellows might get more than their just and legal share. Unfortunately for such happy speculation, someone on the ship got his share early. When the storeroom was unlocked, some of the beer was gone. For perhaps the first time, the crew faced a furious captain. Sanders made a talk about the missing beer over the battle announcing system. He felt that he couldn't trust his own men, and until the culprits revealed themselves, there would be no beer for anyone. And there wasn't. When Sanders gave his word on something he never backed down.

Eventually, it developed there couldn't have been many culprits —probably no more than one—because only six cans of beer were missing. The six missing cans were the subject of especially bitter recriminations down in the CPO quarters, where probably most of the best beer drinkers were concentrated, and where they were prone to point suspicious fingers . . . .

"Goddamitall, you're the only man on the ship with keys to that store room. All you have to do is go tell the old man you took the beer, that's all."

Silence. No confession.

And no beer.

Six months later 399¾ cases of Pabst Blue Ribbon were unloaded from the ship in the Brooklyn Navy Yard. Despite the best efforts of the Japanese Air Force, not a can of it had been harmed. The beer had sailed from San Pedro to Hawaii to Okinawa and Guam to Okinawa to San Diego to Panama to New York. It was probably the best traveled beer ever to leave Milwaukee—and solid proof of the fact that when Bill Sanders said no, he meant exactly that.

The radio shack was another small community set apart from the rest of the *Aaron Ward*. In it the radiomen lived among a maze of black boxes, dials, switches, cigarette trays and stagnant coffee cups, and out of it, insofar as it pertained to *Aaron Ward,* flowed the news of the world. The radiomen hunched over their typewriters, intent on the cricket-like dit-dah-dits and dah-dit-dahs chirped by the big receivers, and pecked out English translations of such gibberish which was often not much more intelligible than it had been in dit-dah talk. On Friday, 13 April, in Guam, the man copying traffic groaned as he typed the heading of what could be a long tedious message:

ALNAV 69 FROM SECNAV TO ALNAV.

Suddenly he grew alert, and other men in the room, sensing his increased attention, crowded to watch over his shoulder as the words formed:

I HAVE THE SAD DUTY OF ANNOUNCING TO THE NAVAL SERVICE THE DEATH OF FRANKLIN DELANO ROOSEVELT, THE PRESIDENT OF THE UNITED STATES, WHICH OCCURRED ON TWELVE APRIL . . . .

Already someone was out the door, spreading the word. This was one message the Captain would not have to publish to all hands. The radio gang stared in dumb disbelief as the words continued:

. . . . THE WORLD HAS LOST A CHAMPION OF DEMOC-RACY WHO CAN ILL BE SPARED BY OUR COUNTRY AND THE ALLIED CAUSE. THE NAVY WHICH HE SO DEARLY LOVED CAN PAY NO BETTER TRIBUTE TO HIS MEMORY THAN TO CARRY ON IN THE TRADITION OF WHICH HE WAS SO PROUD X COLORS SHALL BE DISPLAYED AT HALF MAST . . . .

Men turned away, unable to read any more. Eventually the complete message was posted on bulletin boards throughout the ship, where men stopped again and again, to read what they already knew, and then walked away, silently.

What are we going to do now? their eyes said to one another.

They knew what they were going to do. The war was far from over. That same day, back on the picket lines, kamikazes hit *Purdy, Zellars, Cassin Young, Riddle, Rall, Walter C. Wann, Whitehurst, Lindsey, Jeffers,* and *Gladiator.* Carry on, the man said.

They would go back to Okinawa.

Despite too much heat and not enough beer, Guam was a peaceful interlude the men would long remember. While the repair force worked on the engine and sound gear, most of the crew worked on Blunck, the harried mail orderly.

"Come on, Blunck. Get us some mail. All those other ships got mail."

True enough. But though Blunck went to the fleet mail center every day he always came back empty-handed. After three days, he was almost afraid to come back. But then the whale boat came dashing back to the ship with Blunck waving victory. Mail! The crew made for the post office faster than they went to GQ. Blunck had some mail—ten bedraggled letters, for the entire crew. Ten lucky men dashed off to their private corners with their treasure. The other three hundred all tried to get at the unhappy mail orderly.

"Now see here, Blunck. They got shiploads of that stuff over there. How come you can't get any for us?" That was a good question. Blunck wished he had a good answer. More than that, he wished he could get some mail.

Finally, just before the ship sailed for Okinawa, the boat made one last trip.

"Blunck, either you get the mail this time or you don't come back."

An hour or so later, there came the motor whaleboat. The bridge gang could tell by the very way she leaped and crested on the waves that at last it had happened—the mail had come through. The boat was hooked onto the falls, jerked aloft, two-blocked in the davits, while eager hands hauled the three bulging mail bags out onto deck. People fell all over themselves helping Blunck get the mail to the post office. Blunck was the man of the hour—until the mail had all been delivered. Then he spent the next five minutes trying to explain to the OOD how come he was late relieving the watch.

As the ship headed back to battle, men spent their spare time reading, catching up on what had happened at home since "last time." They wallowed in mail.

"Dear Mom: Guess I had better get started answering your nineteen letters that came yesterday. All in all I got around thirty or thirty-five letters, a couple school papers, several church letters and four magazines and one funny paper . . . . "

Lefty Lavrakas retreated to his room and for once didn't care whether Don Young plugged up the ventilators or tore them out completely. He had three letters from Billye Charleyville in Long Beach, and although all the girl had sent was a few sheets of paper covered with words, she had used words which enabled Lefty to later walk all the way to the wardroom without touching the deck once. In the same mail, Rosy Rosengren learned he had made Lieutenant, junior grade. But not everyone had such grand news. Art Aylworth learned that his brother Charles, a Captain in the Army Infantry, had been killed on Tinian on 11 February.

Aaron Ward returned to Okinawa on 23 April, and the next day DELEGATE sent the ship out on the picket line, to relieve *Cole* on Station Number 1. There was the hottest piece of ocean around the island, fifty miles north of Point BOLO, and right on the track where enemy planes came down from Kyushu. Whenever the enemy hit the picket lines, Station 1 was the first to know it. *Aaron Ward* assumed duties of OTC, and with *Mustin,* and the small boys LCSL 24, LSMR 19, and PGM 9, settled down to watch and wait.

Patrolling on Station 1 was a little like pulling guard duty in a cemetery. The ship steamed around and around, unrolling a white wake across the blue sea, and the blue sky and sparkling sun looked as it did in the recruiting posters. But in the dark depths beneath them were the grim remains of battle. Destroyer *Bush* had been sunk there on 6 April, with ninety-four of her crew killed. *Colhoun* had been so smashed up in the same battle that other ships on the station had to sink her. The kamikazes had hit *Bennett* there on 7 April and made a floating wreck of her. She was in Kerama Retto, waiting for repairs which would not be made until the war was over. On 12 April kamikazes had worked over *Purdy* and *Cassin Young* on that station, and four days later they hit *Laffey* there.

Laffey's struggle was one of the wildest melees a ship had ever survived. Fifty enemy planes jumped her in a battle lasting over an hour. *Laffey* shot nine of them down, but six more smashed into the ship and she had been towed off to Hagushi with pumps battling every minute to keep her afloat.

So the bottom of the ocean around Station 1 held two U. S. destroyers and untold dozens of smashed Japanese aircraft. *Aaron Ward* and her friends patrolled above them, waiting. They had not long to wait.

The Japanese came again on 27 and 28 April, and on the picket lines, at Hagushi, and in Kerama Retto, the guns roared and chattered; dog fights of CAP planes and enemy Zekes, Vals and Tonys growled across the sky; and the "floating chrysanthemums" of the Japanese blossomed into golden balls of wreckage as burning planes tumbled into the sea.

No matter what a man might be doing when the GQ alarm went, manning battle stations took precedence over all else. The enemy planes came fast when they came, and the Japanese had indeed caught more than one sailor with his pants down. The thing to do was, get to the guns first, and then growl about the inconvenience of war. One day Boles dashed out of the shower wearing only a towel and reached Mount 52 wearing only grim determination. There was a check-off list posted in Mount 52, detailing the duties of every member of the gun crew, but it said nothing about their having to wear pants. *Come on, you Nippers, the 5-inchers are ready.*

"MOUNT 51 MANNED AND READY . . . . MOUNT 52

MANNED AND READY .... MANNED AND READY ....
READY .... READY ...."

The 5-inch 38 cal. gun was a beautiful machine. Its parts fitted together as carefully, as delicately, as the parts of a fine watch, yet it was rugged enough to contain the crashing explosion of eleven pounds of powder. That explosion generated enough energy to hurl a fifty-four pound projectile some nine miles. From the mount captain down to the last sweating man in the magazines, each twin mount required from twenty-five to thirty men to service it in action. Gathered in the mount, the gun crew stood ready, each with a specific title, each with a specific task; the mount captain with the phones for communication with the control officer; the pointer who controlled the guns in a vertical plane; the trainer who moved them in a horizontal plane; the sight setter who fed in slight adjustments for wind, and range when the gun fired in local control; the fuse setter who set the shells to explode at predetermined times; the projectile loaders who slammed the projectiles into the open breeches; the powder loaders who heaved the big powder cans in after the projectiles; the spademen who checked the breech closed and dropped the loading spade after the counter recoil; the hot shell-men with asbestos gloves who snatched out the smoking powder cases and heaved them out the chute on deck.

Below the gun room in the upper handling room, from nine to twelve more men worked to keep the ammunition going up the electric-hydraulic hoists, and below them, in the magazine, another crew moved the stuff out of stowage racks and into the "merry-go-round" which took it up to the guns.

Each gun crew had drilled and drilled and drilled, in dead air and stifling heat, with the ship heaving and rolling, until they moved with the precision and timing of a ballet. This was hot, rugged, dangerous work: the twin guns swallowed up and spit out as many as thirty shots per minute.

Once the guns began bellowing, everyone was too busy to worry about what was going on outside; only the mount captain and pointer and trainer could see outside and usually there was so much smoke they couldn't. Control, up above the bridge, kept the guns on target; the gun crew kept the guns fed; the handling room crew passed the ammunition and possibly thought about praising the Lord if they ever got up where they could see blue sky again.

The handling room crews watched the projectiles and powder cases go up the hoist but couldn't see where they were going; the gun crews fed the stuff into gaping breeches but couldn't see what it hit; if a shell knocked a plane down they couldn't see it; if the plane hit the ship they might hear it; and if the magazine went up none of them would ever know it. On the whole, they were a very uninformed bunch of people. Of course, the only information they ever really wanted to hear was "We won!"

The first raid hit Station 1 at 2130. The crew had been at GQ since sunset, waiting for them. During the long night CIC reported thirty-seven distinct raids to DELEGATE. Time after time the planes came in, and time after time *Aaron Ward* and the other ships on Station 1 drove them off, or splashed them. All night long the gun crews stood by their guns while the bridge crew maneuvered the ship to avoid incoming attacks. Picket Station 1 was not the only target; the planes seemed to be all over.

"DELEGATE THIS IS SAGEBRUSH. RADIO CHECK. OVER."

"SAGEBRUSH FROM DELEGATE. I READ YOU LOUD AND CLEAR. YOU KNOW BETTER THAN TO ASK FOR A RADIO CHECK DURING FLASH RED. OVER."

"DELEGATE THIS IS SAGEBRUSH. SORRY, BUT A KAMI-KAZE JUST FLEW THROUGH OUR RIGGING AND WE WANTED TO TEST TO SEE IF WE HAD ANY ANTENNAS LEFT. OVER."

The kamikazes hit *Ralph Talbot, England, Daly, Twiggs,* and *Butler.* One of them caught the hospital ship *Comfort* some fifty miles away from Okinawa on her way to Guam. The ship was lighted, identified as a hospital ship according to the Geneva Convention, but a plane smashed into her anyway. During the raid, *Aaron Ward*'s gunners proved that Dave Rubel's drills paid off. They knocked down two Bettys and one Val and the ship remained untouched. But others were not so lucky.

"DELEGATE THIS IS SLUEFOOT REPORTING A PARTIAL HIT."

"SLUEFOOT THIS IS DELEGATE. INTERROGATIVE PARTIAL HIT."

"DELEGATE THIS IS SLUEFOOT. WE GOT A ZEKE. PART OF HIM MISSED US BUT PART OF HIM HIT."

At 1100 on 27 April the *Wadsworth* swung into position on Station 1 and relieved *Aaron Ward*. Her first go at the picket stations had ended successfully. The only casualty was coxswain Jerry Devlin who had dropped a shell on his foot during a loading drill. *Aaron Ward* hauled off to Hagushi to take on fuel and ammunition. *Wadsworth* had not been so lucky. Five days earlier, out west of Okinawa on Picket Station 10, she had been hit by a kamikaze and had had another brush with one earlier that morning on Station 12.

Aaron Ward swung down south past Iheya Shima, Izena Shima, and Ie Shima, the little island where Ernie Pyle had died ten days earlier, and threaded her way into the crowded anchorage at Kerama Retto. Later that evening she went alongside the *Mayfield Victory* to take on ammunition. In the growing dusk men hurriedly heaved the powder cans and projectiles aboard. No one liked being alongside an ammunition ship any longer than necessary. As the men worked, big Navy PBM patrol planes, their flight ended, came drifting in across the low hills and settled down in the anchorage.

Suddenly there were shouts and strident alarms. There was a PBM coming in to land and sneaking along behind it to avoid radar detection, a Japanese plane. By the time anyone realized what was happening, the plane was in an attack run, strafing, heading right for the ammo ship. If he hit that ship and she went up, the whole harbor might well be wrecked.

For one agonizing moment ships held their fire, hoping not to attract the attention of the raider, but some small spit kit courageously let go a few shots and all hell broke loose. In an instant Kerama Retto exploded into furious action. Thousands of tracers filled the air, zipping in all directions as ships around the harbor fired on the plane.

Now was definitely no time to be alongside an ammunition ship, and *Aaron Ward* commenced that classic naval maneuver known as getting the hell out of there.

"Cast off the lines!" ordered the OOD.

For once Sanders took the pipe out of his mouth.

"Cut the lines!" he roared.

Axes flashed, and there went Shelley's fine manila mooring lines, chopped to bits. *Sorry, chief, no time for regrets now.*

Amidst the uproar, Doc heard someone screaming "The Captain's been hit, the Captain's been hit," and raced to the bridge, only to find the shouting was coming from the *Mayfield Victory.* "Surge, you stay aboard," Sanders ordered and in the same breath, "All engines ahead full!" *Aaron Ward* dug her fantail into the water and leaped as the engineers poured the full power of 60,000 horses into her turbines. All around the harbor ships scrambled to get underway and the sky burned with anti-aircraft fire. Everything seemed to happen in an instant; the plane coming in, the alarms, the gun fire, the sudden rush of ships to get somewhere else. And then the plane wavered in its flight toward the ammo ship, turned, and smashed down on the *Pinkney*, a big hospital evacuation ship 2000 yards away from *Aaron Ward.* There was a dull *whooomph,* and the big ship was wreathed in flames. In the fierce red glow dozens of small boats rushed to her aid. *Aaron Ward* moved up as close as she dared to offer help.

Doc, still on the bridge, felt he was living in a nightmare—a night of raging fires, dead and wounded men, and worst of all, the screams of many battle fatigue patients the *Pinkney* had carried. Eventually the flames were drowned and *Aaron Ward* took off some of the wounded. The patients were all psychos, and before the night ended

153

everyone on board was so jittery Doc warned Sanders he had to get them off before they spooked the whole crew. Early next morning *Aaron Ward* pulled alongside *Terror,* unloaded the poor fellows there and slipped away before anyone had a chance to refuse them. Doc was to feel bad about that, too, because the next day another kamikaze came in and hit the *Terror.*

Later that day, *Aaron Ward* returned to the *Mayfield Victory* to get the rest of her ammo, and Doc climbed aboard to find out what had happened to her skipper. He had been hit, all right—a bullet from the plane had ricochetted around a gun tub and smacked him a good one. Doc treated the wound and wrote him up for the Purple Heart.

"Was it serious?" someone asked in the wardroom that noon.

"Well," Doc replied. "I advised him not to sit down for a few days."

Don Young felt the effect of the disaster on the *Pinkney* more than anyone else; he had left her not too long before. And after he left the *Pinkney* he had been in the *Drayton.* The Japs had bunged her up too, in Leyte. It looked as if they were catching up.

Off Hagushi, *Aaron Ward* went alongside *Daly* to take some of her ammunition. *Daly's* crew was cleaning up the wreckage from the kamikaze hit they had taken. There were blanket covered shapes on *Daly's* decks; she was burying her dead. *Aaron Ward's* people had seen planes burn, explode, and crash; they had seen ships ripped and scarred by kamikazes; they had even seen a couple of bodies drifting in the sea off Okinawa, but this was still the first time they had come face to face with the sobering fact that those impersonal messages over the TBS—"SOFTSOAP HAS MINOR DAMAGE, FOUR CASUALTIES"—referred to people. People like themselves, who had been in the chowline at noon, had perhaps been writing a letter home just before GQ, and who had been standing by their guns when their ship received that minor damage.

The morning of 30 April orders came from Commander Task Force 51, ordering *Aaron Ward* out to Radar Picket Station 10 to relieve *Brown.* The crew was glad to get under way again. The assemblage of wrecked ships in Kerama Retto was a depressing sight, and no one wanted to be there or at Hagushi, anchored, unable to take evasive action, when the planes came in. The Navy had an old saying about that: "He who fights and runs away will live to fight another day." Out on the picket station, at least, one had room enough to run.

And the opportunity. While *Aaron Ward* had been busy with enemy planes up on Picket Station 1, *Little, Brown,* LSMR 195, and LCS 51 had had their problems on Station 10. *Brown* had had a near miss: a plane dived on her and splashed in close enough to the ship to take the gig out of the davits. She headed in to Kerama Retto for fuel and ammunition while *Little* and the small boys stayed on with *Aaron Ward.*

Before *Aaron Ward* had completed her first day more raids hit Okinawa. At 2300 that night CIC reported bogies at sixteen miles, closing.

Instantly, throughout the ship, the alarm broke out in urgent, clamor and men ran to battle as others once ran at Agincourt, at Hastings, at Concord, at Shiloh, at Chateau-Thierry, and not too long before at Ten Ten Dock. They ran, not necessarily because they were eager to fight, but because at that moment they had to fight— and at Okinawa he who struck the first blow stood to win.

There was nothing else to do, nowhere else to go. The enemy was up there somewhere, wheeling like buzzards, waiting to pounce like falcons. Even at that instant the first one might be flashing down, the pilot intent on turning the *Aaron Ward* into one glorious personal pyre. That was his mission; he had sworn by his ancestors that he was not going home. The *Aaron Ward's* job was to make certain he stuck by his oath.

There was nothing particularly personal in the situation. Two machines, one gnat-sized in the sky and the other some two thousand times larger in the sea, were about to play again the old game of irrestible force meeting immovable object. The men in them merely watched dials, pressed buttons, moved control levers a hair right or left, and tried to out guess the other guy. Up to a point it was like playing scissors, paper, and stone—except that here, he who guessed wrong would lose more than the game.

Possibly no more than half a dozen of *Aaron Ward's* men had ever seen a Japanese, and none of them had faced one since the war began. Ten years earlier, one of the crew might have gone to school with the enemy pilot in San Jose, California, and ten years later another might possibly marry his pretty younger sister in Tachikawa. The immediate and pressing fact was, some men out on the picket line were being asked to settle problems which were not theirs. Somehow or other, their learned and superior countrymen, in Tokyo and Washington, had failed in the exercise of tact and statesmanship supposed to go with old family names, university degrees, striped pants, limousines, and frequent mention in the Washington Post. They had all muffed the job, and now they were depending on their loyal subjects, up there in the plane and down there on the guns, confident that each would keep his finger on the trigger just a little longer than the other.

GQ. Ten minutes after the ship went to GQ the planes approached within range and the guns opened up on them. In one minute the 5-inch mounts put out twenty-five shots and the planes turned away. But they were not all turned back that night. In Kerama Retto one dived into the minecraft flagship, *Terror,* to kill forty-eight men and wound more than a hundred. On Station 1, which *Aaron Ward* had left just two days earlier, a plane hit *Bennion* . . . . and that was that, for Monday.

1730 Thursday. *Aaron Ward* still swung around Picket Station 10, followed by *Little.* The first dog watch was nearly over; the crew scattered about the ship, killing time, waiting to go on watch. Section two would take the second dog watch, commencing at 1800, and GQ would go soon after that. Sunset was due at 1907 and the ships always manned battle stations for sunset. Meanwhile, men killed time, waiting.

In the midship's passageway on the main deck, John Marston, one of the bakers, sat talking with Don Jones. Somehow the gloom and inactivity of the past two days had worked on Marston and he was edgy. "I don't like this," he told Jones. "I have a feeling something is going to happen."

Jones had no rebuttal to this. Someone was always expecting something to happen. Bob Couie, for instance, he was always expecting to get killed, somehow or other. Even the Captain, if you looked at it right, expected something to happen.

It had been almost exactly that time, the day before, when the Skipper came on the PA system and gave the crew a little warning.

"This is the Captain speaking. We have had no air activity for two days now. The weather is expected to break tomorrow. I want all hands, especially those on sky lookout duty to be alert for possible breaks in the cloud cover."

In the main radio room, Smiling Jack Martin sat hunched over his typewriter when the Captain spoke. In a few minutes Joe Zaloga came in. Joe was one of several deeply religious men aboard the ship, and in general the less devout crew members respected him for the strength of his convictions. They chewed over the radio news; the war in Europe seemed about to end at any minute. Maybe the whole war would be over soon, Jack said, and they'd all go home again.

"No, Jack. I don't believe I'm going to make it."

Jack argued gently. They had the best gun crews, the best ship, the best Skipper in the fleet. Nothing could sink the *Aaron Ward*. And they had lots of help on RPS 10—the *Little,* the 195, those other little spit kits. Another one, the LCS 83, had reported on station less than an hour ago. Sure they'd make it. But Zaloga was firm.

"I want you to call my mother when you get back, tell her I was ready to die."

"Sure, Joe. Sure." No use arguing with a guy once he made up his mind. No one could possibly know what might happen, even tomorrow.

But Joe Zaloga knew. Tomorrow, aboard the LCS 83, Joe Zaloga would be dead.

And now here it was, Thursday, the day the Captain had warned them of. It was kamikaze weather, all right. Tuesday had been a lousy day until one remembered that kind of weather kept the suicide planes at home. There had been overcast and light rain, and a wind, twenty knots, kicking up the sea. Wednesday had been worse—visibility down to five miles, wind as much as twenty-five knots. Fine for ducks, maybe, but not kamikazes.

But here it was Thursday, and decent weather. Sailors clustered about topside to enjoy it. Only one hour to sunset. The sun dipped toward the horizon, color washed the sky, and as the sea took on the glow the ship seemed to float, suspended in time and space. The white wake still rolled out astern of her and on the foremast the radar whirled unceasingly, peering far out across the sunset horizon, searching.

No contact. Nothing out there . . . . But there was something out there; far in the southwest, too far away for men to see, too far away for the radar to sense, the sky was filled with wings. The ship had waited there three days, her guns ready, but no planes had come to test them. Now, as certainly as the night was coming out of the east, the planes were coming out of the west. Now, the gods of the battle and the breeze looked down with interest as the ship moved across the painted sea. Now the planes were coming; the ship could test her guns. Before darkness arrived the gods would test the ship.

At 1745 the ship's loudspeakers broke the silence.

"NOW HEAR THIS. RELIEVE THE WATCH. ON DECK THE SECOND SECTION."

Again, throughout the ship, the gun crews changed, the bridge watch changed, the engine room gang changed. The men went about their job with the silent ease of long familiarity. It was all routine, no need to hurry. The second dog watch would be over in two hours, at 2000. In the western sky the wings sped on relentlessly. For many men the second dog watch Thursday—everything—would have ended before 2000.

Chapter Six

Second Dog Watch

18-20 Steaming as before. 1822, bogies reported bearing 090°T, distant twenty-seven miles. Sounded general quarters. 1828, all stations manned and ready, condition ABLE set. Bogies closing. 1830, enemy plane making run from starboard, low on water. Commenced firing. From 1830 until 1921, the ship and the formation was under constant air attack. This vessel took at least five direct hits from Japanese suicide planes, at least two of which were carrying bombs, and shot down four others. The engine of the first plane making a run on us came on board on the starboard side of the fantail. *Little* took two suicide planes amidships and went down at approximately 1900. LSMR 195 took one plane and went down. 1922, dead in the water, weather deck and superstructure deck aft of number 1 stack a complete shambles, blazing fiercely, number 1 fire room,

159

number 2 fire room, number 2 engine room and compartment C-203-L completely flooded, six-foot hole at the water line, port side at frame 81, deck and side plating blown loose, port side, from frame 129 to frame 158, and completely open to the sea. Mounts 1 and 2, main battery, still able to fire in manual, guns 41 and 42 still able to fire in local, and guns 21, 22, 23 and 24 still able to fire. Electrical power out, no pressure in fire and flushing mains. Repair parties fighting with handy billies and bucket brigades. Our casualties heavy, but not determined. 1935, LSC 83 tied up to our port quarter and commenced fighting our fires. Other remaining small craft engaged in rescuing survivors from *Little* and LSMR 195.

T. L. Wallace, Lt., U. S. Naval Reserve

Steaming as before. Section two was on deck for the second dog watch. According to the Plan of the Day, the routine for Thursday, 3 May, was nearly finished. About 1837 the ship would go to routine general quarters. The sun would set at 1907. About 1930 the ship would secure from general quarters and the condition watch would take over. Right after secure, they would make eight o'clock reports, the navigator would make another little mark on the chart to show the ship's "2000 posit" and the third section would come on at 2000 to take the night watch. Drink coffee, watch the wheels go around, keep a bright lookout for four hours, and that would be the end of Thursday. As soon as the Exec and his yeoman could get out another Plan of the Day, they would see what was coming up for Friday.

Meanwhile, men killed a little bit of time. In the slanting rays of the sun, some of them perched on the superstructure deck watching the evening splendor spread across the East China Sea. Sunset was still an hour away. Some of them were not going to live that long. On the after deck house, Pete Peterson and Joe Zaloga played checkers. They were on their third game when the general quarters alarm interrupted them. Joe Zaloga never came back to finish it.

On the bridge, Chief Winston waited to help the Navigator shoot the evening star sights. The sky was clear all the way around; there would be a good horizon and plenty of stars. They could get fancy if they chose and shoot them alphabetically; Altair, Antares, and Arcturus would all be in sight. But Wallace and Winston didn't get their star sights. The shooting that night would not be at stars. In his chair on the starboard side, Bill Sanders relaxed, enjoying a last pipe before GQ went. Fifteen hundred feet overhead the CAP—four speedy F6F's—cut circles in the sunset sky. The chickens would be his for another hour yet, and then they would go home to roost.

In the CPO quarters, Shelley, Smith, Salisbury and McCaughey had a big game of hearts going at a penny a point. This was no way to make money enough to buy an avocado ranch; Smitty and Mick had the others down by only a thousand points when the alarm broke up the game and they never remembered to collect. There was a poker game going in the crew's after bunk room; but next day no one could remember what happened to the pot.

Gunner's mate Charlie Shea was in his bunk, reading *The Fountainhead.* He put the book down when the alarm went, and never did learn how it ended. Doc Barbeiri was in his bunk reading; he had been reading a medical text when he heard the war had started on 7 December 1941—but this time it was *War and Peace.* If this war went on long enough, he expected to finish it.

In the armory the minemen clustered around their coffee pot while John Brown tried to talk Medric Armand into swapping battle stations with him.

"How's about it now, Medric? I've had the bridge control ever since we left Pedro, and all you do is ride around back there on the K guns."

"That's all right, Brownie. Me and those K guns get along fine."

"Come on. Mr. Siler will fix it up. Take the bridge control for a while. That's where the suicide planes always hit. It's only fair for you to take your turn up there."

"Nossir. I'm happy right there on the K guns."

Within an hour a plane that missed the bridge would wipe out the men on the K guns.

In CIC the radarman watched the green line sweeping around the oscilliscopes, and suddenly stiffened. There was a blip, some seventy miles west of Station 10. It faded from the screen before they could plot a course for it. More geese, maybe. They all remembered the time, halfway between Ulithi and Okinawa, when a sudden blip on the screen sent the ship to general quarters in the middle of the day. While the gunners waited, ready to do battle, a lookout had suddenly shouted "Look at the planes!" There they came, eighteen of them, in wing tip formation, flapping their wings. *Flapping their wings?* Happy shouts broke out all over the ship. "Geese!" "Wild geese!" "Give the recognition signal, you birds, or we'll shoot you down." The radarmen had been cautious ever since; they were not about to get the ship into another uproar over geese—Japanese geese, Chinese geese, or just plain unidentified geese.

Again in CIC the green finger of the sweeping radar oscilloscope painted a blip on the screen. Geese or not, there it was. The talker pressed the button on his phone and called the bridge.

"Bridge, CIC. Many bogies, many bogies!"

The CIC watch ran a plot—bearing, estimated speed, distance— and called the bridge again.

"Bridge, CIC. Many bogies, moving from south-southwest, will probably pass near next RPS south."

The answer was calm, unhurried. "Bridge, aye."

Throughout the ship the watch still went about its routine duties. In CIC the cryptic symbols on the plotting screen began to take on meaning. "Someone's going to catch hell tonight," said a voice. No one bothered to deny his statement.

Hal Halstead, the CIC officer, watched the plot for a couple of minutes and then called the bridge again.

"Bridge, CIC. Tell the Captain there may be a raid shaping up to the south of us. Suggest routine GQ be moved up a few minutes early tonight."

On the bridge Sanders nodded to Lieutenant Wallace, who spoke to quartermaster Thorpe. "Sound general quarters!" Throughout the ship games, books, letters and coffee cups were dropped as men dashed to their battle stations. By the time Thorpe had scribbled in the rough deck log the entry "1822. Went to GQ." bells and buzzers were sounding all over the ship as phone lines and firing circuits leaped into life.

Within five seconds battle stations began reporting to CIC and the bridge: "MOUNT 51 MANNED AND READY. . . . GUN 44 MANNED AND READY. . . . DIRECTOR MANNED AND READY. . . . SKY CONTROL MANNED AND READY. . . . GUN 42 MANNED AND READY."

In Mount 52 Boles watched Van Paris, the hot shellman, hurriedly cross himself. Van had a big family at home and wanted desperatly to go back to them. Well, he'd done everything he could at this point . . . . "MOUNT 52 MANNED AND READY."

The Exec, Karl Neupert, was in CIC now, watching the plot, keeping all the details of the guns, damage control, fire fighting equipment ready in his mind for instant use. CIC was jampacked with men. Bill Sanders would be there too, at first, intently watching the radar screen. Other skippers fought their ships from the bridge, but *Aaron Ward's* captain fought his ship from both bridge and CIC, with radar and radio to give him an instant picture of the situation. It would have been all right with the crew if Sanders and Neupert had decided to do battle from the ship's laundry room for they had seen their Skipper and Exec in action enough by now to know that they were an unbeatable team, no matter where they fought.

All in the few moments since the alarm went, every man on the ship had moved to a battle station. Still the reports came in: "FORWARD ENGINE ROOM MANNED AND READY. . . . AFTER STEERING MANNED AND READY. . . . MIDSHIPS REPAIR PARTY MANNED AND READY. . . . MANNED AND READY. . . . MANNED AND READY. . . . READY. . . . READY. . . . READY. . . ." In the after engine room Pete Peterson checked his phones and then turned to Duriavig. "Bob, help Macukas light off the other feed pump. They've got about twenty-five bogies up there and we'll need all the speed we can get." Then he started making a fresh pot of coffee. Let 'em come. *Aaron Ward* was ready.

Again, for a moment, time seemed to stop as the white wake rolled longer behind the ship and men turned their minds and hearts to the secret thought which always followed the unspoken "This is it!" even as they automatically checked firing circuits, steam pressure, frequency settings, ammunition supply or plasma bottles. Only the shining gun barrels moved, probing and weaving black muzzled patterns against the sky, and the radar antennaes, silently whirling as invisible electronic beams now followed the unseen enemy.

Radarman Hosking, standing near the Captain, watched the blips which showed that "Freddy" was vectoring the fighter planes to meet the enemy. The bogies were still circling, way out. Topside, the fire control director searched the sky and the six 5-inch guns swung with the director as one. *Aaron Ward* had encouraged enemy planes to keep their distance before; the gun crews were confident they could do it again. Then, while Hosking was still panting from his dash to CIC, one of the blips headed in toward the center of the screen. Attack!

"CONTROL, CIC. TARGET BEARING 250 SPEED 180 CLOSING RAPIDLY!"

"CONTROL, AYE. TRACKING, TRACKING!"

On the bridge Thorpe logged the time. 1829. Seven minutes since GQ went. Bright eyed bridge lookout Gerald Simons spotted the plane first and shouted the alarm. It was away out at 22,000 yards—eleven miles away—but coming in.

"ALL GUNS. AIR ACTION STARBOARD. AIR ACTION STARBOARD." In Control, Rubel and Lavrakas watched the guns slue around in automatic control to follow the director. The main battery guns lifted their muzzles, ready, all pointing at the target the director had picked up for them.

On the guns, men stood with ammo clips in their hands, with tense fingers on firing keys, with quick eyes on target cross wires, with their pulse beating in their ears and with unspoken thoughts now pushed to the back of their minds. *Ready. Be ready.*

Suddenly in the sunset sky a dark pinpoint appeared, took on substance, grew solid, *moved.*

"Oh, boy!" shouted Tom Whelan in Mount 51. "Here he comes!"

"All engines ahead flank!" ordered Wallace, on the bridge. The engineers spun the throttle valves, the turbines howled, and *Aaron Ward* leaped ahead at thirty-two knots.

Ten thousand yards out on the starboard quarter now, the plane, a Val, headed in. The others wheeled in circles, waiting. First it was merely a dot creeping across the back drop of the evening sky, then it was moving, moving fast—3000 feet high and coming in.

"RANGE NINE 0 DOUBLE 0 . . . . RANGE EIGHT 0 DOUBLE 0 . . . . RANGE SEVEN 0 DOUBLE 0.

"COMMENCE FIRING, COMMENCE FIRING!"

The main battery guns roared into action at 7,000 yards. Below decks, engineers who fought without ever seeing the enemy judged the course of battle by the sound of the guns. While the 5-inchers slammed out their shells with a dull ba-ROOM ba-ROOM, the enemy was still too far off to worry about. Topside, men watched the fiery tracers streak up and out in red curves, fade to hot points of light and then hover in space until the plane flew into the cone of fire.

Hit! Smoke trickled, then poured from the plane, but it kept coming, and in the director the range dials spun madly down—6,000 yards, 5,500 yards, 5,000 yards, 4,500 yards. *Four thousand yards!*

At 4,000 yards the smoking plane dipped over into its suicide dive, and the 40mm guns opened up with their stacatto a-WHOOMP a-WHOOMP a-WHOOMP. Below decks men grew tense; the sound of the forties meant the plane was maybe a couple of miles away, due to arrive in less than a minute, and the next shot had damn' well better be a good one.

"RANGE THREE 0 DOUBLE 0 . . . . RANGE TWO FIVE DOUBLE 0 . . . . RANGE TWO 0 DOUBLE 0!"

Two thousand yards! Now or never! All along the starboard side the little 20mm guns burst into their frantic y-APPITY! y-APPITY! The plane skimmed the water, coming fast.

"RANGE ONE 0 DOUBLE 0 . . . . RANGE EIGHT DOUBLE 0 . . . . RANGE FIVE DOUBLE 0."

Get him! In Mount 53 gun captain Dial and his crew pumped out a 5-inch projectile and the plane blew up almost in their faces. SPLASH!

"We got him!" yelled Dave Rubel in Control.

"CEASE FIRE! CEASE FIRE!"

The flaming wreckage tipped into the sea a hundred yards from the ship, and as the plane ended its death dive, startled gunners saw the pilot catapult from the cockpit. With an unopened parachute trailing behind him, he hurtled high across the ship and smashed into the water on the opposite side. To Bill Rader, about to feed a clip of shells into gun 42, it looked like a mess of raw hamburger. One kamikaze pilot had met his ancestors.

Most of the plane disappeared on impact, but the engine, propeller and right wing section skittered the last hundred yards to crash into *Aaron Ward*. The engine slammed into Mount 53, which had shot the plane down, while the propeller twanged into the after deck house like a giant harpoon and pinned shut the door to the after passageway. Later, as men cleaned up the wreckage there, they found a pilot's boot with a foot still in it.

The men in Mount 53 were still bouncing from the sledgehammer blow of the airplane engine crashing into their mount when the thing suddenly crunched to a halt.

"Training gear jammed!"

Shorty Abbott, gun captain on the left hand gun, jerked open the hot shell hatch, peeked under the mount, and saw a smashed airplane engine almost under his feet.

"Get it out of there!" yelled Dial.

Like a pack of frenzied ants, the men swarmed out of the mount and attacked the smoking engine, then jerked back in pain.

"Damned thing's hot!"

"Heave on it. Get it out of there!"

They went after it with bare hands and dragged it out of the way, then piled back into the mount nursing their blisters. But the engine had given them more than blisters. No power!

"CONTROL! MOUNT 53. HYDRAULIC-ELECTRIC SYS-

TEM OUT. SHIFTING TO MANUAL CONTROL." This meant the pointer and trainer now had to move the 10,000 pound mount themselves by hand gears, blisters or no. This was no time to stop, the fight had just started.

"On target!"

"Load!"

Keep that ammo coming!

The crash set the after battle dressing station on fire and completely destroyed it, but somehow the chief, Tedford, and his helper Fletcher got out. Tedford made it to the main station in the wardroom. Fletcher was killed before he had run a hundred feet. Doctor Barbeiri was already there; he had brought *War and Peace* along with him in case he needed something to help pass the time. Kennedy had borrowed a book from the wardroom library and had a soft chair by the time Doc arrived. Chief Shelley and Gunner Siler hurried in —the early arrivals all got the best chairs—and settled down to wait until the midship repair party had need of them. Not until they heard the phone talker in number two handling room shout "Action starboard!" did they know this was anything more than routine sunset GQ.

Then the guns began. The 5-inchers. The forties. When the twenties opened up they put down their books and waited. This was getting close. Suddenly they felt the ship tremble and shake as the engine from the first Val hit the after mount. The damage control people rushed out on deck. Doc and his helpers put down their books and commenced preparing the wardroom table for surgery. Under their feet the ship twisted and turned and above their heads the guns roared again. The second attack was coming in.

Time 1830. In CIC Glenn Newman on the ground search radar was checking positions of other ships on the station when he heard radarman Beadel, on the air search radar yell, "Here comes another one!" Beadel began calling out the range while topside the director wheeled around to face the attack coming in on the port bow.

"ALL GUNS ACTION PORT, ACTION PORT!"

"RANGE EIGHT 0 DOUBLE 0 . . . . RANGE SEVEN 0 DOUBLE 0 . . . . RANGE SIX 0 DOUBLE 0."

"COMMENCE FIRING, COMMENCE FIRING!" Again the 5-inchers opened up, followed by the forties and the twenties. When the range closed to 4,000 yards, Beadel jumped off his seat and as the plane moved in to 2,000 yards, he crouched behind the radar, still calling the range. On the bridge, Winston watched the intense cone of fire reaching out to port, and felt that the plane, another Val, was riding directly down the stream toward him.

"RANGE ONE FIVE DOUBLE 0 . . . . RANGE ONE TWO DOUBLE 0!"

SPLASH! Mount 52 got that one.

"CEASE FIRE, CEASE FIRE."

A few cheered as the flaming wreckage tumbled into the sea. In the gun tubs, gunners kicked empty cartridges aside and checked the ready ammo racks. In CIC men watched the green fingers sweeping the radar scopes; around that sudden battle ground more enemy planes were waiting.

Time 1831. Short seconds after the last plane had disappeared, men on the bridge and in control were startled by a furious burst of fire from Mount 42, the port twin 40-millimeter just aft of the bridge. Gun captain Larson had spotted the plane before radar picked it up and opened fire without orders. Frantically the director and the main battery guns swung around to fire on this new attacker, a Zeke, 6,000 yards out and already in its suicide dive. The guns zeroed in, all the 5-inchers, the port side forties and twenties, and the plane started smoking. Hit! Hit!! Hit!!!

Still it came on, growing larger, seeming to increase speed. There was a bomb, a big, mean looking one, hanging under the plane's belly, and in the last hundred yards it dropped loose, curved down and hit the port side of the ship under gun 44 just as the plane flamed into the superstructure.

Willand, the pointer and one lucky man on gun 44, watched the plane coming in, and watched the tracers from his gun slicing into it, right into it, but it kept coming, the prop spinning slower and slower. Although the flash of fire from the twin 5-inch mount on the fantail reached out in front of gun 44, Willand was so busy keeping the gun on the approaching plane he never noticed whether Mount 53 was firing or not. Finally the plane loomed up and Willand yelled "We're not going to get him!" He started to jump out of his seat but it seemed as if a hand touched him on the shoulder and pressed him down again. An instant later the plane hit and a big ball of fire went up in front of him. The explosion blew him out of the seat; he crashed into a ready ammo rack which kept him from going overboard and bounced him back on deck minus both shoes and one sock.

The vast, dull thud shook the entire ship. Lavrakas in the director felt the ship tremble and watched a mass of flame tower above the superstructure deck. Under it was only black smoking wreckage and crumpled bodies. Almost every man around gun 44 had been killed instantly.

On the bridge Winston had spun the wheel for a hard left turn and suddenly felt it go dead. The ship had lost steering control, with her rudder jammed hard left, and commenced chasing her tail in tight port circles like a mad dog.

Except for Rawlins and Willand the gun 44 crew was wiped out —smashed, burned, or blown overboard. The gunners on the four after 20mm mounts had the plane blow up in their faces. Ladon Jones, on gun 28 to starboard, had his gun jam just before the plane struck. He started to dash forward, fell to the deck, looked back, saw Rawlins who had been blown off gun 44 jump up and take over his gun.

"Damn' thing's jammed!" Jones yelled, then grabbed his phone talker, Hendrickson, whose forward dash had suddenly ended when he reached the end of his phone cord, and it jerked him back again, and together they helped Rawlins slam a clip of shells into gun 27 and started firing. The next crash blew Rawlins off that gun too and he was never seen again.

The bomb smashed through the ship's hull below the water line, exploded in the after engine room and ripped a hole fifty feet long through her port side. The ship reeled and shook under the blast. The engine room and fire room flooded, the port engine stopped and the ship soon slowed to fifteen knots. Ruptured oil lines poured more fuel into the fire raging topside, and ammunition commenced exploding in the fierce heat. Telephone and power lines were broken, circuit breakers and fuses went out, and trouble lights began flashing all over the fire control switch boards.

Pete Peterson, in the engine room where the 500 pound bomb exploded, somehow failed to hear it. He was leaning against the cruising throttle waiting for his coffee to perk when he saw a sheet of flame ripple across the forward bulkhead and felt himself sailing through space. He woke up seconds later slumped against a piece of machinery ten feet away. Everything was dark. Instantly he knew that with the emergency lighting system out the after emergency diesel was gone and decided it was time for him to go somewhere else. He scurried for the escape trunk, found it, and clambered up, the last man out of the engine room alive. On the way up Pete passed Ensign Paine who was helping Stole up. Topside, Paine felt that everyone in the black gang had walked up his back bone on the way out. He had lost his right shoe on the way up. On the main deck he met Harry Salisbury, from the damage repair gang, who had lost his left shoe.

"Here, Sal," said Paine, handing over one shoe. "You can wear mine but I can't wear yours." He went barefooted the rest of the night.

The main deck was almost as bad as the engine room. It was sheer catastrophe: wrecked gun mounts tipped at crazy angles, torn steel plates, twisted cables, fire, smoke, exploding ammunition, sprawled dead bodies and men with broken arms or legs trying desperately to crawl out of the way of shipmates battling the roaring flames.

Right in front of Pete lay Moose Antell and Duriavig, who had passed him in the mad scramble to get out of the engine room.

Moose had had every bit of his clothing blown off, was wearing only his shoes and a belt with a big sheath knife on it. The next time Pete saw them would be in a hospital. In the same instant he took in the scene around him, he looked outside of it to see a plane crash into the *Little*, a mile or so away, and a big ball of fire unfold above the ship like a deadly blossom.

Pete's shirt and pants were nearly ripped off his body, and as he methodically took his ring, lighter, pen and pencil out of the pockets so he wouldn't lose them, he saw Stefani, who must have made it up from the after fire room, standing beside him.

"Here, Steve," he said, "hold this for me."

Steve put the stuff in his pocket, and just then another explosion lifted him off the deck and he went over the side like a Roman candle.

Steve lost his shoes when he hit the water. The ship was still making plenty of knots and the helmet cut his head. One hand was full of shrapnel, one leg was injured, and his life belt had been torn apart. His biggest worry was the sharks which followed the ship, waiting for the garbage the mess cooks threw overboard every evening just at dusk. He devoutly hoped they had been fed that night. Several hours later Steve was fished out of the water by a rescue ship, but by that time Pete's belongings were at the bottom of the East China Sea.

Just ahead of Pete, Coltra had crawled to the ladder top and "Sparky" St. Clair took his arms to help him on deck but the burned flesh came off in his hands. Silently, Coltra shook his head and painfully made it by himself, then dropped to the deck as wildly exploding ammunition sent everyone diving for shelter. Next, Sparky saw Coltra crawling, inch by inch, toward the sick bay, and with another man he helped carry Coltra there.

When the bomb exploded in the after engine room, electrician's mate Allan Curr was standing by the switchboard there. Chief Mann had just borrowed his flashlight to check the reduction gear—right where the bomb hit—and Jerry Smith in the emergency diesel room had asked for a repeat on a phone message that Mount 53 had been wiped out. Curr had a momentary impression of standing within a gigantic bell while someone slugged it with a mighty hammer, then the lights went out, someone walked over him in the dark, and he heard a voice yelling down the starboard escape hatch to get out. Curr made it. Mann and Smith didn't.

Amid the topside chaos, Curr stood watching more suicide planes diving on destroyer *Little* a mile away. The red hot tracers from *Aaron Ward's* guns zipped into the night like furious bees, slowed, then seemed to hover in space before they floated down past the planes.

In the few seconds after that bomb explosion, many men had fleeting glimpses through fire and smoke of *Little* valiantly fighting off her attackers, but to each of them the immediate danger was so great that *Little's* battle was unreal and of little import, as if it were a movie sequence.

In the forward engine room the whine of the turbines was suddenly interrupted by a thumping noise when the bomb went off and the ship seemed to shudder and jump three feet sideways. A fine sprinkling of dust from overhead beams sifted down on their heads.

Machinist's mate Berry whirled on chief McCaughey, and shouted in fury "Mick, that sonofabitch hit us!"

"Yeah!" Haubrick added "If this keeps up we may have to leave her!"

Mick laughed at him. "Are you crazy? Until the water gets up to our chins we ain't going to leave her. The ship won't sink—the old man wouldn't stand for it."

But she was slowing down. They stood there with the Chief Engineer and watched the revolution indicator for the port engine in the after engine room unwind, all the way down to zero revolutions. Weyrauch, on the phones, automatically checked the circuits.

"AFTER ENGINE ROOM?" *No answer.* "EMERGENCY DIESEL?" *No answer. They were in trouble.*

"AFTER FIRE ROOM?"

"AFTER FIRE ROOM AYE." The voice was gasping, choking. "WE'RE FILLED UP WITH SMOKE BACK HERE. PANERO THINKS THE ENGINE ROOM IS ON FIRE. NO ANSWER IN THERE."

"SKI? THAT YOU? MR. YOUNG SAYS SECURE THE BOILERS, GET OUT OF THERE, HELP TOPSIDE."

Topside could use help. On the bridge, with the view aft blanked out by fire and billowing smoke, no one could see what had happened. There was no communication aft. The phones were knocked out.

"MOUNT 53! CONTROL." *No answer.*

"They got the after mount," Rubel shouted to Lavrakas. Just then they saw a plane start a run on *Little*. "Here we go again!"

"AIR ACTION PORT. ALL GUNS, AIR ACTION PORT."

Again the 5-inchers opened up, the forties joined in. Mount 53, not having heard Dave Rubel announce their destruction, swung around to port, the men cranking frantically by hand, and joined in.

While the guns barked and roared above their heads, the damage control and repair gangs on the main deck rigged fire hoses, ran emergency phone leads where they could, fought fire, and helped wounded men to the battle dressing station.

First to reach the wardroom was Moose Antell, stark naked, skin hanging in shreds from his arms, hair and eyebrows gone. Behind him came a gruesome parade—Coward, Peterson, Parker, all in nearly the same condition. The medics prepared themselves for a long night.

Wounded men seemed to be flooding into the wardoom by that time. Doc sent Kennedy aft to help with minor first aid cases on the fantail and Kennedy worked alone there for part of the night. Ensign Rosengren came down from the sound room to help. Eddie Gaines, who had only been trained to wait on tables and clean staterooms, worked with the doctor the whole night long, a medic like the rest of them. Eddie's big hands were gentle and tender. Men remembered him later as the blackest angel they ever saw.

Soon the wardroom was jammed with wounded. Doc sent Tedford down to set up another emergency station in the mess hall, and as men were treated in the wardroom those who could make it were moved to the mess hall and laid out on deck. Others were dropped into convenient bunks in the officers' rooms. One of these was Paine, who sometime during the night woke up, looked around, and stared in dismay. He was in the Captain's bunk.

"What the hell am I doing in here?" he asked himself, and without waiting for an answer jumped up and got out of there. He spent the rest of the night huddled in a corner on deck, cursing those who stepped on him in the dark, and being greeted in kind.

In the wardroom dressing station, Doc and his helpers worked as hurriedly and efficiently as possible, but certainly not according to the teaching of Lister.

"Plasma!" "Right here." "Sulfa." "Coming." "Penicillin." "I'll get it." "Morphine." "Here 'tis." "Another morphine." "No more needles!" "Use the one you have!" "It's not sterile!" "Sterile hell! Wipe it on your pants."

By that time their pants were not sterile either. By the following morning Doctor Barbeiri, his assistants, their pants and the entire wardroom would have created antiseptic dismay in the Navy's Bureau of Medicine and Surgery. But none of their patients died of infection, that night or later.

Neupert, in CIC, with communications out aft, sent messengers scrambling through the flames and wreckage with word for Biesmeyer and Rainey, and to check on the after engine room. Rubel in Control set up his own emergency system. Brown, on the bridge, could whistle louder than any man in the Pacific Fleet; each time an attack came in Control passed the word to Brown who whistled at the nearby guns and pointed out the target to them.

Yeoman striker Deacon, phone talker for the Assistant Gunnery Officer, Ensign Ferguson, was still in touch with the radar room and CIC, and over the next several minutes began to gain a fair idea of their plight as messages trickled in . . . . after engine room flooded . . . . after fire room flooded . . . . port engine out . . . . fire out of control aft . . . . fighter director radar out of commission . . . . fire in the after clipping room . . . . steering control lost.

The phones to after steering were also out, and the Exec started another messenger back there, but the sudden eruption of fire on the main deck stopped him. Ten minutes passed before he worked his way aft with the word for Flinn to take over the steering control. During the rest of the battle, locked in their stifling hot steel box, Flinn and his gang steered the ship by hand.

The bomb that wrecked the after engine room knocked out the gas ejection system for the 5-inch mounts and they filled with hot choking fumes. Stacy, hot shellman on Mount 51, passed out and slumped to the deck. Whalen motioned another man into his place, opened the side door and dropped Stacy out on deck. The guns kept on firing. In other mounts men choked, retched, stumbled.

"Open the door. Throw him out!"

"It's against regulations to open the door when firing!"

"Hell with regulations. Open the door." Out they went.

The guns grew hot. With the gas ejection system out, unburned gases rolled into the mounts when the breech blocks flew open, and erupted into thin wisps of flame. If a powder can split or spilled, a flashback would roast them all crisper than potato chips.

"Flashback!"

"Damn the flashback! Keep on loading!"

With the loss of power, the Mark 14 director was out of action. Mr. Tiwald sent Eves down to the clipping room a deck below to help pass out more 40mm ammunition. By this time the stench of burned flesh and ruptured bodies filled the air, and as he felt his way down the ladder Eves stepped on something horribly soft and yielding. He couldn't see what it was, and he didn't want to see;

sheer dread of what it might be filled him with unreasoning terror. Then a roaring fire broke out just aft of the ammo storage. Frantically, he began heaving the cans overboard, as far from the ship as he could. Two men usually handled the heavy cans, but Eves was all alone there; he had to do it by himself. The next morning, he forced himself to go back to the ammo storage to see what he had stepped on. Only a couple of life jackets.

In CIC, Neupert and the "Freddies" watched the green fingers of the search radar. The blips had moved well out of gun range for the moment. The lull was welcome, but suspicious. *Watch them— they're up to something.* The planes circled the formation, like Indians around a wagon train, getting up courage for the next attack. The night was far from over; they were bound to come back. With *Aaron Ward* heeling to port and still steaming in a circle, the Japanese figured she had had it. They would reorganize, bore in for the kill. Quickly, quietly, Sanders and Neupert went over the situation. The Exec had every detail of damage, destruction, and casualty on the tip of his tongue . . . . port engine out, rudder jammed, fire mains out, loss of power, Mount 53 in local, the Mark 14 director out, fire in the after clipping room, the port quad forty wrecked and most of the crew killed, Doc and his gang swamped with wounded men.

Bill Sanders decided that although the ship was still fighting, she had perhaps a little more fight than she could handle, and that some assistance would be more than welcome. He put Woody Woodside on the TBS to call Commander Task Force 51 back in Kerama Retto.

"DELEGATE, THIS IS MONGOOSE. OVER . . . . DELEGATE, DELEGATE, THIS IS MONGOOSE. OVER."

Finally DELEGATE came up on the circuit. "GO AHEAD MONGOOSE."

"DELEGATE, THIS IS MONGOOSE. WE ARE IN TERRIBLE SHAPE AND ARE SINKING. WE HAVE BEEN HIT TWICE AND ARE STILL UNDER ATTACK."

The voice came back in calm, measured tones.

"WE KNOW IT MONGOOSE, WE KNOW IT . . . . BLUE-NOSE IS ON HER WAY TO HELP YOU."

BLUENOSE! That was *Shannon,* with Commander Edward Foster as skipper. *Shannon* was supposed to be blessed with the luck of the Irish. "Uncle Ed" and his boys were on their way, and *Aaron Ward* needed all the Irish luck the *Shannon* could carry.

Shannon had just put in to Hagushi Roadstead, on the western coast of Okinawa, when she got the word. Snoopers were about, and the familiar old FLASH RED, CONTROL YELLOW had sent all hands to general quarters. Five minutes later, she got the word from DELEGATE. Guns bristling, *Shannon* plowed out and headed for RPS 10, out beyond Kume Shima. She had a couple of hours to go before she could be of any help to the hard pressed *Aaron Ward*; enroute, *Shannon* sailors prepared for anything—fire fighting, transfer of casualties, rescue of survivors, towing—whatever it was *Shannon* could do it. Whatever it was, *Shannon* had done it. *Shannon* first got into the rescue business on 26 March, when a kamikaze got the destroyer *O'Brien* out near Kume Shima, and she escorted the wrecked ship into Kerama Retto. A week later, *Shannon*'s crew watched kamikazes hit three transports—*Henrico, Dickerson,* and *Goodhue,* all at once, and had again helped fight fire, treat wounded, and care for the dead.

As *Shannon* plowed westward, her bridge crew listened to the TBS. Out on the same station with *Aaron Ward,* the *Little* had been hit and had gone down. *Aaron Ward* was damned near to sinking too . . . . no, belay that last word. She was still afloat, and still fighting, too. The Japs were all over the place, holding a field day. *Aaron Ward* had already knocked down five of them. This last news put the *Shannon* definitely in second place, so far as *Aaron Ward* was concerned, for although *Shannon* had fought at lots of enemy planes, so far she had only managed to fight one of them down for a kill. Oh, well, the night wasn't over yet.

"*Shannon*'s coming to help. *Shannon*'s on her way." The word ran around the ship to a few people who still had phones tied in to

CIC. But *Shannon* was a long way off. Time was fast running out on Picket Station 10.

In what time there was, *Aaron Ward's* men fought fire and flood. Doc and his men got the wounded a little better disposed and the repair parties on deck moved some of the dead out of the way of the living. Neupert in CIC, Biesmeyer in damage control, Sanders on the bridge matched information, played what they had against what they could expect. It was going to be close. DELEGATE ordered the small boys to move in and support *Aaron Ward* and *Little* with gun fire as possible. The small boys had anticipated him and were already on the way. The CAP still orbited overhead, but time was running out for them too. "Freddy" sent up the warning about 1855.

"BRIDGE, CIC. SUNSET DUE IN A FEW MINUTES. I CANNOT HOLD PLANES ON STATION MUCH LONGER."

"CIC, BRIDGE. ROGER. GIVE US ALL THE HELP YOU CAN."

The sun was nearly down now, but there was plenty of light from fire still leaping up above the wrecked engine room, and in the red glow the damage control and repair gangs worked like demons, dumping hot ammunition, rigging emergency circuits, getting portable fire pumps onto the flames.

Here was a chance, Doc decided, to get back to the mess hall and see how Tedford was making out with the patients there. With Crider, he hurried out, checked over the men, started back to the wardroom. They were just at the galley when the next plane hit and the explosion threw them all the way to the wardroom and through the door. Crider was knocked out. Doc stretched him on the deck and left him there; he was busy. An hour later Crider finally woke up and went on tending the wounded as if nothing had happened.

Time 1859. The lull was finally over. The kamikazes had been milling about, some five miles off the starboard quarter, 10,000 feet high. Now they broke it up and suddenly swooped down in a vicious, well coordinated attack which hit the entire formation. Guns on all the ships roared into action, but the planes plummetted down and nothing could stop them. *Little* got it first. She had taken one hit on her port side, several minutes earlier, with no great damage, and she had knocked one down. But this time they rushed her, one right after another. Nothing could stop then. all.

The first plane hit. The second hit. The third flashed down in a vertical dive—hit—and vanished amidships in a tremendous explosion. Lefty thought perhaps *Little*'s torpedo warheads had exploded. Actually only their air flasks went up. But the plane's engine or a bomb went into *Little*'s after engine room and her boilers blew up. The high pressure steam ripped the ship open like a sardine can. She blazed brilliantly from stem to stern for a few moments, then folded up and disappeared. In less than ten minutes it was all over for *Little* and thirty of her men.

Among the men who watched *Little* go down, none felt quite like Harry Salisbury. He had originally been detailed to the *Little* in Norfolk, but uncompleted dental work made him miss the draft when they left for Bremerton to put the ship in commission and he got the *Aaron Ward* instead. Only the grace of God and a lucky toothache had kept him from going down with *Little*.

"CIC, bridge. *Little* has gone down," reported Deacon.

"We're not interested in *Little* now. We're trying to keep ourselves afloat," Neupert shouted back to him.

As the planes smashed into *Little,* the small boys, LCSL 25, and LSMR 195, were racing toward her, steaming side by side. Another plane loomed up out of nowhere, just cleared the 5-inch mount on 195's fantail, and then crashed amidships. The "R" in LSMR's designation stood for rockets, and she was loaded with them. They went off in all directions like a Fourth of July celebration. But when the show was over LSMR 195 was gone.

"There goes the '95!" shouted someone else on the bridge. Lavrakas saw a ball of fire float up from the little ship. He watched for an instant, then turned to look at *Little* but she had nearly disappeared. Only a bit of her bow pointed to the sky and that slipped out of sight as he watched. Next a plane went to work on LCSL 25, whose guns killed the pilot, for it zoomed, wobbled, and then overshot the ship but sliced off her mast. LCSL 25 stayed afloat, but the next time Lavrakas thought to look for the '95, she had gone to join the *Little*.

About this time it seemed to Deacon on the bridge that all hell broke loose. A Val, buzzing about the amphibs, suddenly turned on *Aaron Ward* and commenced a suicide dive from about 8,000 yards out. Again the guns ran through their gamut of defiance, the 5-inchers roaring, the forties barking, and twenties yapping. The plane started smoking as the shells smashed in, but it came on until several hits by the 5-inchers blew it to bits and it splashed, 2,000 yards out. Four down! . . . . but more to come.

In Mount 52, the twin breeches were eating up the big 54 pound projectiles when suddenly one of them refused to slide into the firing chamber. The fuse in its nose had jammed, the shell would not go in. Boles and his crew looked at one another in a lightning flash of understanding. The fuse had been set down in the handling room under instruction from Control. No one in the mount knew how many seconds the fuse had been set for, or if it would wait to go off until it was fired, but they all knew if the shell was still in the gun when it went off, Mount 52 would have had it. Together Boles and Van Paris wrestled the shell loose and dragged it out of the gun. Boles undogged the side door. Van stood there, holding the thing in his arms while it counted seconds to itself. The other men just stood there; either Van heaved it out or he didn't. Finally Boles wrenched the door open and Van heaved the shell overboard. *All right, you guys. Don't just stand there. Didn't you ever see a loading casualty before?*

Load! Load! Load!

Boles was glad Van Paris had taken time to cross himself before the action started. There hadn't been any time for it since, and certainly whatever grace Van had won for himself had been spread very thin in Mount 52.

Time 1904. On the air search radar screen in CIC, another blip started for the center. Attack! The ship was still circling and the plane seemed to be maneuvering for a run-in from astern. Finally CIC got the control crew looking in the right direction and they spotted the plane, a twin-engine Betty, 14,000 yards off. The 5-inchers began firing at 10,000 yards, a long five miles, but had difficulty keeping on target, due to the smoke still rolling up amidships and the constant turning of the ship.

The forward mounts continually slammed into the stops which limited their field of fire aft, over the ship, and the gunners had to franctically whip their guns all the way around to the other side to take up fire again. This could be as dangerous for the bridge crew as for the enemy; a couple of weeks earlier, in the same situation, Sanders had been knocked down by the muzzle blast of a gun firing almost directly into his face.

Finally, at 5,000 yards a 5-incher made connection. The plane smoked, flamed, and went into its death spin. "Such a beautiful sight," Rader thought, while around him men who had sweated at their guns for half an hour yelled and cheered. Five down!

Just then a flight of Marine F4Us, sent out to help *Aaron Ward,* came in low over the sea with their running lights on to show they were friendly, but a nervous gunner opened up on them anyway, the other guns joined him, and the Marines fire-walled their throttles getting out of there. *Aaron Ward* was still ready, still fighting. The battle was not yet over. In a few minutes the sun would slip below the horizon. A mile or so away the remaining amphibs huddled together in the dusk, and around the rim of night the kamikazes still droned. *Would the damned things never stop coming?* The fight had gone on just a little more than thirty minutes, yet it seemed like hours—days—an eternity—an eternity filled with the clamor of guns and roar of planes, the stench and reek of burning oil, powder and flesh. For some of the crew eternity had already come; for more of them it was surely to commence in a few short minutes.

Time 1908. "AIR ACTION PORT, AIR ACTION PORT!" There they came, two Vals, with a pair of the Marine fighters hot on their tails. The planes mixed up in a brief dog fight out of which one Val plunged in flames, but the other one slanted down in a very steep dive, coming fast. Again the guns took up their chant as the range dials whirled down—the computer said this one was coming in at almost five miles a minute. The guns hammered and roared but the plane jumped and rocked through the storm of fire and kept coming, heading for the bridge and the main battery director, *kept coming, kept coming!*

"Hit the deck!" yelled Sanders, and men piled into corners, behind equipment, anywhere but where they had been. Everyone had the same impression, that the plane was heading right at *him.* Lefty Lavrakas watched the stream of tracers burning into the sky and stood transfixed as the plane seemed to lock onto them and ride them down to the ship. When it was 300 feet away he turned his head from the sight and made his peace with God.

Danny Danford on top of the wheel house knew he was a goner and said his prayers. Ladon Jones, on one of the twenties, knew the plane was going to hit him; in the last fleeting instant he snatched up his shrapnel shield and heaved it at the pilot's face. Brown, on the bridge, knew the plane was going to hit him; it loomed up suddenly as big as a house, right on him, with two exhaust pipes spitting blue fire. He hunched his shoulders and waited for the crash. In CIC the assistant "Freddy" Lieutenant junior grade Fred Koehl, could see nothing but he listened as the roar of the plane drowned out the guns and thought to himself "Why in hell didn't I stay in Ashland, Ohio, where I belonged, instead of volunteering for this mess?"

Then the plane was on them, the roar of its engine filled the night, its wings spread across the sky. *Here he comes!* Suddenly as if a mighty hand had pushed down the right wing, the plane twisted in flight. It banked slightly and roared flat across the bridge. The left wing ripped out the signal halliards, clipped the port forestay, carried away most of the radio antennae, smashed the top of the forward stack in a tremendous metallic scrunch and the whole thing went cartwheeling into the sea to starboard. Larson, on gun 42, almost had his hair parted by the landing gear as it roared past. The broken forestay lashed Rader across the face. He saw it coming, but was too frightened to move—too frightened, in fact, to feel it.

In the plane's wake, bits and pieces of wreckage rained down and men stared at each other, dumbfounded, in a perfect bedlam of noise. The crash had opened steam lines to the whistle and siren and they joined in the tumult to deafen everyone.

Even men floating in the sea where the *Little* had gone down could hear the whistle bellowing, although they could not see what had happened. By that time, what men could see and hear, and what, in the shock of battle, they believed, made for oddly contrasting viewpoints. Weeks later, an *Aaron Ward* sailor who came from the same town as a *Little* sailor received a news clipping from home. The *Little* sailor got home first, and gave the press his account of the battle at Picket Station 10. After his ship sank, he reported, all those *Aaron Ward* sailors did was sail around in a circle, tooting their whistle. Fortunately, for him, the *Aaron Ward* sailors were still in Kerama Retto when he said it.

In the hideous uproar of escaping steam and bellowing whistle, the gunners seemed to be doing a grim pantomime, firing their guns silently. A sheet of flame flashed through the radar room and many of the radarmen, with nothing better to do at the moment, rushed out to help the gunners. They were none too soon.

Time 1913. There came another Val. This one streaked in from ahead and again aimed at the nerve center of the ship, the bridge structure. Despite the steam and smoke swirling around the ship and the fact they had no warning from director control, the eagle-eyed gunners on the after 5-inch mount picked the plane up visually and opened fire. Larson's gun joined in furiously. The plane streaked in, maybe seventy-five feet off the water, and 2,000 yards out its machine guns commenced spitting death. A strafing run! No one could see the bullets coming, but a man could hear the WHACK PINNNG after they went by.

At that instant the pilot raised its nose slightly, aiming right at the upper bridge and director. Dave Rubel, in the director, stood and watched it come—there was nothing else to do and nowhere to go—and shouted to Lefty "This is IT, boy!"

Gun 42, below and in front of Rubel, was pouring out a solid stream of fire—that gun alone fired a thousand shots during the entire battle—with thirty-four-year-old Larson working as calmly as if it was just another drill. Frozen by the thought of what he knew was about to happen, Rubel watched the enemy pilot's goggled head coming nearer and nearer and braced himself for a flaming death. And then he saw Larson do something he would remember all his life. Larson raised his gun until the stream of fire flowed just above the wing of the onrushing plane. And then coolly, as methodically as if he was back home slicing cheese in the kitchen, he lowered the gun again and the fiery stream of hot bullets literally sawed the wing off.

That man deserves the Congressional Medal of Honor! Rubel said to himself. The crippled plane faltered, swerved, tumbled, just missed the bridge and ended up in a fiery furnace on the main deck near the forward stack, very nearly on top of gun 42.

In the instant before impact, the plane released a bomb which exploded a few feet from the side of the ship, blasted the port side with a hail of shrapnel and blew a hole into the forward fire room. The fire room flooded, the boilers drowned out, the last engine stopped, and *Aaron Ward* was without all power, coasting to a dead stop.

Flames from the burning plane leaped as high as the top of the director and the concussion knocked some men off gun 42 and injured others. Out of the fire and smoke a man scurried forward, unharmed, but with the entire seat of his pants missing. Again the switchboards lit up like Christmas trees with circuit overload lights. Men were still picking themselves up from that explosion when another plane, four seconds later, hurtled out of the cloud of smoke and fire and crashed on the main deck. Absolutely not a man on the ship saw that one coming; what with the exploding bomb and raging gasoline fire from the prior crash it made little difference— some of them never knew what hit them.

At that moment, the chaos and destruction topside seemed to have reached an absolute peak. But at least a man could *see it*; he had something to worry about. Things were worse below decks. Down there, all men knew was that terrible things had happened or were undoubtedly about to happen, but no one knew what, when, or where.

In the wardroom, each time the roar of the guns began as another plane came in, a whole mass of humanity—patients, corpsmen, volunteer assistants, the Doctor, everybody able to move— piled under the operating table in one big bloody heap. Men who had been burned left skin and flesh in their tracks, the deck grew sticky and slippery with blood and worse. There were no lights except the small portable electric battle lanterns. In the midst of the noise and confusion, in the fetid air and faltering light, the door opened and Kennedy found himself facing a ghastly apparition, a man with anguished eyes but no face. His mouth and nose were torn away, his jaw hanging loose on one side; he was choking to death.

Again the guns roared, the ship shook. Doc, Kennedy and the bloody man all crouched under the table. Doc could find no surgical scissors in the insane clutter. Kennedy held a bandage over the man's eyes. Doc wiped his shark knife on his pants, and cut away tissue so the man could breath through the gaping hole where his face had been.

As they sought to stop the gush of blood, another sailor burst into the wardroom!

"Hey, Doc! Ballard's up by Mount 52, bleeding like hell!"

185

"You, Kennedy," said Doc. "Go fix him up."

Kennedy grabbed soap, sulfa powder, gauze and ran up and out into the battle. Wounded men were all over on deck, he jumped over and among them. As he passed underneath the muzzles of Mount 52, the guns opened up on another plane and nearly blew his head off. He grabbed Ballard, dragged him feet first back to the spray shield, bandaged a gash in his upper arm, and then hauled him aft toward the wardroom. At the moment they moved in off deck a plane hit number one stack and fire and wreckage came down all over the spot where they had been.

In the forward magazine, Philip Rapalee and his four man crew were completely isolated from topside and without any knowledge of what was going on. They had been worried enough and the last explosion very nearly spooked them; Rapalee tried again to find out what was happening.

"Hey, you guys in the handling room! What the hell's going on up there?"

"You just keep that ammo coming, Rap! Keep that damn' ammo coming!"

"Okay, so they want ammo! We'll give 'em ammo!"

Everywhere below decks, where they could see nothing, hear very little, and only surmise what was happening by distant thumps and a few terse words over a phone now and then, men lived in a dreadful state of suspense, trying not to let their fears overwhelm their hopes. When the plane wrecked the forward fire room, the men working in the magazines and handling room under Mount 52 were as close to it as they could be without actually being in the crash. All they knew was, something terrible had happened. They never stopped passing out ammunition; Marquoitt just had time, between shoving powder cases into the hoist, to say sadly to himself, "You aren't going to see home again."

Wayne Schaefer, who was also handling ammunition for Mount 52, had nearly the same thought. His wife Marjorie was back home in Fort Wayne, Indiana, with their young son Thomas who was just exactly two years old. He had seen the baby only once, Schaefer said to himself, *only once.*

Down in the forward emergency diesel room, Cezus and Lunetta also fought without ever seeing anything. They were sealed up in a steel compartment below the water line with a diesel driven 150 KW emergency generator which automatically cut in if all other power went out, as happened when the forward fire room flooded. When their generator lit off they knew things topside were bad. Laboring to supply power to the guns, the generator was running in overload condition and should have automatically tripped out, but Cezus held the overload trip in by hand—if the gun crews needed juice, he would give them juice until the generator blew itself to bits. He knew that if the ship sank he and Lunetta were going down with it, for they couldn't get out until someone came to let them out.

The shock of the crash rattled things all over the radar room, and Pete Aitchison yelled at Beadel.

"Beadel! You know what? Here we are getting the hell beat out of us and I bet they don't have a dime's worth of insurance on this ship!"

When the radio and radar antennae were wrecked, Reichard, Phillips, and Thibodeau scrambled out of the radar shack and set about trying to rig an emergency antennae. They were working by the forward stack when the second explosion blasted the area with shrapnel. Reichard was pinned to the stack by a splinter of steel through what he thought was his sleeve, until he ripped away and found his arm dangling loosely with blood pouring down over his hand. He watched a gunner, still too young to shave, cruelly burn his hands dragging a wounded shipmate from the flames around a wrecked gun. The boy tried to hold a fire hose but his hands were too raw to manage that, and when a bullet whizzed through the hose and punctured it, he plugged the hole by sitting on it while someone else fought the fire. Rader, blown off his gun and wounded, dashed to the bridge. Then he thought, *no, they'll hit the bridge next,* and ran back to his gun. He was still scared stiff, but he felt safer there.

Seaman Thomas Erin had been in CIC, but with the TBS wrecked he had nothing to do, so went out on deck and took the place of someone on a 40mm gun. Fighting was better than nothing.

The wardrom filled with smoke after the last explosion and the wounded men were near panic. Doc called the bridge for "the word."

"Bridge, battle dressing. Ask the Captain are we going to abandon ship."

"Sir, the Captain says, hell no!"

But somehow, in the chaos and confusion, someone misunderstood someone else and the word did get out.

"Skipper says we're going to abandon ship!"

A couple of men ran from the forward superstructure deck all the way to the fantail and jumped overboard. That they could have jumped from where they were, without scrambling through fire, explosions and torn wreckage, somehow never occurred to them. Before the battle ended a few more went overboard intentionally, some through accident. Later, as the ship floated and refused to sink, some of them gave up waiting to be rescued and climbed aboard unaided.

Mount 42 got the word on abandon ship too. It never occurred to Blunck that he might abandon ship, but he was certain the rest of the crew would go. "Don't leave me," he kept telling Larson. "Don't leave me. I don't want to be left here all alone."

"Who the hell's going anywhere?" said Larson.

Brown, on the bridge, was still hunched over waiting for that first plane to hit him when the second one crashed four seconds later; more 40mm and 20mm ammunition blew up and a rain of fire and hot metal washed over the ship. A red hot jagged piece of the plane, perhaps the size of a silver dollar, pierced the back of his neck and Brown said to himself "I'm dead!" But it went on burning like hell's own ashes, so he decided he was alive after all and tore it off. By then there were so many badly wounded men needing care far worse than he did that Brown refused to bother Doc for treatment, and so he never got the Purple Heart medal he should have had.

Instead, he asked Sanders for permission to disarm the depth charges—if the ship did sink, they might detonate in the water and kill more men. With Hitchcock and Mogensen he hurried aft, pulled out the arming pistols and heaved them overboard; then the depth charges, each loaded with hundreds of pounds of high explosive, followed. There went one hazard for a ship which needed all the luck there was if she was to survive. Suddenly they became aware they were not the only men on the fantail; there were dark shapes, stretchers filled with wounded men, where the medics had placed them to keep clear of the fire and destruction amidships. Brown nearly stumbled over the nearest stretcher.

"Who the hell is this?"

Someone bent down, peered into the face. "Zaloga."

Even in the darkness, they could see he had one arm shattered, one leg hanging by a tendon, a piece of steel speared through the other. But he stirred, recognized Brown's face bent over him.

"Brownie, look at my legs for me," he pleaded. "They hurt. Tell me how badly I'm hurt." Brownie felt sick all over. No wonder the poor devil's legs hurt; both feet were gone, the legs so badly mangled there was no place to put a tourniquet. A great pool of blood glistened under the stretcher.

"You're Okay, Joe," Brownie lied. "You'll be up and around in a month."

Joe would have been okay if he had stayed back on the fantail, but there was nothing to do there, and he had tried to get forward to help, just as a plane hit the port quad 40 and the exploding ammunition cut him down. The campaign was finally over for Zaloga.

The other men held a battle lantern while Brown sprinkled some sulfa powder in Zaloga's wounds. Then someone yelled "Lights out!" and the guns opened up again.

Time 1916. That one was a Zeke, coming in astern at high speed in a steep glide. None of the 5-inch guns could bear on him.

Gun 42, with the indomitable Larson still shooting, took him under fire but without result and the plane slammed into the ship near gun 43.

Gasoline from the plane's belly tank sprayed the area and started another raging fire. No man from 43 was ever seen again. Larson on gun 42 was hit in the face by what he thought was a slab of bacon until he remembered that bacon didn't bleed. Many men on nearby guns were killed outright and some of them were blown overboard. Those who did not die in the blast floated around in the dark ocean until the "picker uppers," the small amphibs, fished them out. Lefty Lavrakas looked down at the smashed gun which gunner's mate Long had kept always ready and thought to himself *I've lost a fine shipmate and the best gunner the Navy ever had. If there is a Valhalla, Long has earned it.*

By now the ship was dead in the water, the weather decks and superstructure aft of the bridge were a complete shambles, dead and dying men were tumbled in the wreckage, fire raged uncontrolled and in the inferno exploding ammunition made existence uncertain for those still left.

Through the chaos the repair parties fought fire, rigged pumps, and dragged out the wounded. The repair gang, Lieutenant Biesmeyer, Chiefs Offins and Gains, St. Clair and James and others, were bruised, burned and bleeding; they had already out-labored Hercules but there was still work to do. The ship was low in the water, going over to port, but she was still afloat, still fighting, and they intended to keep her so. The enemy had other plans.

Time 1921. "Here comes another one!" yelled Beadel in CIC.

"God, we can't take another one!" groaned Neupert.

There he came, out of the darkness, low over the water, masked by the smoky haze drifting away from the burning ship.

"AIR ACTION STARBOARD, AIR ACTION STARBOARD."

Guns still on power from the forward emergency diesel trained around but the crew could see nothing. Baffled, they stood waiting.

They knew that this time they might have only a few seconds to get the plane before it got them.

"FIRE AFT, FIRE AFT," ordered Control. The forties opened up, shooting blindly.

Suddenly the plane loomed into sight and all the remaining guns trained aft in one supreme effort to knock it down. Relentlessly it bored in, while the gun crews fed shells to the bellowing guns.

For the tenth time in less than an hour they stood at their stations and looked death right in the eyes. "The way to handle enemy planes," Bill Sanders had told them the first time the ship went into combat, "is to shoot them down, one at a time." *Aye, aye, Sir. One at a time it is! Number ten coming down!*

Down it came, down the stream of tracers, down the length of the wrecked ship, and down right into the gunners' faces, with the big bomb under its belly looking bigger every second. The plane crashed amidships, at the base of the after stack, with a blasting, searing flash of exploding gasoline and bomb, and then plane, stack, searchlight tower and guns leaped into the air and smashed back on the shattered deck with a great tumultuous din as if the world had ended. For more of *Aaron Ward's* men, it had.

On the main deck, Tony Macukas, who had escaped fiery death earlier by scrambling out of the blazing engine room, yelled "He's coming in!" and pointed. All around him men dived for shelter, but Tony was still standing there, pointing, when the plane smashed down on him. Some of the men dived the wrong way and went overboard. The first thing Frank Ceckowski remembered after the crash was Tony pleading for help, and a man kneeling nearby praying. Frank prayed too, but stayed on his feet, just in case.

Jack St. Clair rushed to help Macukas—the plane had pinned him down by his left leg—and yelled at the top of his voice for help but no one heard him. Then Jack realized he couldn't even hear himself, and thought for a second he was dreaming, until he realized that a steam line had broken and the roar of escaping steam was so loud it had absolutely stopped all sensation of sound. Only later did he notice the search light tower had smashed on deck near him without his hearing it.

The tower fell on Jim Berkey; it was on fire and so was he until someone drenched him with a fire hose. When they lifted the tower off, Jim jumped up off deck, ran, and passed out. An hour later, he woke up with someone shooting morphine into him. As he helped lift the burning plane to rescue Macukas, Ceckowski's feet slipped and skidded. He suddenly realized he was standing in the middle of what had been a Japanese pilot a moment before and hurriedly stepped aside. Grim men were frantically pushing and heaving the wreckage overboard and Ski saw a man pick up a leg and toss it into the sea without even noticing what it was.

Gunner's mate Charlie Shea, standing with Macukas when the plane hit, could think of nothing better to do than crawl under a portable quarterdeck desk. Burning gasoline ignited his dungarees and he jumped overboard—the ship was so low in the water all he did was walk off to douse the fire. In the water he remembered his flashlight didn't work, but the burning ship made light enough for one of the "picker-upper" boats to find him soon afterward.

The time was now 1922—exactly sixty minutes since the first bogies had been reported. The once trim *Aaron Ward* resembled a floating junk pile from the bridge aft. Stacks, guns, searchlight tower, boat, everything was smashed and battered beyond recognition. Fires raged on deck, in the officer's and chief's quarters, in both clipping rooms, and in the after engine room. The main deck was only inches above water, both fire rooms flooded, after engine room flooded, after diesel engine room, machine shop, shaft alleys, crew's bunkroom, all flooded. Dead and wounded littered the wardroom, mess hall, sick bay, fantail and passageways.

The night was black and deep, except where the *Aaron Ward* burned like a devil's barbecue. There was no electricity, no lights, no power, no pressure on the fire mains. Men fought fire the way they fought fire in Homer's day, with water. There was still plenty of water.

The wrecked decks weren't much of a place to be, but better

than where they would be if she went down . . . . "All right, sailors. Over here. Grab a bucket and get in line. Keep them buckets coming. There's lots more water in the ocean . . . ." and plenty already in the ship, too. Back aft another party worked at bailing out a flooded compartment. "But chief, we ain't got no more buckets" . . . . "Use empty shell cases, we got plenty of them."

And by that time it certainly looked as if she might go down. Water was lapping across the fantail where some wounded men had been carried out of the way. Sanders had sent messengers scurrying around the ship to find Biesmeyer and Doc, and the three of them met just outside CIC so Neupert could join in the discussion. About the only thing in their favor was that the sea had calmed down until it was like a black mirror. But the stability factor was critical. Biesmeyer ticked off the damage—forward fire room flooded, after fire room, after engine room flooded, after diesel flooded, the big after crew's compartments flooded, machine shop, shaft alleys, all flooded. If a bulkhead gave, she'd be a goner.

"What do you think, Surge?"

"We still have some life rafts. We can load patients onto them. They'll be as comfortable there as anywhere else."

"Good. We stay with her."

Doc and his men bundled some of the badly wounded onto life rafts, and tied them alongside so they wouldn't get lost. They didn't have to reach down to the rafts; the ship was so low in the water they just reached across. The fire fighters, the repair gang, everyone able to help, fought fire, dumped hot ammunition, pushed weights overboard in an effort to help keep the ship afloat. They were going to stay with her.

One of the helpers was Bill McKanna. Bill was a sonarman but his GQ station was in the handling room for a twin forty. When the last plane crashed in, debris put the gun out of commission, so Bill went down to the wardroom to see if he could help with the wounded.

Doc needed no more help then, so he sent Bill up on deck to help Kennedy. The wounded men were all over the place, it seemed. It was dark, except for flickers of light from the fire, and the ship had a sluggish feeling about her. There were some life rafts in the water alongside, looking very small and inadequate.

"Here, Bill," said Kennedy. "We gotta get these men onto the rafts. See if you can get someone to go with them."

Bill yelled for help, but the few men he could see failed to hear him—either they were furiously fighting fire, heaving around on wreckage, or they were just standing there, filled with momentary hysteria.

"I'll go," Bill said, and climbed up on the rail. Just as he tensed himself to jump, someone yelled "Take off your helmet!" That was a good idea. Stefani had been nearly knocked silly earlier when he went overboard with his tin hat on and it konked him a good one. So Bill threw the helmet on deck and jumped.

His feet had no more than left the railing when the voice yelled again: "Look out for sharks!"

It was too late. Bill was on his way down. He hit the water and piled out on the raft so fast his shirt never got wet. Then Wayne Schaeffer jumped down to the raft with him, and between them they got Turner and Viega on board. Viega looked as if a 20mm projectile had gone right through him. It seemed awfully lonesome down there on that raft.

Suddenly there was a hail out of the darkness: "AARON WARD, AHOY THE AARON WARD!" and there came the crummy, dirty, lovely little LCS 83, creeping into the circle of fiery light with her fire hoses streaming water and her crew ready to duck in case *Aaron Ward's* gunners still had itchy fingers. She eased up on the port quarter—the ship was now so low in the water that once her bow slid right up on the deck—and men piled on board the stricken ship to help. Among them were a few *Aaron Ward* sailors who had been blown overboard, had been picked up, and were now coming back for more. There was a fierce fire burning forward, and the 83 boat pushed her nose into the middle of it. Just then ammunition in a 40mm magazine commenced exploding and the men on the 83's bow dropped their fire hose and ran. McCaughey wished he could have got hold of that hose, but he didn't need to; the skipper of the 83 boat, Lieutenant Faddin, jumped off the bridge, ran forward, and took the hose himself. Just in case the ship did decide to go down, Doc and his helpers moved a few wounded men from the deck of the *Aaron Ward* to the 83.

A sailor needed lots of friends on a night like this, and there came some more—the little LCSL 14 snuggling up to the starboard side of the ship. More fire fighters. More pumps. *Aaron Ward*'s medics hurriedly slung a couple of stretcher patients aboard the LCSL 14 too. One of these was Turner, gun captain of the starboard quad 40. As Boles helped lift him aboard, Turner whispered "Tell my mother my body wasn't mangled."

"Sure, Jack. Don't worry. You'll be fine."

But Turner wasn't fine. His legs had been nearly torn off in the explosion. No doctor could help him. He died aboard the LCSL 14 a couple of hours later.

The time was 2000. The second dog watch was over. The battle was finished. The enemy had gone. Yet men still fought, silently, desperately, against man's fiercest enemy, fire; against the sailor's greatest enemy, the sea; against the one who had taken many of them and still might get the others before the night had ended, death.

Black night crowded close around the wounded ship, a backdrop to a Greek tragedy. Leaping red flames painted crazy shadows against the sky and exploding ammunition rocketed toward the stars. But finally the planes were downed and the guns were stilled. The gods of the battle and the breeze marched back to their celestial mountains to consider what they had seen. *Aaron Ward* had met the test and *Aaron Ward* had won.

The sea lay black and flat in the night. The ship hung there, motionless. The routine had run out. The wheels had all stopped. Time had ceased to exist there, long ago; now even the wind had gone. In the stillness, in the silence, men at last had time to think. Radarman Bell had been too busy to know fear for the past hour, but now he knew he was scared as hell. He was not alone.

The time was 2000. No one passed the word to relieve the watch.

No one made eight o'clock reports. No one stopped for a cup of coffee or a game of cribbage. There was no coffee and no time for it. No one knew how much time they had left, but in what time there might be they fought to save the ship.

A century had passed since Lawrence said "Don't give up the ship." This night Bill Sanders and his men gave the words meaning for another century. A century had passed since John Paul Jones said "Give me a fast ship for I intend to go in harm's way." In the respectful silence of the crypt at Annapolis where his bones still lay, one might almost expect the little fighting man to step out of the shadows to study those thunderous names immortalized around his tomb: *Ariel* . . . . *Alfred* . . . . *Alliance* . . . . *Providence* . . . . *Serapis* . . . . *Ranger* . . . . *Bon Homme Richard* . . . . and then say "Boatswain! Another name here. Make it read *Aaron Ward*."

The time was 2000. The second dog watch was over. For most of the crew, it was the longest watch they would ever live through. It had been the last watch for the rest of them.

Chapter Seven

Night Watch

20-24 Dead in the water. 2005, listing five degrees to port. All fires under control except one on the fantail. Some casualties have been transferred to LCS 83. 2019 Began making preparation for towing. USS *Shannon* (DM 25) reported coming to our assistance. 2024 all fires out. List is steady at five degrees to port. 2026 fire broke out again on fantail. 2045 all fires out. 2049 forward diesel generator commenced furnishing some electrical power. Gyrocompasses back in operation. 2120 *Shannon* 200 yards off our starboard quarter, maneuvering to take us in tow. 2120 listing six degrees to port. 2220 tow line from *Shannon* secured. *Shannon* began taking out slack. 2242 commenced making headway. Steering control is aft (manual). LCS 83 still following alongside. Repair parties are attempting to pump out all flooded compartments.

T. L. Wallace, Lt., USNR

20-24 Dead in the water. That just about described it. The ship was still afloat. No one wanted to guess how long she would stay that way. She had no lights, no steam, no power. Biesmeyer and his men were still pumping water into a fire on the fantail. In the darkness on the forecastle, Shelley and what was left of his deck force worked at making up a tow line. The gunners still stood by their guns, those which could be fired, and Dave Rubel was bumping around the ship checking on them. If another plane came they would be ready for it. If another plane came they had to get it. If one more plane got them first, more than the ship would be dead in the water.

Meanwhile, until help came, men helped themselves as best they could, with bare hands, axes, flashlights, gasoline pumps—whatever they could find in the dark and put to use. Their clothes were ripped and burned; they were cut and bruised and bloody; they were tired and hungry and thirsty, but they kept working. No man slept until exhaustion forced him to the deck; one bunk room was flooded, many more bunks were burned, still more had been torn apart to provide for the wounded. With the ship low in the water and listing to port, no one wanted to go below unless they had to. The ship which had been their home two hours before was now dark and flooded and filled with strange sounds, and terror could suddenly lurk in old familiar places.

But men had to go below, to hunt out needed gear; to check into damage, and finally, to get something to drink. As the Ancient Mariner once pointed out, thirst at sea can be a terrible thing. Men had been heaving ammunition, fighting fire, battling for their lives for a couple of hours without time to take a drink. Now they had time but no water. Pipes were fractured, tanks were ripped open or contaminated, there were no pumps to get the stuff up anyway. Many of the wounded had lost blood, and those who were burned

198

had lost still more body fluid. Thirst raged in their burning bodies.

Somewhere on the main deck, Shelley mentioned the lack of water to Boles. Shelley was thirsty enough himself, but Don Jones, following him around like a lost pup ever since Doc had operated on his torn jaw, must have been suffering insufferably.

"I know where to get something," said Boles. In a few minutes he was back, carrying bottles of warm Coca-Cola, and Shelley poured some into Jones. It must have gone down his tortured throat like ambrosia. Boles went back and got more, and more. Other men, that night, too badly bunged up to help themselves, drank the tepid stuff with tears of gratitude in their eyes. Boles and other men pack-ratted off dozens of bottles of the precious fluid, from the locker where he knew it had been stored ever since the ship left the states. If he had taken it the day before, he would have been stealing from an officer. That night he simply took it and to hell with the consequences. There were none—except that Jim Berkey, who also drank the stuff, would go to work for the Coca-Cola Company years later, but never again would he taste another coke like the one he had that night off Okinawa.

Soon after the action ended, Dave Rubel left Control to check on gunnery casualties. He disappeared into the after section of the ship and that was the last Control saw of him for some time. There were no phones, and no word had come to the bridge from him.

"Tiwald," said Sanders, "You'd better go find Dave and see how he's making out back there."

Like everyone else that night, Tiwald had the baffling experience of getting lost on the main deck of a ship he had known well a few hours before. Strange shapes loomed up ahead of him in the night and he banged his shins on objects that had not been there before. Limp fire hoses twisted about like dead snakes, there were places where his feet slipped in something probably as well unseen in the dark. Almost as bad as the fear of running into something was the chance that he might stumble into a hole ripped in the deck and fall into something—what, he would rather not worry about.

Slowly he felt his way aft, calling "Mr. Rubel? . . . . Mr. Rubel!"

Suddenly a voice answered. "Hey, is that you, John? Can you swim?"

That was Don Young. Maybe he had found one of his engineers in the water alongside and needed help to fish him out. In the darkness Tiwald finally made out Young's form near the port rail. "Don? Sure, I can swim. Why?"

Young motioned over the side, where the sea should have been some eight or ten feet down. The water was nearly on a level with the deck. "You probably will have to very shortly."

In the hour after the battle ended, the damage control and repair parties worked with grim determination, doing all they could to save the ship. They especially sought to jettison topside weight—ammunition, loose wreckage, anything which could be dumped overboard to lighten the ship, whose sluggish motion in the water showed that she was close to the critical point.

If she did go down, the ability to swim was going to be a decided asset. According to the Ship's Organization Book, *Aaron Ward* had a motor whaleboat which could carry 16 people, and six life rafts and eight floater nets which could carry 25 each, for a total of 366 men. But the Ship's Organization Book had become sadly out of date during the past hour. All that was left of the whaleboat was her stem and stern posts, still dangling in the davits. A few of the life rafts and floater nets had been blown overboard, others of them had burned.

From the bridge of a ship some 35 feet above the sea, with 60,000 horsepower under foot, one could regard the Pacific Ocean with a certain degree of contempt. But with both engines dead, and several hundred tons of water in the after engine room and fire room, restlessly seeking a way into the rest of the ship, the ocean looked black and dangerous and deep, ready to swallow the ship in one gulp if anyone so much as stepped heavy on the deck.

Why she didn't go down, Biesmeyer and his damage control experts never did quite explain. Maybe Cooper, the oil king, was the man who saved the ship through not completing the job he was supposed to. Just before general quarters he had pumped oil from the after wing tanks into the service tanks. Then, according to routine, he should have ballasted the wing tanks down with salt water—perhaps 20 or 25 tons of it. But the alarm went before he made the connection, so he shut the intake valves and went to his battle station. The extra buoyancy of those two tanks may have saved many lives that night.

Or there may have been more than empty tanks holding the ship up. Willand, after being patched up in the wardroom dressing station, had been strapped into a stretcher and carried to the fantail along with other wounded men. He laid there in the darkness, unable to move, burning with thirst, listening to water he could not drink lapping at the sides of the ship only inches from his head. Once, someone came and let him sip some warm Coca-Cola and he felt a little better. Later, Willand felt hands reaching for his, and a voice said "Here, Chuck, take this." Chuck was too far gone by that time to recognize the voice, but he knew what the man had put in his hands—some shipmate had given him his Rosary.

Somehow in the chaos topside Bull Weyrauch and Pappy Berry found a P-500 pump. They lugged it about in the darkness, through wreckage, for what seemed like hours until they found a spot where they could get a suction hose into a flooded compartment. Then the gasoline motor turned obstinate. They cranked, sweated and swore, and each time the motor sputtered and died again, bystanders wilted, but finally it roared into action and everyone cheered as it began spouting a torrent of water over the side.

"We're gaining on her," Weyrauch announced, just as Mc-Caughey came past.

"What's going on here, Bull?"

"We're pumping her out, Chief."

"Yeah! Well, take a look over the side. There's a hole forty feet long in her and the whole damned Pacific Ocean's coming in just as fast as you pump it out."

Slowly, slowly, the flames subsided. Men, faced with the chance that the stuff might blow up in their hands, still heaved ammunition overboard. By 2045 the fires were all out. The ship was a blackened wreck in the black night, and her crew liked it that way, for a burning ship was a beacon for roaming enemy planes. But the enemy was gone. The Japanese had sent at least 25 planes against Radar Picket Station 10 that night, and *Aaron Ward*'s gunners had made certain that 10 of them were never going home. Bill Sanders had been right. His men—everyone of them—had known what to do.

Years after Okinawa, the Navy would be subjected to a fancy-pants investigation of the qualities of leadership which would result in more weighty orders on how to improve it than in, possibly, actual improvement. The whole situation had been plainly stated down in the CPO quarters of the *Aaron Ward* soon after Bill Sanders took command: ". . . . the old man ain't going to put out any crap . . . . and he ain't going to take any . . . . " Respect down the line, obedience up the line, and devotion both ways to hellangone. That was exactly how the Skipper brought his ship through her last battle, and if the gates of hell had suddenly yawned open on the deck of *Aaron Ward* that night and Bill Sanders had yelled "Come on men, we're going in," he would not have had to look back to know that every living man on the ship was crowding on his heels.

In the first hour of the watch it had been a distinct possibility. The weary fighters would never forget flames leaping in fury at the sky, and exploding ammunition snarling at the stars. There had been moments when men were not certain whether they were going up, or going down. They were too weary, sometimes still too frightened, to care.

By 2030 *Shannon*'s bridge crew could see flickers of light several miles ahead, where *Aaron Ward* was still fighting fire. "Uncle Ed" took his ship in with caution. *Aaron Ward* had no radio, so he couldn't tell her he was coming and she had no radar, so she wouldn't know he was coming until he got there. If she had any guns at all in commission, someone might well starting shooting at anything bigger than a seagull. Playing the Good Samaritan in the night off Okinawa was a role one didn't want fouled up by some sailor with a still itchy trigger finger.

Time 2106. Out of the night came a hail. "AARON WARD, AHOY THE AARON WARD;" and there came the *Shannon*. Men on *Aaron Ward*'s main deck, by now standing almost at water level, looked up at the ship looming above them in the night. She seemed as big as a battleship, and almost as welcome. *Shannon*'s crew peered down through the dark unbelievingly. Was that a ship? The hulk was unlighted, except for the fitful glow of battle lanterns shining out through ragged holes where men struggled to clear away wreckage. Emergency pumps still racketed in the night, and there was the sudden screech of tortured metal plates. It was difficult to make a ship out of that crazy mess of wreckage. The port side aft was just a heap of rubble. Scraps of wood dangled from the davits where the whaleboat had been. The forward stack had been smashed almost flat. Pieces of what had been Japanese aircraft cluttered the deck, pieces of what had once been guns still pointed at the sky, and around them sprawled what once had been gun crews.

Shannon's crew stared, silently. They needed no light to tell them what had happened. The night was rank with the stench and stink of battle—spilled fuel oil, blistered paint, overheated guns, empty cartridges, burnt mattresses, sweat, blood, and fire seared flesh.

Carefully, cautiously, *Shannon* worked into position with her fantail ahead of *Aaron Ward*'s bow. The small craft, the "picker-uppers" were still roaming about in the night, looking for survivors. Someone on *Aaron Ward* called over, "There's a man in the water off our starboard bow. Please pick him up." Between the ships there floated a life raft, empty; a body, face down; a man, face up, explaining to friends on the *Aaron Ward* "I can't climb up the ladder, my legs are broken." Somewhere a picker-upper boat flashed her searchlight across the scene and furious voices shouted "Put out that damned light!"

Several men who had been blown overboard and were floating around keeping each other company began helpfully blinking their flashlights and again nervous sailors roared, "Turn off those goddamn lights. We know you're out there."

In complete darkness, *Shannon* set about towing *Aaron Ward*, a job difficult enough for skilled seamen in broad daylight. On both ships, men worked in darkness, shouting commands and a few threats into the night.

"*Aaron Ward*! Heads up!" A heaving line slapped on the forecastle and sailors grabbed it, hauled it in.

"We're sending over our twenty-one thread messenger. Let us know when you have it."

"*Shannon*! We have the messenger." Now, *Shannon* bent on the big four-inch line and started it across.

"Let us know when you have the four-inch." Weary sailors heaved and tugged, snaking the heavy line across between the two ships, while on board *Shannon*'s fantail the crew fastened the tow wire to the line.

"*Shannon!* We have the four-inch."

"Roger. We're paying out the wire now. Heave 'round slowly."

"Aye, aye."

On *Aaron Ward*'s forecastle, Chief Shelley and the ragged remnants of his deck force toiled in the darkness, manhandling the heavy lines, wires and chains which could make a wife a widow almost as quickly as could an enemy bullet. There was no need for Sanders to hurry them up from the bridge; this was an operation in which every man took a great and personal interest.

On *Aaron Ward*'s fantail while this was going on, Offins and Winston snagged a floating life raft, lowered two wounded men to it, and Martin paddled them over to the *Shannon*. Coming back he picked up a couple of survivors. No point in a man spending the night out there doing nothing—there was plenty of work on board.

One long hour after *Shannon* arrived, a shout went up from *Aaron Ward*'s forecastle. "*Shannon*! we have the wire." Now both crews were tense. The ships were dead in the water, and until the wire was fast to *Aaron Ward*'s anchor chain, *Shannon* could not move. Until *Shannon* was able to move, *Aaron Ward* would not move. Minutes dragged like hours while a man rained sledge hammer blows on the connecting shackle of the anchor chain, while others heaved and strained to make the wire and chain fast. Finally there was a triumphant shout: "Connected up!"

"Roger" from *Shannon,* and on the bridge her annunciators jingled over to one third. The *Shannon* inched forward, paying out the rest of the tow wire. But still the *Aaron Ward* did not move. Her own anchor chain had to be run out to 45 fathoms, to provide the catenary necessary for the tow, and she had no power. So *Shannon* crept ahead and the chain clanked slowly out.

"*Shannon.* Forty-five fathoms on the capstan."

"Okay!" Now the ship could move a little farther. Impatience strained the voices of both crews. The operation had to go slowly if it was to go safely. If the wire parted, or if it slacked off and fouled *Shannon's* screws, there would be two more dead ducks on RPS 10.

"*Aaron Ward*! Let us know when you have way on."

By now the *Shannon* was definitely moving, and the *Aaron Ward* was almost lost in the blackness astern. Then, faintly, a voice carried across the night: "*Shannon.* We have way on."

"Roger." *Shannon's* crew finally took a deep breath. They'd done it again. Well, nearly . . . .Only forty-five miles more to go. "If the Japs are as fouled up as we are," muttered Lew Witmer to himself, back in a 5-inch mount, "we just might make it."

"Ease her ahead a few turns at a time," Uncle Ed told the OOD. A couple of hundred feet behind him in the night, the tow wire ran back still a few more hundred feet to the *Aaron Ward*. If it parted, *Aaron Ward* would have had it. If it slacked off and fouled *Shannon's* screws, she too would have had it. Slowly, cautiously, *Shannon* worked up speed to eight knots, while her wounded companion, floundering around in the night like a harpooned whale, dragged the average down to five knots. As the ships crawled through the night, Uncle Ed nursed the tension on that tow wire with all the care a concert violinists would have devoted to a C-string. That was the only wire he had, to haul a 2,500 ton ship forty-five miles into Kerama Retto. It was going to be a long, slow ride.

Still *Aaron Ward's* crew worked. The only men not on their feet were the wounded. No one on the ship had slept since five that morning. The men in section one, who had been on watch when the day began, were still on watch when it ended. The day had been a full twenty-four hours long for them, but at least they would be there to see Friday arrive. Not everyone had been that lucky, on Radar Picket Station 10.

In the dark, now silent sea where Radar Picket Station 10 had been, ships prowled the night, searching for survivors. One of these was the destroyer *Bache,* which had been patrolling on Radar Picket Station 9, some thirty miles southeast, when the raid first came in. *Bache* had logged the raid at 1809, when her radar picked up a large group of aircraft nearly seventy miles away to the southwest. When the planes closed to seventeen miles she went to GQ, and at 1828 sighted them and opened fire with the 5-inch battery. One Tony went down smoking. Two more planes started suicide runs on the ship. *Bache* got one with her 40mm battery; he crashed into the sea close aboard with slight damage to the forecastle. The other one headed for the *Macomb* astern, hit her after 5-inch mount and killed seven men, wounded 14 more. At the same time a friendly fighter made a crash landing nearby.

Bache ordered the LCS 111 to pick up the American pilot and maneuvered to help pick up men blown overboard from *Macomb.* While she was at this, DELEGATE ordered her up to Picket Station 10 to help there. *Bache* took off at 25 knots, but by the time she reached RPS 10 there would be nothing to do but look for survivors.

The LCSL had come alongside *Aaron Ward* immediately after the battle ended, picked a few swimmers out of the water, and took on eleven badly wounded men, one of whom soon died. Later, as other ships arrived, she backed clear and began hunting *Little's* survivors. Before the night was over, LCSL 14 had fished 150 men out of the water, thirty-five of them wounded.

Soon other craft arrived and began searching through the night for survivors. By midnight, the water around Station 10 was being combed by *Bache, Bennion, Sims, Pavlic,* LSM 167, PCE 855, and the LCS 85. The ships crept back and forth across the sea, at five knots, with bridge watch and lookouts straining their eyes and ears for a glimpse of a light or the sound of a cry in the darkness. Once during the night a bogie came within 23 miles and they went to general quarters, but there was no attack.

In the first light of dawn *Bache* found one body which was brought on board and identified as that of gunner's mate first class Hale from the LSMR 195. A little later they saw what had once been a body before the sharks found it. There was no use in taking what the sharks had left. At 0740, Friday morning, the search was called off and the ships headed for the transport area off Hagushi.

The little LCSL 25 had reported to RPS 10 late Thursday afternoon; in fact, she had just had time to march twice around the five mile square with the other small boys when the battle started. Ten minutes after her crew went to general quarters, she charged off with the other craft to assist *Aaron Ward*. On the way to where the big fight was, she got into a small one. Her gunners winged a plane, but it came on in, hit the mast and conning tower, and wrecked one gun. Flames seared the area. The gunners, a typical all-American crew named Smith, Dressel, Brunner, Echels, Bloomfield, Klimowicz, Lean, Nordhausen, and Raile were all burned. Mancini and Paczkowski went overboard.

But still LCSL 25 charged on in. The small boys were there to help the big boys when they got into trouble, and right then the big boys had plenty of it. *Little* sunk before LCSL 25 got there, but she managed to pick up sixty-six survivors. They were all from *Little* but one; somehow, in the darkness and confusion, some sailor who had been blown overboard from *Aaron Ward* got himself rescued with the *Little* crowd.

On board the LCS 83, Lieutenant J. M. Faddin and his crew were so busy their log of the action looked like shorthand:

"1827 GQ 1830 Plane crashed into DM 34. 1832 planes hit both *Aaron Ward* and *Little*. 1845 both ships burning. LSMR 195 fell behind because of engine trouble. 1848 *Little* burning. 1855 *Little* appears to be broken amidships. 1902 *Little* sunk. 1906 plane hit 195. 1910 plane took off mast of 25. 1912 picking up survivors. Plane approached from port side, fired at by all guns. Plane out of control, crashed about 50 feet over bow. LSMR burning furiously.

Plane coming in astern, shot down astern, fired at ship as it hit water. 1920 lowered life rafts. 1926 another plane hit DM 34. 1942 195 sunk. Still picking up survivors. 2030 Came alongside starboard quarter of *Aaron Ward,* put P-500 pump over. Took some men for medical attention. 2105 backed away starboard side, came alongside port quarter, put another P-500 over. Pulled away, returned to give *Aaron Ward* gasoline, they said they had gasoline. 2242 Under way to area where *Little* and LSMR went down."

All in all, the LCS 83 had spent what could be called four busy hours in any man's navy. Her night was not yet over. Loaded with survivors from the *Little* and *Aaron Ward,* she went alongside the PCE 855 for medical aid. For one of them, it was too late. The tag on Joe Zaloga's stretcher was marked "Died at 2337." By half past one in the morning LCS 83 had unloaded all her wounded, and just in time. There came another plane, and the weary men dashed for their guns again.

Hours after the battle, the LCS 83 roamed around Picket Station 10 while her weary crew scanned the dark waters for survivors, but finally Lieutenant Faddin called off the search. By that time, either the rescue ships had found the men in the water, or the sharks had. LCS 83 pointed her nose toward Kerama Retto and started in after the *Shannon* and *Aaron Ward,* now miles ahead of her.

Then someone saw a faint light in the darkness and LCS 83 swung over to starboard to investigate. There it was again . . . . blink . . . . blink. "Give him a light," ordered Faddin, and a signalman sent a few quick flashes that way with a blinker gun. Men could almost hear the light answer frantically . . . . BLINK . . . . BLINK . . . . BLINK! There was someone out there yet, still swimming, still blinking. The ship eased alongside, slowly, and men hauled the swimmer aboard.

There is a standard greeting among men in the Navy. It is used whenever strangers meet, and is appropriate whether they meet in the men's room of the Commodore Hotel in New York or in the middle of the night in the East China Sea:

"What ship, sailor?"

"*Aaron Ward*. James Fields, seaman first, USS *Aaron Ward*!"

Fields was the last man fished out of the sea that night. If LCS 83 had passed a half mile farther away from him, if she had turned a few minutes earlier or later, if some lookout had yawned at the exact moment Fields blinked, if a shark had come along . . . . there was no doubt about it, Fields was a lucky sailor. He had been crowding his luck for several hours.

Several hours earlier, Fields had been sitting on his bunk, writing to his wife back in Greensboro, North Carolina:

"We feel that so far our luck has been extremely good, and are just hoping the cards aren't stacked so we receive something like that. All the others feel the way I do and that is to survive and get home with our families. If God will look after us as He has so far we'll have nothing to worry for.

"Sweetheart, the weather the past two days has been terrible as far as physical comfort goes, but it eases our minds just a little towards air attack . . . . It's good though in the sense of keeping the Japs away . . . . Only one other ship patrols this area with us and that is a 1850 ton destroyer *Little* . . . ."

General quarters went then and Fields wrote no more that night. His battle station was on the superstructure deck, with 20mm Mounts 25 and 27. The third plane to attack hit the superstructure deck just below Mount 44 and the explosion threw a life net over Fields. As he fought himself clear he could see Mount 44 wrapped in flames, and the director crew, Good and Olmeda, sprawled on deck. With his guns damaged, Fields ran forward to Mounts 26 and 28, on the stack, and helped there for a few moments, until someone sent him down to the clipping room to help pass up ammunition. Just as he slid down a ladder to the main deck an explosion blew him overboard. The ship was still making about 20 knots and the suction of the screws took him under but he missed them, and when he came up the ship was 50 yards away and still going.

The ship was on fire. There was a patch of fire on the sea, too, so Fields swam away from that. After swimming for maybe ten or fifteen minutes he found another sailor floating in his life jacket; Steinhilber, who must have been blown over when Mount 44 was hit. But Steinhilber was dead, so Fields swam away again.

A mile or so away, Fields could see the ship still fighting, still burning. Two more planes started their attack, roaring in past Fields, and as *Aaron Ward's* guns opened up on them the projectiles spurted into the water all around him. He was certain one of them would get him. Then he saw a plane hit the ship and more flames billow into the night. He was pretty certain the ship was a goner then, and started praying. For a bit he prayed that the *Little* would pick him up, but then he saw her burn and sink and things looked mighty hopeless. But he kept on praying, and flashing his little one-cell flashlight, for hours and hours.

Finally he saw a light. But he was afraid of it. Other nights out on Station 10, they had seen a light over on the Japanese island of Kume Shima, and Fields feared that was what he saw now. But a light was better than nothing when a man was out in the ocean at night all by himself. Japanese or not, he swam toward it. It almost disappeared at times; it must have been five miles away, but he swam toward it. His own light was growing dim. He was growing cold. Cramps knotted his legs. His throat ached from the salt water he had swallowed.

And then suddenly, he could see the dark shape of a ship looming up against the sky, and hear voices calling.

"Standby to recover survivors."

Someone had seen his light. Someone had heard his prayers. He was saved.

"Anyone else out here with you?" they asked.

"Steinhilber was." he said. There was no use looking for Steinhilber now.

Two days later Fields got himself sent back to the *Aaron Ward*. Not until then could he conceive of the damage that had been done to her. Not until then did he have any idea of how many of his shipmates had lived, or died. Not until then did the ship know Fields was alive. He had been officially listed in the ship's log as missing.

Back aboard, Fields went down to his locker, got out his pen, and the unfinished letter to his wife, and went on where he had left off Thursday evening.

"It's hard to explain how thankful I am this Sunday morning just to be able to write . . . . Guess it was just God's wish to have me here and I am hoping not to forget Him for that. What happened to me last Thursday is hard to believe. GQ was early in the evening, about 6:30, and only a few minutes later . . . "

Fields was not the only lucky man. Eight others besides himself came back to the ship that day. The ship's log had declared them missing; their shipmates had mourned them. Mr. Rosengren logged them all in: Foster, Schaefer, Moxley, Greenoe, McKanna, Martin, Gross, Schofield. The Captain came down to greet them. They were in the Navy again, and very glad of it.

Midnight. On Picket Station 10, the battle was over and the battleground was cleared. The sea around looked as it had a hundred years before, as it would a thousand years later. At Ypres and Austerlitz, the grass that covered scars of battle took years to do its work; on RPS 10 the sea cleaned up the mess in minutes. There was nothing left to show that battle had flamed around Picket Station 10 hours earlier; no evidence of the twenty-five planes shot down; no sign of the two ships sunk; no trace of the eighty men dead or missing; no mark to show that two damaged ships were limping away for repairs and that more than one hundred and fifty men would spend days, weeks, sometimes months in painful hospital beds because of that night. Where the "floating chrysanthemums" had come with the sunset, there remained for the midnight moon only silence, and desolation, and dim night.

. . . . a deed whereat valor will weep. — SHAKESPEARE

Chapter Eight

Additional Remarks

Salvage and repair. Reports to next of kin. "Stateside!" Victory and decommissioning. A last tribute.

In the weary, dreary hours past midnight, *Aaron Ward* followed *Shannon's* towline through the night. The compass repeater on the bridge clicked slowly as the bow of the ship swung from port to starboard and back again. There was power again; Cezus and Lunetta had finally fired up the forward diesel generator. In the dim binnacle light, the compass heading read 090—east. That meant stateside, Uncle Sugar, the United States, home again. If one got that far. But they weren't going that far at the end of a five-knot towline. If another plane caught them before they reached the doubtful refuge of

Kerama Retto, they weren't going anywhere at all. Except down.

And the night had just begun. Around midnight the moon came up and there they were sailing along just like in the song, except they were sailing right past the Japanese island of Kume Shima. If the planes came back, there might not be enough of *Shannon's* Irish luck to do for the both of them.

But until the planes came, *Aaron Ward's* people worked to save their ship. Dazed, confused, weary, they toiled. Neupert, Rubel, Biesmeyer, Young, the other officers, the CPO's, encouraged and inspired by the unconquerable Sanders, kept their men at the work of saving the ship. Men later remembered they had seen Offins and Shelley in more places at one time than men could rightfully be— fighting fires, clearing decks, dumping wreckage, tending wounded, calming frightened men. These were not necessariiy the duties of a mineman or boatswain's mate, but they were what the Skipper expected of a good chief, or any good man, and no one ever thought of letting the Skipper down.

The gunners, what were left of them, still stood by their guns, what were left of those. They still might have to use them. Before the ships had moved many miles, the sky behind them again filled with tracers and shell fire. Snoopers were in the area, prowling, looking for crippled ships, and had jumped the small craft still searching for survivors. The threat of another air attack, in their nearly defenseless condition, was almost more than men could endure. Especially so, with their SC radar out. A ship without radar, at night in enemy waters, was really going it blind, and her crew stood a very good chance of being clobbered before they knew what had hit them.

Once a snooper flew within four miles of the ships. *Shannon* watched him on the radar, all guns trained out, men with their fingers on firing keys. But *Shannon's* guns stayed silent. If they didn't shoot, maybe he would miss them. The plane flew on. Still safe, and they breathed easier.

On *Aaron Ward* radarman Reichard labored painfully despite his torn arm and finally got his radar operating again. Just at that moment Karl Neupert came by with a dish of ice cream, scrounged from the wardroom refrigerator by a considerate messboy. Like many other men in the crew, he hadn't had time for supper the night before, and no one had eaten anything since.

"Commander," said someone in CIC. "Reichard's got the SC4 on the line again."

Neupert turned and looked at Reichard. "You fixed the air search radar, hey?" Reichard nodded.

Neupert handed him the ice cream, silently, and walked away. Reichard licked up every drop of it. "The Brain" might be a little hard to understand at times, but he was a great guy.

During the night Shelley and Rapalee ventured into the cold storage room under the forward crew's quarters—three decks down in a dead and darkened ship—for some crates of oranges. Each time they went down through another hatch it was like taking one more step into a tomb. They found what they wanted and scrambled up topside; anything was better than that. By this time reaction to the battle had set in. Frank Ceckowski ate his orange, huddled on deck; he was dirty, covered with oil and blood, and trembling so he had to hold it in both hands.

0440. *Shannon's* radio broke into the silence. An air raid alert at Kerama Retto. They were heading right into it. Again they saw AA fire streaking into the sky over the island refuge. For a moment the sky glowed, some fifteen miles away, where some ship knocked off a plane. *Shannon's* luck was still with them; the planes moved off southward, probably headed back to Sakashima. They were, by God, maybe going to make it after all. And by the grace of God they did.

As the warm light of 4 May flooded across her charred and twisted decks, *Aaron Ward* drifted to a stop outside the submarine net gates at Kerama Retto. This was the place she almost didn't reach; this was the day some of her crew never expected to see. On the forecastle, covered with canvas bunk bottoms, were those who wouldn't see it. *Shannon's* crew could see the wreckage plainly now, and stared silently. "How do we look?" Sanders called across the water to her Skipper. "Uncle Ed" had difficulty thinking of a heartening reply.

The little tug *Tekesta* came bustling out and made fast to *Aaron*

Ward's starboard bow. Her crew passed over big pots of steaming coffee, loaves of bread, chunks of cheese, and *Aaron Ward's* crews wolfed the stuff down with burned and bloody hands. Such a breakfast was a luxury granted only to the living.

Even as they ate, signal flags whipped to yardarms throughout the anchorage and on nearby ships men pounded to their battle stations. *Shannon* dropped the tow line, sounded GQ, buzzed off on four boilers.

RED ALERT! The damned Japs were coming back again. *Well, let 'em come. The crew had held them off for an hour last night on RPS 10. Someone else could have the honor now.* The ship had a few guns that could still fire, but the chances were good that if they did fire the shock would break her back and she would go down like a rock. The only thing to do was pretend they were in a nice fox hole and hope the raiders weren't shooting at fox holes that morning . . . . *Another hunk of cheese, anyone?*

Slowly *Tekesta* shoved her crippled charge through the crowded anchorage. On larger ships, silent sailors looked down, like spectators at a theatre, on the dirty, ragged, bloody crew; on the indescribable wreckage; on covered forms on the forecastle; on burned bodies still trapped in the debris. A swarm of boats from *Gosper* clustered around as medics clambered aboard to prepare patients for transfer. Thirty-nine badly wounded men were sent off the ship. But many who stayed behind were cut, burned, and bruised.

As the most seriously wounded were being transferred, men hunted among them, checking on friends. Eves, from Hagerstown, Maryland, found his buddy Floyd, whom he considered practically a next door neighbor since he came from Lancaster, Pennsylvania. Floyd was lashed into a stretcher.

"How are you, Harry?" he asked.

Harry's right hand and left foot were swathed in bandages, but he could still talk.

"I won the Purple Heart," he said.

At that moment, there were more men among the crew who qualified for the Purple Heart than who owned a clean shirt.

One of these was George Coward, burned from head to toe. It

was a hell of a way to spend a birthday, he thought to himself, but certainly better than being up on the forecastle, stretched out under a piece of canvas. There would be no cake or candles for him, no one to sing "Happy Birthday," but he was lucky, plenty lucky. George spent many long painful days in a hospital ship before his wife's birthday card finally reached him.

Through no fault of his own, a man who happened to be facing the other way when some ammo blew up was peppered with shrapnel which more or less ruined his dungaree trousers. This affliction was the source of considerable merriment—for everyone but the victim—as the medics, in days following the battle, spent tedious hours prospecting for tiny bits of metal in what a man rightfully considered highly personal property. Comments by passersby were always variations on the same old theme: "Hey, Doc! I see he's finally getting the lead out . . . . !"

On the flagship *McKinley* nearby, a signal searchlight blinked and Kellejian and Zagone began recording the message. Before the last word had been scribbled on the message pad, everyone on the bridge knew what it said:

> "WE ALL ADMIRE A SHIP THAT CAN'T BE LICKED X CINC-PAC ADVANCE HQ SHOUTS ACTION TO AARON WARD X INFO TO COMMANDER FIFTH FLEET COMMANDER TASK FORCE FIFTY ONE X CONGRATULATIONS ON YOUR MAGNIFICENT PERFORMANCE . . . ."

In case there was someone on the ship who didn't know who CincPac was, Zagone printed the last word in big letters: "NIMITZ."

Fleet Admiral Nimitz! The boss man himself. Through the long night the news of their heroic fight had flashed all the way back to the Headquarters, Commander in Chief, United States Pacific Fleet, and the Admiral had taken time to let them know he was proud of them. *Magnificent! Admiral Nimitz said so. How's about that, men!*

The message went on the crew's bulletin board, to be followed by others:

"WE ALL ADMIRE YOUR JOB X NO ONE COULD HAVE
DONE ANY MORE."
"CONGRATULATIONS TO YOU AND YOUR CREW FOR
BRINGING THE GRAND SHIP BACK TO FIGHT AGAIN."

And one from the Skipper of the *Robert H. Smith,* hit by a suicide
plane on the first day of the operation:

"MY SYMPATHY IN YOUR LOSS OF WHAT MUST HAVE
BEEN FINE MEN."

Aye, Captain Waldron. You never miss them until you lose them.

A boat pulled alongside and an officer wearing two gold stars
clambered on board. An admiral's visit to a ship usually involved
scrubbed paintwork, polished brass, and spotless uniforms, but not
this time. This was Rear Admiral Alexander Sharp, the minecraft
boss. His own flagship, the *Terror,* had been badly damaged by a
kamikaze only three days earlier; he could understand what *Aaron
Ward* had gone through, and came to personally commend her captain on saving the ship.

"It was close, Sir," said Sanders. "The mine tracks were all that
held her together."

The wounded were no more than off the ship before she caught
fire again. This time, in daylight and with some pumps in use, they
doused it in a hurry. A boat came from the repair ship *Zaniah,* to
arrange sleeping space and meals there. It was no go—Sanders had
said they'd stay with the ship last night; they were going to stay with
her today, and so long as she floated. They didn't exactly have many
bunks, or much chow, but they'd make out.

Weary, hungry, sleepy, bloody, men dragged about the ship, faced
with the horrible task of trying to create order out of black chaos.
After the ship anchored, Flinn came blinking up out of the steering
engine room, dumbfounded at the desolation around him. He had
seen a lot of wrecked ships, but never anything like this. The ship
had been in perfect condition when he went below 14 hours earlier.
Now she looked like a floating junk pile—and among the junk

Flinn saw the broken bodies of men he knew. He talked for a moment with Tedford, lining up blanket covered shapes on the fantail, and as "Doc" checked off names—Fletcher, Macukas, Olmeda, Dial, it seemed to Flinn that the battle had indeed come out like a classic tragedy.

"It's always the good guys who get killed. The bad ones, the miserable ones, they are the ones who survive."

Miserable they were, the bad guys, the survivors, as they hunted through the debris. Near the twisted wreckage of Mount 44, they found a pair of shoes still standing at Lieutenant McKay's battle station. Farther aft on the superstructure deck was another pair of shoes, standing side by side, neatly laced, as if Medric Armand was still in them. In the wreckage of the after port quad 40 they found the dog tags which had belonged to Rawlins. Pepoon they found with his arms around the body of a much smaller man, as if he had tried to shield him from the blast which got them both. Bob Couie, who had told his friends he wouldn't make it to the end of the war, had been right. Couie didn't make it.

The after emergency diesel room had been ripped open. Anderson, whose battle station it was, was gone, washed out by the sea. The body of Smith, who manned the diesel with him, was still there. Smith had never had time to remove his headphones, and the telephone cord had kept the body from going with Anderson.

That day, and the days that followed, as they pried through the blackened ruins and the increasing stench of death, remained in the memories of many men like scraps of horrible nightmares, nothing a man wanted to remember, but something he could never forget.

. . . . there was a shapeless mass, a burned life jacket, slumped at the hatch to number two fire room. "Hey, Shelley! Here's another one, over here!"

"Who is it, son?"

"Damn, chief. I can't tell . . . . He ain't got no head."

. . . . there was a hand on the deck near number one stack. Nothing else.

"That's all there was, Doc. Look, there's a high school ring, Class of 1943. Do you know who it was?"

"Yes, Mac. I know."

. . . . there was a body on the superstructure deck. Just a body.

"All right, men, let's have a blanket over here."

"Hell! We can't bury him this way . . . . no arms or legs?"

They put four arms and legs in the bundle . . . .

. . . . there were two bodies in the burned out 40mm clipping room. One was the dead Japanese pilot whose plane had set the fire. It was unmarked. Only the eyeballs were missing. As Brown climbed back out on deck, a friend met him. "Brownie! You okay? What the hell you got in that pillow case?"

"Follett."

. . . . there was a body, down in the engine room. No one in this world could have identified it. But in what had once been a dungaree shirt pocket, McCaughey found the little silver ear clips Stu Mann had been happily making for his wife in Palo Alto.

. . . . and there was a body, clothing burned off, but with a tattoo.

"Two bluebirds, Doctor, right on his chest."

"Oh. I know him. That's Tony Olmeda."

"Doc, why's a guy want bluebirds tattooed on him?"

"Didn't you know? Bluebirds are supposed to bring happiness."

But not on the picket line.

By early afternoon they had sent off the wounded, identified most of the dead, held quarters for muster, and tried to determine who was missing, but there was always the chance of a mistake. Karl Neupert climbed to the bridge and handed quartermaster third class Michael a list of names. "Pass the word," he said, "if any of these men are aboard, or anyone knows their whereabouts, report to the bridge at once."

Mike warmed up the PA system. It was a long list.

219

"Now hear this! Lay up to the bridge, Anderson, Armand, Beattie, Bruna . . . ." Mike's voice broke. This was the toughest job the Navy had ever handed him . . . .

" . . . . Cain, Carpenter, Carrick, Coltra, Connell, Couie . . . . " Along *Aaron Ward's* burned and twisted decks the living stood silently, listening to names of men who had been their friends . . . .

" . . . . Dalton, Dart, Dial, Dulin, Fletcher, Follett . . . . " The names went out across the sunny sea, and tired men turned to look at the horizon with unseeing eyes . . . .

" . . . . Good, Harris, Hendrickson, Lepon, Long . . . . " Yesterday *Aaron Ward* was a proud fighting ship; now she was a wreck, but the proudest wreck in the fleet . . . .

" . . . . Macukas, Mann, Marshall, McCoy, McKay, McLaughlin . . . . " *Aaron Ward's* guns were silent now, her gunners deep in the sea . . . .

". . . . Morgan, Niwinski, Olmeda, Pepoon, Rawlins . . . ." For them the war was over; they had dreamed the last dream, stood the last watch, fired the last gun . . . .

" . . . . Schroeder, Schroeter, Smith, Spradling, Steinhilber . . . . " They had fought together and died together, and now they were named together in a final roll of honor . . . .

" . . . . Stole, Symes, Turner, Wagner, Zaloga." The last echo died away. On the main deck a sailor in torn pants savagely kicked a piece of a burned plane. Later would be soon enough for tears.

Mike turned off the PA system. He would never forget the silence that followed. No one came to the bridge.

After the crew's compartment had been pumped out, Sanders went down to take a look. A handful of sailors were cleaning up the indescribable mess. Shelley had located and opened the lockers of those men killed or missing, and "Doc" Crider and a few helpers were stacking the contents up on empty bunks, picking and sorting, making inventories, getting the gear ready to send home. Gaping open, the lockers were pitiful reminders of the men who had once "lived" in them. By regulation, they were all alike; each contained the same items, each was stowed in the same way. There was not much room for individuality in a gear locker. It was a sad state of affairs that, looking at the lockers of two men he had known well only a day or so before, all he could see to make one different from the other, now that they were gone, was that one rolled his clean socks and the other folded them.

Unnoticed for a moment, the skipper stood and listened to his crew as they went about their unhappy task.

"How's about this picture here. Is that his sister or his girl friend?"

"Her? That was that babe in San Pedro. Deep six it!"

"Hey, looky this! Smell what he had in that big old bottle of dandruff cure. No wonder it's damn' near empty!"

"For cripes sake, watch what you're doing—don't send a pair of dirty socks back to his mother!"

A sodden piece of paper on deck in front of an open locker caught his attention and Sanders picked it up. It was a page torn from a small pocket notebook. Printed in pencil, here was one man's crude attempt to fox the censor and let his family know where he was: "If I sign *your son,* it means I am in the Solomons. If I sign *your faithful son,* it means I am in China . . . ." The little code sheet named other salutations for Australia, India, Hawaii, New Caledonia. The man who had written it had probably never heard of Okinawa until it was too late. The Skipper crumpled it up and tossed it into a trash can, and just then one of the men looked up and saw him.

"Hell of a mess, ain't it, Sir?" he said.

Sanders nodded. He knew the man wasn't talking about the after crew's compartment.

Poking and prying through the fire blackened wreckage officers and men found strange things. A burning plane had smashed into Doc's room, incinerated everything there. His binoculars were melted into a lump. Doc scraped aside the ashes of his mattress, under which he had kept a prized bamboo bass rod, and there it was, in perfect shape. But when he picked it up it collapsed into dust. All that Tiwald and Dillon saved out of their room was the clothes they had worn to GQ that night, everything else had burned. Tiwald's billfold, with forty dollars in it, had burned in two, and so had the bills. He eventually recovered twenty dollars for the pieces from the Bureau of Engraving and Printing.

Dillon and Tiwald shared their room with a big safe in which the registered publications, the secret and confidential communications codes and tactical manuals were stowed. The intense heat had blackened and charred them beyond all recognition. Regulations required that all registered publications must be accounted for to the Chief of Naval Operations, and in case of damage the register numbers were to be salvaged where possible. Even the FBI couldn't have found register numbers in that mess, and Woodside and Tiwald didn't try. They carefully shoved the entire collection into an incinerator and then truthfully reported that all publications had been destroyed by fire.

Late on Friday the tug ASR 34 came alongside and moved *Aaron Ward* over to the repair ship *Zaniah*. That ship had arrived in Kerama Retto from Ulithi only two days earlier, and almost immediately had been treated to a FLASH RED alert. Now her crew was to find out what happened out on the picket lines when the planes didn't get into Kerama Retto. The wrecked ship, her tired men, and their tense silence, greatly impressed these newcomers. They piled aboard and commenced cleaning up wreckage, pumping out water, patching up holes, but they worked without chatter. *Aaron Ward's* sailors didn't feel like talking much yet.

After the flooded crew's compartments were pumped out, they had to be cleaned out. This was a task only slightly easier than cleaning the Augean stables. Personal gear, blankets, mattresses, everything had been soaked in salt water and collected a heavy coating of fuel oil. The stuff could never be used. They couldn't dump it overboard because it would float and foul up boat screws. Finally someone borrowed a small landing craft and all hands turned to, loaded the filthy mess into the boat and took it over to a nearby island and burned it. They spent several days stoking up the fires on their private dump, before the trash was all gone.

A few days later, the crew watched with great interest as a group of landing craft came charging past, loaded to the gunwales with Marines in full battle array. The Marines headed for *Aaron Ward's* trash-burning island, stormed ashore, and occupied it. No one had gotten around to securing the island until then, and the *Aaron Ward* trash burners, had, technically, been burning their trash on enemy ground.

On the Sunday after the battle Bill Sanders gave himself a few minutes for a luxury he had not enjoyed during the past week—a letter to his wife. In his last letter he had mentioned briefly the holocaust when the *Pinckney* was hit. There was another one to write about now.

"Now we have a rest after what was the most horrible hour of my life just a few days ago . . . . I thank God I am alive, for I hardly expected to be after the battle was underway. I'd hate to ever go through it again. Tonight as we were going over some of the mail I read one letter from one of the boys to his mother. It was written just a few minutes before the attack and later found in his effects after he had been killed. He had written a Mother's Day message in his own way and it was beautiful and now to think that soon after she receives it she will also hear from the Navy Department in its cold official manner . . . . "

There was one way to take off a little of the chill in Navy Department communications. Bill Sanders wrote to the man's mother himself. During the next week he wrote to the mothers and wives of every man he had lost. These were no stereotyped "regrets," but deeply personal letters, each one bearing the stamp of an officer who knew his men intimately:

" . . . . Henry was one of the more cheerful men aboard ship. His watch station was close by my cabin. His cheerful daily 'Good Morning' will be missed by myself and his comrades."

" . . . . Joe was buried with appropriate military honors and now rests in a well-kept American Military Cemetery over which the flag of his country proudly flies. His grave is marked with a plain white cross bearing his name."

" . . . . Farrell did splendid work while aboard, both in the sick bay and in his capacity as spiritual director . . . . Although your sorrow is undoubtedly great, I know that you must be proud that he followed the example of Christ as a healer of soul and body until he was lost from us."

" . . . . Medric was at his battle station on a forty millimeter machine gun, amidships. This gun crew earned the admiration and respect of all hands by destroying one plane and firing into another until it crashed into their mount. The explosion that followed cleared the deck of all personnel and material."

" . . . . Junior was well liked by all hands. He was never moody and the music of his guitar, even in the most trying times, was pleasant to all. In his capacity as ship's tailor, he showed great skill, and the ship still carries many useful products of his handiwork."

". . . . Your loss was also ours, for like all good Navy cooks, Frank was a favorite of the crew's, and his appetizing meals, shy smile, and helping hand will long be missed on board the *Aaron Ward*."

" . . . . Jerry was at his battle station . . . . when the ship was struck by a suicide plane, carrying a bomb. Jerry was instantly killed. His body was found at his station, bearing mute evidence to the fact that he did all in his power to help his shipmates in their fight."

Here was surely one of the most difficult duties ever required of an officer in command. Forty-two times he wrote that last line: "With kindest regards and deepest sympathy." Bill Sanders meant every word of it.

"FLASH RED! CONDITION YELLOW!"
Air attack imminent. Fire on any plane in sight!
This was an emergency signal, but in Kerama Retto it was a routine emergency. The planes came every night. Everyone expected

them. Sunset announced the witching hour, the time the bats came out, and gunners stood by their guns. Maybe this time they'd get one .... There was always the distinct possibility that things would work out the other way around, too. Enemy planes came in low, depending on the mountains of Zamami Shima and Ada Shima to hide them from radar until almost the last instant before they flashed over the anchorage. If only the chickens—the Navy and Marine fighters—didn't go home to roost too soon.

Ships at Kerama Retto hid too, as best they could, under smoke screens. Each night smoke boats roamed the anchorage, pouring out clouds of thick chemical smoke. But men who gasped and choked for hours in the stinking stuff would just about as soon have shot it out with attacking planes. The thing to do was lie doggo and keep the guns silent; let the planes buzz right on past. *Aaron Ward* had to keep quiet; there was still the prospect that shock of firing the 5-inch guns would shake her to pieces.

"ALL HANDS, GENERAL QUARTERS!"

That was the *Zaniah*, carrying out her nightly routine. Her smoke boats would be in the water, smoking, and her skipper would be on the bull horn, shouting at them in the darkness and confusion to make still more smoke. "Smoke boat, make smoke! .... Smoke boat? Where in hell is my smoke boat!" The show was better than some movies they had on the *Aaron Ward*.

"ALL HANDS TAKE COVER. MOVIES WILL START IMMEDIATELY."

That was how *Aaron Ward* spent the witching hour. She couldn't fight, so the crew piled into the mess hall and had a movie. A good lively cartoon or Fitzpatrick Travel Talk helped pass the evening, helped one forget for as much as a few seconds at a time that there might be another plane up there in the dusk, loaded with bombs and gasoline, pulling over in a dive, heading in, aiming right at them. Either he would miss or there would be the dull thump they all recognized now, the blast of heat, the smash of high explosive, the slash of razor sharp steel plates, the searing superheated steam, and again the sickening sweet smell of burned flesh and sticky blood

225

. . . . Hey, a Mickey Mouse cartoon tonight! Laugh like hell, every-one.

The best show of all, in Kerama Retto, took place in CIC. This was no Hollywood fantasy of underdone plot and overdone characters, but a real drama played out to the frequently bitter end—the battle on the picket line. There was no film, nothing but the terse voices of men on the picket stations coming from the radio loud-speakers, but for those who had been through battle on the picket line nothing else was needed. Their still vivid memories supplied all the picture one could want.

During alerts men crowded into the CIC room, more men jammed in the door, others hung around outside, to follow the course of battle they could not see. They listened silently, each one imagining the hurried words of other men working in a CIC room miles away where the planes were coming in, the sudden roar of guns, the snarl of aircraft engines, the explosions, the tower of smoke day by day, the pillar of fire by night marking again the place where men had fought and died on the picket line.

Four more big raids hit the picket lines while *Aaron Ward* lay licking her wounds in Kerama Retto. Four more times battle swirled around those distant outposts where a few ships stood between the raiders and the main forces at Hagushi and Buckner Bay.

On 9 May they hit *Oberrender* and *England* on the inner screen. The next day they hit *Brown* west of Hagushi, and *Harry F. Bauer* on Station 5, out east of Okinawa. In the next three days they hit some big boys—the carriers *Enterprise* and *Bunker Hill,* the battle-wagon *New Mexico,* and the *Evans, Bache* and *Bright.* Up on Station 15, *Hugh W. Hadley* got it from a Baka, a piloted bomb. In isolated actions over the next week, only *Douglas H. Fox* and *Sims* were hit. Then, on 20 May, they hit five ships between Kerama Retto and Ie Shima—*Thatcher, John C. Butler, Tattnall, Chase, Register,* and the LST 808.

The Navy has a saying, "When in danger or in doubt, run in circles, scream and shout." As far as the *Aaron Ward* sailors were concerned, danger was all about them at Kerama Retto. Everyone had a fair ration of doubt, too; doubt that they still would get out of it without taking another kamikaze; doubt that the ship ever would actually make it stateside; doubt that, even if she did, they would be allowed to go along instead of being sent off to some other ship remaining behind. But a man could still grin a little, after the nightly raid was over, and enjoy a bit of light verse before he piled into the sack, clothes, shoes, and all . . . . just in case.

Bill Shakespeare, who might have gone to sea a few times himself before he wrote:

". . . . overboard
Into the tumbling billows of the main.
Lord, Lord! methought, what pain it was to drown!
What dreadful noise of waters in mine ears!
What ugly sights of death within mine eyes!
Methought I saw a thousand fearful wracks;
Ten thousand men that fishes gnaw'd upon; . . . ."
. . . . Richard the 3rd
Act I, Sc. IV

could have penned some immortal lines about Okinawa. The local talent did the best they could, with Lieutenant Winfrey in *Gosper* heading the list:

"Now I lay me down to sleep; I pray the Lord my life I keep,
Until the morning rolls around, keep me healthy, safe and sound.
About this vessel lay some smoke until the time when we're awoke.
Grant no Baka bombs intrude into our private interlude.
Keep our chickens up on high; splash all bogies in the sky.
If buzz bombs come before I wake, I pray the Lord a raft I make."

Unlike Shakespeare, Lieutenant Winfrey needed no footnotes to his text. Everyone knew what it meant: *You may be next.*

Almost worse than being under way at night and waiting for a

227

raid on the picket station was being at anchor and helpless at night in Kerama Retto. After the enemy planes had either been shot down or driven off for the night and the smoke boats had found their way home through the stinking mess they had made earlier, men who went topside in the dark did so with more than a little caution. The crew had been warned when they first entered Kerama Retto to be alert for Japanese who swam out to the ships at night and climbed up anchor chains, to knock off weary watchstanders.

There was some basis of fact for the warning. The ships were anchored so close to the beach that snipers could hit them. At least twice ships had been boarded by the enemy, and a man on board LST 884 had been shot by one of the midnight marauders. Of course, no one among the crew ever missed any of his friends in the morning, and no bodies were found floating alongside, so no one believed the story too seriously, but just seriously enough so most of them were jumpy as cats.

Bull Weyrauch didn't believe in Japanese swimmers, but he carried a big knife anyway. Coming off watch one night, he spied "Jesus" Cezus mooching along the dark deck and decided to liven things up a little. He hid by the mine shack until Cezus passed, then jumped out and shouted "Banzai!" What Weyrauch didn't know was that Cezus had an even bigger knife. Cezus leaped into action and Weyrauch very nearly got himself sliced up before he could convince Cezus he was friendly.

For five weeks *Aaron Ward* laid in Kerama Retto while her crew put her back together as best they could. *Aaron Ward* was going home if they could keep her together long enough. But the ship was going to have to limp home on one engine. The first thing the repair gangs did was to pull off the propeller, the only salvagable part of the damaged port engine, to use on another ship. Sanders knew if he didn't get the ship out soon she would never leave; in their frantic rush to put damaged ships back on the picket line the repair crews were liable to pick the ship to bits and leave them nothing to go home in.

Ships only slightly damaged were hurriedly patched up and returned to duty, but *Aaron Ward* had received what was known as a "Stateside hit"—her damage could only be repaired in a mainland navy yard. Sanders was going to get his ship back there even if she did have to go on one engine.

In ten days the engineers had steam on the boilers in the forward engine room. There was some doubt about whether the boilers would hold pressure after the fire room had been flooded, but they did, and that was when Bill Sanders put out the word. "We'll take the ship back—and everyone with her." All but the Fighter Director Team which came aboard in Ulithi. They went on another picket ship. The war on the picket line was far from over.

The telegrams went out from the Navy Department building on Constitution Avenue in Washington, every morning. They always began with the same words. "I DEEPLY REGRET TO INFORM YOU . . . ." and were signed by Vice Admiral Randall Jacobs, the Chief of Naval Personnel. The stars Admiral Jacobs wore were small recompense for the fact that in thousands of homes grief and despair arrived in a telegram bearing his name.

This was a quiet, sunny afternoon on North Laurel Street in North Hollywood, especially at the McKay home. Mrs. McKay, feeling poorly, had been in bed for a couple of days. Her daughter Betty had come to spend the afternoon. Possibly a part of Mrs. McKay's trouble was the news that one of Bob's friends had been killed, and the unwelcome telegram from Washington had reached the bereaved family on Mother's Day. The news from Bob had been sparse, after his ship left Long Beach, but there was a letter, at last, received only the day before, and still on a table in the living room.

It didn't say much about where he was, but at least now they knew where he had been . . . . " . . . . I am sending you a gift from Hawaii." And, in the same letter, "I can't tell you where I am, but I'm a hell of a long ways from home . . . . "

When the door bell rang, Betty went to the door, took the yellow envelope, opened it, and cried "Oh, Mom!" Clutching the yellow sheet, Mrs. McKay ran outside and down the walk to her neighbors, the Bolsers, crying "My son is missing." Then Mrs. Tressel came out to comfort her, and in a few minutes she returned to the house. She went through the living room, the dining room, and down the hall to Bob's bedroom where medals, ribbons, honors, certificates, and photographs covered the walls . . . .

"Bob will rise to great things," one of his teachers had once told Mrs. McKay. And one of the officers on the ship, just a few months earlier, had prophesied that he would sometime become governor of California. Mrs. McKay sat there for a long while among the mute remembrances of what Bob had been in high school, college, and officer training. What Bob McKay might have become, no one would ever know.

Just a few blocks east of the gleaming towers of the City of the Angels, the little houses of Boyle Heights huddled together in close companionship on the steep hills. Geraniums brightened the air outside, peppers and frijoles brightened it inside, for many Mexicans lived in Boyle Heights. Chickens basked contentedly under fig or loquat trees out back, and in more than one of the houses, stars in the front window spoke silently of young sons gone to fight a war in strange and distant lands.

In the neatly curtained Olmeda window there were two stars. One of them should have been gold, because elder brother Robert was never coming back to Boyle Heights. Only a month earlier, the yellow envelope had come from the War Department, bearing the sad news that Sergeant Robert Olmeda, "Tudi" to his dark eyed sister, had died in a place called Luzon.

This left only one son for the Olmeda's—Augustine, named for another brother who had died long ago at the age of two weeks. For this last son, on this sunny May day, Mrs. Augustine had walked over to the Central Market, all the way to Third and Broadway, to buy the pinion nuts that "Coochi" especially liked.

Coochi graduated from Roosevelt High at 18, joined the Navy, and married just before the *Aaron Ward* left for the Pacific. His new wife, Pina, was visiting in Mexico and it was up to Mama Olmeda to see that Coochi had some little goodies from home.

When Mrs. Omeda returned from the store, there, again, was the dreaded yellow envelope. Already Papa Olmeda was in a state of shock. Younger sister Isabel had dashed down the street to find elder sister Theresa, and they read the words together . . . . "I DEEPLY REGRET TO INFORM YOU THAT YOUR SON AUGUSTINE OLMEDA . . . ." Tudi had died in Luzon, now Coochi was gone, and they didn't even know where, in the wide Pacific, he had died. This war had become more than Mama Olmeda could bear.

Wordless, she went to the window, took down the flag with two stars on it, and folded it away. Mrs. Olmeda would need the flag no longer to remind her of what she had done for the United States in this war. The people on her block already knew she had sent all her sons to the war, and for the next six months Mama Olmeda wore black, to show that they were never coming home.

On Tuesday, 29 May, the eighth grade at Washington School was going ice skating. Their teacher, Violet Good, would go with them. Washington School was just up Leahy Avenue and across on Bellflower Road from where the Goods lived in Bellflower, California. Her son, Rae, had gone through that school not too many years earlier. Now, with a neighbor boy, Harry Abercrombie, he was in the Navy.

Only a few weeks earlier one of her students had read, as a current events item, a story from the local paper about Rae Good and Harry Abercrombie going overseas on a minelayer. The eighth grade kids knew them, they had visited in her classroom as late as December.

Rae had sent his mother some gladiolus for Mother's Day. Harry sent his mother flowers too, and both women compared notes on them when they next met. Mrs. Abercrombie was one up on Mrs. Good, though, because she had had a letter only a few days earlier. The last letter Violet Good received from her son, Rae, was written on her birthday, 3 May, and it was still on the desk by the window. She looked at it as she went to answer the door bell . . . . Now who could be calling at this hour? She had to leave for school in a minute.

"Mrs. Good?" said the pleasant, soft voiced woman, and handed her the yellow Western Union Telegram envelope. There were three black stars stamped on it. Violet Good tore the envelope open, walked inside. The woman had delivered other envelopes with black stars on them, and knew what might happen. She followed Mrs. Good into the living room while she read:

"MR. AND MRS. MATHEW L GOOD
240 LEAHY AVE BELLFLOWER CALIF
    I DEEPLY REGRET TO INFORM YOU THAT YOUR SON RAE GERVAIS GOOD FIRE CONTROLMAN THIRD CLASS USNR IS MISSING FOLLOWING ACTION IN THE SERVICE OF HIS COUNTRY. YOUR GREAT ANXIETY IS APPRECIATED AND YOU WILL BE FURNISHED DETAILS WHEN RECEIVED. TO PREVENT POSSIBLE AID TO OUR ENEMIES PLEASE DO NOT DIVULGE THE NAME OF HIS SHIP OR STATION UN- LESS THE GENERAL CIRCUMSTANCES ARE MADE PUBLIC IN NEWS STORIES
              VICE ADMIRAL RANDALL JACOBS
              THE CHIEF OF NAVAL PERSONNEL"

Violet Good folded the sheet up and tucked it neatly into the envelope.

"I didn't even know he was in action," she told the woman.

"Do you want me to phone your husband at the shipyard?"

Mrs. Good shook her head. The place to learn of this was at home. She picked up her things and went up the walk to school. This was the day she had to take the eighth grade skating.

At the school she handed the telegram to Mr. Ferebee, the principal, and said, "I'll be all right if you will just go in and tell them. I can't talk about it." The kids were wide-eyed, but silent; war had never come into the eighth grade room before. All that day she too was silent, words would do no good, tears would do no good. At five in the evening Lincoln Good came home from the Navy Yard and she handed him the telegram, still silently. She could not talk about it. Together they read it. They knew that when the Navy said "missing" there was nothing more to be said.

For Violet Good, there was nothing to be said for a long time. There came the final official notice from the Navy Department, a personal letter from Bill Sanders, a touching note from Joe Queior who had been with Rae in the battle. Finally, after casualty lists were published, there came a letter from Teresa Olmeda whose son Coochi had gone with Rae: "please tell me if your son comes home." There was a memorial service at the First Christian Church, and a medal from the Navy Department. At last Harry Abercrombie came home, and Glen Good, and eventually Lieutenant Kelly of the *Aaron Ward* came to talk about the ship's last fight. But Violet Good had locked up her emotions the day she learned her son was missing and she could not talk about him.

It was painful not to say Rae's name, not to be able to mourn him with tears, but all those things had been locked away, with his match covers, election buttons, and bird feather collections, and they grew dusty with the years.

It was painful to see the birthday marks on the kitchen door, showing how tall Rae had grown, but years passed before she could paint them out. It was painful ever to be alone all day, so she always carried something to read, and in July 1950 opened up the *Reader's Digest* to find Hanson Baldwin's account of the fight for Okinawa —the "Last Battle" of World War II. It was painful to see that the Battle for Okinawa could be described without mentioning the *Aaron Ward*, which had also been a last battle, for Rae Good and forty-one others. And it was painful most of all each year when 3 May arrived and someone would wish her "Happy Birthday." There had never been a happy birthday after the one her son wished her from the *Aaron Ward*, an hour before he died.

On 22 November 1955, Glen Good phoned his mother with the news she had been waiting for for months. "Elaine is all right. You

233

have a new grandson. His name is Rae—Rae Good." At long last there were tears, but these were tears of joy. Violet Good could finally say the name of Rae.

On 21 May, at the Macukas farm out near Argos, Indiana, there came a note from Felke, the florist in nearby Plymouth. Mrs. Macukas spelled the words out to herself as best she could—she had first learned to read and write Lithuanian and still had to put the English into her native tongue before it made much sense. Even so, there didn't seem to be much sense about the message and it worried her. It said Felke, the florist, had some roses for her for Mother's Day and she should come to the shop and pick them out.

Now, Mrs. Macukas was the last person in Indiana to need roses, or any other flowers. Even as a girl, as Veronica Elizabeth Latvenas in distant Kaunas, Lithuania, she had had a green thumb. Here, in Indiana, she was known all around Argos and Plymouth for her beautiful flowers. People came out from town to drive past the beds of blossom, and admire them, and try to buy them, but Mrs. Macukas didn't sell flowers, she gave them to anyone who liked them. Except Felke—she sold him African Violets.

But the note said these flowers were from Tony. This worried Mrs. Macukas too. Tony never bought flowers. When he used to give her presents, for her birthday or for Christmas, he gave nice sensible things, like a garment to wear or a new kitchen kettle, something lasting, because she was a practical woman. Something was wrong with Tony, Mrs. Macukas knew it. All day she worried about this.

Next day, her daughter, Beatrice, came out from Chicago and explained the roses. Tony was thousands of miles away, somewhere in the Pacific, and there was a war on and he couldn't buy anything out there to send her. That was why he had arranged for Felke the florist to send roses. Mrs. Macukas pretended to believe this, but she was not convinced. Flowers from Tony was too unusual. Something was wrong. Together, they went to the florist. Mrs. Macukas finally decided on the roses, but not just a bouquet of them—being a practical woman, she took a rambler rose bush. That would be much more lasting. They took it home and put it in the good black Indiana soil, so when Tony came home he too could enjoy the roses he had sent his mother.

Two days later the telegram came from Washington. The postmaster in Argos knew what such things meant, and he also knew Mrs. Macukas. Among the people who made up her world, telegrams came just a little more often than absolution by the priest, and were nearly always as final. So he delivered it, in person. This was the sort of news a good woman like her must share with friends.

On the way he picked up several women, all friends of Mrs. Macukas, and by the time the car reached the Macukas farm with its load of sad news and grief, party telephone lines were ringing all around the county. As certain as she had been that something was wrong with Tony, even when Mrs. Macukas saw the car and the women she only assumed they were collecting for some cause or other and wanted to know how she could help them, who had only come to help her. At this all the women broke down in tears.

"I'm sorry, Mrs. Macukas," said the postmaster, handing her the yellow sheet. "It's from the Navy, in Washington. It's about Tony. Tony is dead." For Mrs. Macukas the full meaning of the message never quite came across. Tony, dead! Tony couldn't be dead. When people in her world died, they died decently at home, with weeping women in the parlor, not in some outlandish place no one ever knew where it was.

May is a beautiful month in Indiana, even as it once was in Lithuania. Lilacs bloom and meadow larks sing above the green fields, and around the neat farmhouses are roses. Especially roses—and now in the warm earth only two days were Tony's roses. Tony couldn't be dead. Mrs. Macukas called her daughter Bea again, in Chicago. Bea could explain this.

At the Sherwin-Williams Company where Bea worked, the superintendent came to her during the lunch hour, his lips trembling, tears in his eyes, and Bea knew what had happened. Tony was dead. Her husband, Charlie, was also in the Navy, but Bea and Tony had grown up together and there was an affinity between the two. She knew, before the man spoke, that Tony was dead. She left the office, went home, and neighbors used precious gas coupons to drive her the 110 miles out to Argos to be with her mother.

"Maybe he is not dead." Mrs. Macukas said, when her daughter arrived. "Maybe the government made a mistake." Beatrice told her the government didn't usually make this kind of mistake. There was no doubt about what the telegram said. Anthony Macukas, Fireman second class, United States Navy, was dead.

But Tony didn't die for Mrs. Macukas, not until one day in April, three years later, when the casket finally came to Chicago from distant Okinawa, escorted by a sailor with bright ribbons on his jumper, the same ones Tony would have worn. The flag-covered casket waited at the mortuary, with an honor guard of Legionaires from American Legion Post 49, and Mrs. Macukas touched it and said "Tony is home."

The Legion gave Tony a military funeral, with guns and bright uniforms, and when the casket went into the ground at St. Casimir's Cemetery, they removed the flag and gave it to her. Mrs. Macukas folded it proudly against her breast. She had given her son to the United States, and the people of the United States had given the flag—their flag—to her, Mrs. Macukas, as a tribute to her Tony. When she took the flag back home to Indiana, the roses—Tony's roses—were in bloom. They were still blooming, eleven years later, when she died.

Frank Bruna had sent his mother flowers for Mother's Day, too, but there was a foul-up somewhere and they did not arrive in Chicago until the day before Decoration Day. The telegram from Washington, saying he was dead, came several days ahead of the flowers. His sister Blanche was still waiting for the surprise he had mentioned in one of his last letters. She never found out what it was. The old dog, Brownie, frantic with joy when Frank arrived home for a few days in January, was still waiting for him to come home again. How could one explain the telegram to a dog?

By the time a year had passed, Brownie and the Bruna family had

236

reconciled themselves to the fact that Frank was not coming home. But fate and the U. S. Navy moved in odd ways to awaken old memories. On the day before Mother's Day, 1946, there came a package. It had been carefully packed up abroad the *Aaron Ward* in distant Kerama Retto, and methodically inventoried and shipped and logged in and receipted for through no one knew how many warehouses and supply depots. The last worldly possessions of Frank Bruna finally came home, and it was like losing a son and brother all over again.

Out in Elgin, Illinois, when the telegram reached the local Red Cross Office, Mary Cramer took one look and knew what it was. LaVerne Schroeder! She could look out the front window and see the garage where Harry Schroeder worked. She took the yellow envelope and hurried across the street. Mrs. Schroeder was finishing up her housework for the morning, in the old-time farmhouse on Walnut Street, out near the edge of town. On a sofa in the parlor was a decorated pillow just received from LaVerne in Hawaii. He said he sent two, but only one came. On a stand near the piano was a stuffed ring-necked cock pheasant he had shot when he was fifteen. Mrs. Schroeder was proud of that bird, had had it mounted for LaVerne. When she looked at the bird's shining plumage, she could remember that LaVerne had been home from the *Aaron Ward* for a brief visit with them, only five months ago . . . . *Goodness, how time flies. It seemed only yesterday he had been learning to ride Fanny, the old white horse, and him only knee high to her. He'd be eighteen in just a few more days, on the 12th of June. Next time he came home he'd be taller than the horse.*

The screech of tires broke into her thoughts and she saw Harry Schroeder's old Hudson Terraplane skid into the yard and stop in front of the house. Now why would he be coming home in the middle of the forenoon? He had Mary Cramer with him. He leaped out of the car, faltered, and fell to the ground. She rushed to help him, and when he was on his feet again he handed her the telegram:

"I DEEPLY REGRET TO INFORM YOU . . . ."

LaVerne's younger brother, only four years old, came out of the house and saw his mother crying. He didn't know why she was crying, but he cried anyway. The next day the mail brought another pillow top from Hawaii.

The first *Aaron Ward* sailor to go on to new duties, after the battle, was one the ship had depended on most, and would miss most if ever they needed him again—Karl Neupert, the Exec. His orders—to command the destroyer *Aylwin*—had come in before the battle. Sanders had particularily recommended Neupert for command; winning a combatant command was a high point in any officer's naval career, and he felt Neupert deserved the chance. Yet it created a real hardship for the man whose unfaltering courage, strict devotion to duty, and unlimited attention to detail at all times had undoubtedly saved the ship. Certainly he should have returned stateside to share in the honor and glory of bringing back a fighting ship. But orders were orders; he had wanted them and there they were: *proceed and report and assume command of USS Aylwin.*

When Karl Neupert left the ship on 23 May, every man who could make it was at the railing to see him go. If they said nothing, but just stood there silently and watched him go, it was because there was nothing to say. There was no going away present; what could the grimy crew of sailors in Kerama Retto give an Annapolis man who had been number one in his class? Yet *Aaron Ward's* fighting Exec left the ship with a tribute more touching than fine words, more treasured than a medal. As his boat pulled away, as his crew turned their heads, and silently watched him go, their eyes filled with tears.

The tedious paperwork; action report, war diary, recommendations for commendations and citations, letters to next of kin; was still incomplete when Neupert left the ship. Dave Rubel stepped up to relieve Karl Neupert and when *Aaron Ward* made her triumphant return to the United States, he was her Executive Officer. But he was an Executive Officer whose ship never fired a gun, never tracked a bogie, never faced action or danger. When the bands started playing back home, weeks later, and the news about *Aaron*

Ward and her battle made newspaper headlines in August, it was sometimes difficult to remember that some of the praise belonged to Karl Neupert, whose brilliant performance under stress of battle had helped make them all famous and who was still out there in the Pacific, a long, long way from home.

A sailor could always think of home, even at Okinawa. He might not say much about it, but the thought was always in the back of his mind, somewhere between "Wonder if I really will get shore duty when we hit the States?" and "Gotta remember that Chuck owes me five bucks if he ever gets out of the *Gosper* sick bay." *Gosper* sailors thought about home also, and between air raids and sniper scares Lieutenant Napier put their thoughts into a brief parody which was considerably funnier in Okinawa than it would be back in Oklahoma:

> "Oh, give me a home, far away from the foam,
> Far away from this smoke and this bay,
> Where seldom is seen FLASH RED CONTROL GREEN
> And the sirens are silent all day.

> "We watch all the night with no sign of delight
> For the bogies are coming they say,
> If it rains we get soaked, if it's dry we get smoked;
> We get dinged by the Japs either way.

> "Home, home, take me home
> Get me there and I'll never more stray.
> Get me out of this plight so I sleep some at night
> And relax just a bit through the day."

Home, home, take me home. It finally came true for the *Aaron Ward.* Monday morning, 11 June, was the morning the master at arms didn't have to make reveille. That was the morning everyone was already up. Everyone made chow, everyone made quarters, everyone helped get the engine warmed up, everyone stood by the lines. Everyone, that is, who was going home. It was impossible to watch the green slopes of Zamami Shima slipping astern without remembering that a lot of good friends and brave men were going to have to stay behind, for a long, long, time.

Despite an undercurrent of sadness, subdued excitement filled the air. *Stateside! We're finally going stateside!* The ship would have to make it on one engine, but they were taking her home, back to the land of no GQ. At 0800 *Aaron Ward* steamed proudly out of Kerama Retto. After five weeks she had escaped the boneyard.

On the signal bridge Leahy, Harris and Zagone scribbled down farewell messages sent by ships they might never see again:

From *Grady*: "OUR HATS ARE OFF TO YOU."

From *Tolman*: "BON VOYAGE."

And from *Shannon*, who had towed her in to the refuge five weeks earlier, two words, filled with deep meaning for the *Shannon* crew, deeply understood by the *Aaron Ward* crew:

"GOOD LUCK."

The ship stood out northward around Kuro Shima, swung south, and joined up with Convoy OKU 7, an assorted group of transports, combat ships, and merchantmen bound for Ulithi. For an hour or so the mountains of Okinawa loomed up to port, but they were too far away for one to hear the shooting, too far away to see the fire, too far away to smell death. Slowly they dropped into the sea, and when the convoy turned east at noon Okinawa had become only a bad memory, lost beyond the limitless horizon of the Pacific Ocean.

Somewhere in that vast ocean, growing farther away at every turn of the starboard screw, was the place known as Radar Picket Station 10. No one in the *Aaron Ward* crew would ever go back to RPS 10; no one in the crew would ever forget RPS 10 or the men whose last fight had been made there. From skipper to mess cook, they had all been there together, and thanks to *Shannon* and her Irish luck, most of them were going home together.

From *Shannon* to *Aaron Ward*: GOOD LUCK . . . . to all *Aaron Warriors*, wherever they might be: Bon voyage, good luck.

In Guam, a few of the wounded men, evacuated out of Kerama Retto earlier, returned on board for duty. These common "white hats'' were forever impressed by the fact that their Captain met them at the quarterdeck, shook hands with them, and welcomed them back to the ship.

Here, Lefty Lavrakas left the ship to fly on ahead, to arrange for her repairs. Technically she no longer had a gunnery department and Lefty could best be spared for the mission. Besides, Sanders knew about Lefty and the cute blonde in Long Beach and could see no harm in giving Lefty a chance to get in a few more words for himself as soon as possible.

So, armed with plans of the ship, photographs of the damage, orders to report to ComServPac and ComMinePac in Pearl Harbor and to the Brooklyn Navy Yard in New York—and the telephone number of Billye Charleyville in Long Beach, Lefty hopped eastward across the Pacific.

In Hawaii, he put through a call to California, to Miss Charleyville in Long Beach.

"Billye! I'm calling to see if you'll marry me."

A girl doesn't get called out of bed at 2 A.M. every Saturday morning to answer questions like that, but she had the right answer:
"Yes, I will."

The important points settled, she began pressing Lefty for details, but their romance had already became a triangle—phone calls from Hawaii were monitored by a censor and most of the questions she asked were answered by the censor—"Sorry, you can't say that." *Oh, well, Lefty had really said enough.*

In fact, as the plane winged eastward to the Naval Air Station at Alameda, Lefty debated privately as to whether he had said too much. He was elated that Billye had said yes, but perhaps a little dismayed that she had said yes so soon. It had been as easy as getting a haircut—maybe too easy. A guy hadn't ought to walk into situations like this with his eyes closed. *Careful, Lavrakas!*

While the passengers debarked from the big seaplane at Alameda, Lefty slowly picked up his gear, thinking. He was 85 per cent sure he wanted to marry the girl, but the other 15 per cent urged caution. He purposely tailed up to the passenger transportation office at the end of the line, thinking. *If I fly on to New York, I can call her up and say "exigencies of the service" and then think this over; if I go down to Long Beach now its going to be too late.*

Lefty was right—it was too late. For the handsome young officer, bronzed like a Greek god, the oracle was about to speak. A Japanese plane had spared his life at Okinawa. An American plane changed it at Alameda.

Lefty lugged his bags to the desk, explained his primary and secondary destinations—New York, or Long Beach—to a pert Wave.

"Sorry," she said. "No planes out to the East Coast until tomorrow. But if you want to go to Long Beach, we have a C-47 loading in five minutes, and one seat still empty." The oracle had spoken. Lefty dragged his gear out to the C-47. He was convinced now, 100 per cent.

From Pearl Harbor to Long Beach, from bachelor to benedict, from the BOQ to the Wedding Chapel, Lefty Lavrakas made the trip in seventy-two hours. In that time Billye Charleyville and her mother rounded up bridesmaids, fitted a white bridal gown, and sent Lefty out to comb the waterfront for enough officers with swords to stage a proper military wedding.

One day later the happy pair boarded a plane for New York. And a couple of hours later, in Dallas, Texas, an Air Corps pilot whose travel priority was considerably higher than that of a new bride was put aboard the plane and Mrs. Lefteris Lavrakas watched disconsolately while the plane and her new husband went off to New York without her. She sat in the passenger lounge and cried for six hours, until the airline located another plane headed for New York and put her on it. A day later Lefty and his new wife finally found each other, in the lobby of the Hotel Pennsylvania. They lived happily ever after.

Sunday, 8 July. The old shellbacks knew they were nearing home; long streamers of brown kelp floated past, and in the early dawn

California's traditional greeting committee—the white winged sea-gulls—came out to swoop and clamor about the ship as they escorted her in. The radar scope showed the first faint return from land—a thin finger reaching across their path, miles ahead. Point Loma! Shelley found a bugle somewhere below decks, turned on the PA system, and shook the whole crew awake with "California, here we come."

Aye. Here we come. The fighting Aaron Ward . . . . *Anastasio, Kellejian, Fitzpatrick, and me. She was a fast ship and we took her in harm's way, like the man said. We took her out and we brought her back . . . . Gaworski, Van Paris, McCarthy and me. Look here, you shoreside sailors, we're back from the picket line; tell the Rich-field News we're home and tell them in San Anselmo, in Santa Maria, in Merced Falls, and all those other places—we're sorry everyone didn't make it, but we're proud as hell and we're never going to forget . . . . And that's the word, mates, from Sanders, and Shelley, and Storey, and me.*

Slowly the blue mountains lifted out of the sea, the hump-backed Coronado Islands became visible, the long low arm of Point Loma grew distinct. Sanders grinned to himself as he recalled the unmentionable name Point Loma went by among San Diego based tin-can sailors in the peaceful thirties, when they went to sea every Monday morning and came in every Wednesday afternoon for "rope yarn Sunday." Point Loma drew abeam to port and the ship rounded the sea buoy marking the channel entrance, with its bell tolling mournfully for the ships which were not coming back from Vella La Vella, or Leyte, or Okinawa, and started up the channel. Stateside!

Happy homeward-bound sailors excitedly picked off the landmarks they had feared they might never see again . . . . the old Spanish Lighthouse; the light low on Ballast Point; to starboard, the Silver Strand and the tower of the Hotel del Coronado, the reference point by which at one time or another probably every ship in the United States Navy had plotted its anchorage in Coronado Roads. Beyond, there were the high frequency radio towers out at Chollas Heights, the distant loom of Mt. Miguel, and spread along the hills from Old Town to Golden Hill, the gleaming white walls and pink tile roofs of San Diego. Among those men whose families lived in San Diego, eager eyes tried to pick out certain private landmarks. They were *home*!

As the ship neared Ballast Point, she met a couple of big, fast new destroyers standing down the channel to sea. They were trim and shipshape, jaunty and business-like, guns bristling, crew at quarters; one would almost expect them to lift their bows in a dainty sniff as they passed the beat-up, patched-up, still somewhat stunk-up mine-layer, limping home from the picket line off Okinawa. But they didn't. To the surprise of most *Aaron Ward* men and the everlasting pride of many, the lead destroyer piped "ATTENTION TO PORT," her companion followed suit, and both ships rendered honors as they passed, as if she had been a battlewagon, or the President's yacht, or something . . . . *By God, Mac—did you see that! They saluted us like we were a flock of star spangled admirals . . . .* To the *Aaron Ward* crew, pleased at getting home again, proud of having brought their ship back with them, there came at last some realization of what they had done, although no one yet had put it in words. The essence of it was there, in almost forgotten promises each one had made in the past, upon enlistment, or on being commissioned: "I . . . . do hereby swear . . . . to bear true faith and allegiance to the United States . . . . and to defend her against all enemies . . . ." So had they done. So had they become heroes.

The warm California sun beat down on the bridge. The Training Center was abeam to port, on North Island to starboard the drone of aircraft engines rose to a roar. Dead ahead lay Broadway Pier, the U. S. Grant Hotel—stateside! Bill Sanders looked across the bridge at Mr. Dillon whose red beard by now covered tie, shirt, and the top button of his blouse. They were home at last and the war was close to being over. He could ease off a little.

"Sky, you can take your beard off now."

"Captain, I think I'll keep it on."

"Oh, come on now, Sky, we're home. Take off your beard."

Mr. Dillon reviewed the last four months in the case of the red

244

beard; the act, the ultimatum, the sentence, the punishment. "No, Sir, Captain. You gave me the prerogative of taking it off or wearing it. I choose to wear it."

Bill Sanders let the matter drop. There was one thing in favor of young men from the Ivy League; even when they made unwise decisions they used proper grammar.

The ship steamed slowly across San Diego Bay, nosed up to Broadway Pier. Somehow or other the word had gone around; the women who had spent long months at home waiting and hoping were on hand to wave and smile through their tears and welcome the ship home. Their wishes had gone out, farther than they knew across the sea, had taken the ship through a battle they could never imagine, and had brought her safely home. The ship was proud, but so bedraggled and worn it hurt to look at her. They knew they could only wonder about what had happened, until their men found the time to tell them, if they ever did.

Sailors who returned from the war zone had seen strange things, and they were liable to go ashore and do strange things. San Diego was used to this. The boys deserved a little fun, so long as they didn't try to climb the palm trees in the Plaza to shake down coconuts. That night Marvin Vermie swaggered up Broadway, no longer a seasick recruit, looking for something he had thought about all the way across the Pacific and back. When news of the Japanese raid on Pearl Harbor reached Iowa on 7 December 1941, Marvin had been milking a cow on his father's farm. He had missed cows in the Navy. At the first one-arm joint he came to, he went in and ordered two quarts of milk.

"You want it to take out?" asked the waitress.

"No, I'll drink it here," said Vermie, and he did.

Farther up town that night, Doc, Sky Dillon, and some other unattached officers assembled around a table to enjoy a few of the niceties of civilian life. There was no doubt about one thing; while the food and service in the wardoom was good, the surroundings in the El Cortez Sky Room were certainly somewhat different. When someone needed cigarettes in the wardroom they could have sent

245

Eddie Gaines for them, but here they merely had to wave a finger at the cigarette girl.

"Do you have any Pall Malls?" asked Mr. Dillon.

"Sorry, I'm out of them," she replied. And then she took a look at the magnificent chin whiskers he had decided to wear. "But I do have razor blades," she added.

The ship stayed in San Diego for seven days. Half the crew shoved off on thirty day's leave. Tiwald, Paine, and Dillon were all promoted to Lieutenant (junior grade). Blunck brought mail back to the ship every day. No one worried about watching the radar scope for bogies, or listening to the TBS. The latest papers were on the quarterdeck every morning and evening, with the latest baseball scores and comics in them. But just under the surface, memories of Okinawa were still there and easily aroused.

Sally Gross came down from Long Beach to be with her husband, Norm. Next morning when her alarm clock went off he piled out of bed and was in his clothes before she knew what had happened. It took a little bit of talking to convince Norm they didn't hold morning GQ at the Pickwick Hotel.

On 15 July *Aaron Ward* gave the customary three toots on the siren and long blast of the whistle which had echoed around the San Diego waterfront every time a destroyer got underway during the past twenty-five years, took in her lines, and backed out into the stream.

Escorted by the usual crowd of optimistic seagulls, she rounded North Island, passed Whaler's Bight, and poked her nose into the slow Pacific swells rolling in past Point Loma. A couple of miles past the Point, the sea buoy lifted and dipped, still tolling its bells for the ships which had gone that way during all the years, never to return.

In 1939 the first *Aaron Ward* had sailed out that way, for Panama and the East Coast, and never came back. In 1943, the second *Aaron Ward* had headed out for the Solomon Islands and never came back.

246

Now the third *Aaron Ward* was laying her course south, for Salina Cruz and Panama. As she rounded the buoy and swung her bow to port on the long slant down to Panama, the first half of her passage to the Navy Yard, in New York, the sea buoy tolled again. The men on the bridge did not know it yet, but *Aaron Ward* was never coming back.

In Panama the *Aaron Ward* picked up a detachment of Army troops for transportation to New York. As the ship moved up the east coast of the United States, the troops hung over the port rail all the way, watching the coast slide slowly past. Finally, a Colonel caught Sanders down on the main deck and commented on this pleasant arrangement.

"Captain," he said, "on behalf of my men and myself, I'd like to thank you for taking us so close to shore on this trip. Everyone certainly is enjoying it."

Sanders took the pipe out of his mouth and looked down at his feet. There was a crack in the deck there, and if one looked at the crack closely he could see the ship moving on each side of it.

"Well, Colonel," Sanders replied, "This isn't exactly a pleasure cruise, you know. I'm keeping her close in to shore like this so if she breaks in two I can beach the front end."

The Colonel turned white, and never slept below decks again.

On 30 July, less than six months after she left the United States for the first time, *Aaron Ward* returned to the United States for the last time. In the early dawn she crept up Ambrose Channel, still a dismal wreck from the war zone, hardly recognizable as a destroyer with her stacks amputated and guns missing. The most thrilling way for combat ships to come back from the Pacific was to enter San Francisco Bay, because when a ship passed under the Golden Gate Bridge she was officially home and all hands could shout their joy at a definite point. But the entrance into New York Harbor was almost as good; there was a certain satisfaction in seeing the lady over on Bedloe's Island, still holding her torch. The men from the Western states had never expected to see the lights of New

York; a few of those from the East had had moments two months earlier when they didn't expect to see them again.

The ship stopped and offloaded her ammunition; they wouldn't be needing that in the Navy Yard. A barge came alongside and sucked her oil tanks dry; there would be no more steaming until she was again as fit as a fiddle. In the late afternoon tugs nudged her into Berth 9 at the Navy Yard. One of the first visitors aboard was was an old time merchant skipper, Captain Mahoney, who peered about the ruined ship and exclaimed "You rode this thing in from Okinawa? I wouldn't ride it across the East River!"

Aye, Captain Mahoney. But you could walk across the East River if you were so inclined. It was a long way home from Okinawa, and the only way guys like Buschbacher, Clingenpeel, Wittenberg, and me were certain we could make it was to keep the ship together 'til we got here.

And no matter what people said about Brooklyn the ship was safe at last. They didn't have to worry about her breaking in two and sinking under them; they didn't have to worry about getting blown on the beach by a typhoon; they didn't have to fear that a floating mine or lurking submarine would blast out her bottom and half the crew with it; they no longer had to suspect there was a suicide plane behind every cloud waiting to pounce down and incinerate them. No more kamikazes .... No more kamikazes. They had made their last flights the day before, in far-off Okinawa: one had damaged the high speed transport *Horace A. Bass* off Hagushi; the other hit the *Cassin Young* in Buckner Bay and killed Tom Wallace's brother Mike. Tom wouldn't know this yet for another two weeks.

The next day an Army bomber splattered itself against the Empire State Building and created the biggest headlines any single aircraft had made since Lindbergh flew to Paris. Down in the CPO quarters on the *Aaron Ward*, where there were still vivid memories of the night when six Japanese aircraft had smashed into the ship, Winston tossed the papers into an empty chair and growled: "Look at those headlines! Imagine all that excitement over one lousy kamikaze!"

Tuesday, 14 August 1945. 00-04 Resting on keel blocks in dry-dock number 2, New York Navy Yard, Brooklyn, N. Y., under-going repairs. Receiving fresh water, electricity, fire main pressure and telephone services from the dock.

There wasn't much to writing a log in drydock. The ship wasn't going anywhere, nothing was going to happen. One could write the log for the rest of the day, with the same three words each watch: "Drydocked as before."

By 1600 the liberty party had shoved off and the few men in the duty section poked about the nearly deserted ship, disconsolate. She was cluttered up with the usual navy yard hamper—air lines, steam hoses, welding machinery, grimy navy yard workmen with tool boxes, and looked more like a broken down boiler plant than a ship. Supper over, the duty section hung over the rail, shooting the breeze. Suddenly all hell seemed to break loose in the yard, along the river, clear over in Manhattan . . . . whistles, sirens, horns joined in the tumult. The men listened for a moment, then pounded each other, shouting. *Japan had agreed to surrender. The war was over!* MacPherson rushed to the bridge and grabbed the whistle lever; *Aaron Ward's* boilers were dead and she had no steam of her own, but there was enough steam coming through the shore lines from the Navy Yard for a few good healthy toots.

It was her victory salute, her last shout of defiance; her "Aloha" to the sparkling and once more pacific sea where she had fought; her "So long" to the men who brought her back; her "Goodbye" to those who didn't; her "Adieu" to the memory of Admiral Aaron Ward; her "Farewell" to the fleet with which she had triumphantly sailed; and her "Bon Voyage, and fair winds" to the ships which would now sail on without her.

All across the United States, and out in the Pacific, men and women took the news of victory in their different ways. From his bed in a hospital ward, overlooking Pearl Harbor, where it had all started nearly four dreary years earlier, Pete Peterson heard the sudden hammering of 20mm and 40mm batteries, and leaped to the window to see tracers as jubilant sailors shot holes in the sky. His first thought was, "The damned Japs are back again." And then he realized the war was over. His body was still covered with the scars of 3 May, but the war was over.

At Okinawa, on VJ day, the guns all spoke for the last time. At noon, every gun ashore and every gun on every ship all let go together, in one jubilant, final "hell of a big noise." And that was the end of that. The war was over.

In San Francisco, Dayle Aylworth was driving down Van Ness Avenue in their old jalopy. The engine had died on her and some passing sailor had helped her get it started: she was going to haul him down to Market Street for his trouble. At the corner of Fulton Street she heard church bells ring out in a wild tumult and knew instantly what it meant. She pulled the car over to the curb and turned off the engine. She didn't care if it never ran again. The war was over. Her husband was three thousand miles away in Times Square, but he'd be back home. The war was over.

Tom Wallace was going home on leave, riding the Lousville & Nashville Railroad from New Orleans to Gulfport, Mississippi. His father met him at the station with the old family car, happy at having one son but sad about the other. The day before, Mr. Wallace had received that telegram from the Navy Department which began "I DEEPLY REGRET TO INFORM YOU . . . " Tom's brother Mike, whom he had last seen in June had been killed on 29 July when a kamikaze hit the *Cassin Young*. That was the last day the planes had come to Okinawa. And now, the war was over.

Hal Halstead was on the ship, waiting for his wife Virginia, who arrived in New York that evening. They had a room at the Taft, but didn't get to it until four the next morning. For hours they milled around Times Square with the great happy excited throng. Despite having his wife with him, Hal must have kissed at least a hundred other girls that evening. Man, the war sure enough was over.

There were others caught up in the whirl of Times Square that evening. Shelley was there with his wife, Mary, but his mind was far away. All around him were cheering men in uniform. Shelley felt they had a right to their exultation. But how could civilians make merry at a time like this, when they had never learned the meaning of valor?

Who among the noisy crowd was cheering for Armand, Bruna, Niwinski, or Zaloga? Who among them had ever heard of the picket line? Among the bright lights, the shouting, the celebrating, who could know that Shelley's mind was half a world away, on a distant place, a bitter battle ground the charts had once called RPS 10? There the blue Pacific spread, once more serene and peaceful. There the sound of battle had long since faded away on the wind, and only the cries of sea birds winging over the sparkling waves broke the long silence. There the bones of victors and vanquished alike rested beneath the eternal sea; there the men who had ended their short years in war would forever sleep in peace. For them, too, the war was over.

The war was over. In distant Kerama Retto, the sun beat down on long rows of white crosses. One of them wore the dogtag of Stu Mann, who stayed behind in the engine room to secure steam valves the night *Aaron Ward* was hit. In Palo Alto, California, on that joyous day of victory, Mary Mann bore the son Stu Mann would never see. And in Brooklyn, New York, Leon Woodside completed the 16-20 log of the USS *Aaron Ward*:

"1902, Word received of Japanese acceptance of Potsdam surrender terms."

That made it official on board the *Aaron Ward*. The war was over.

Midnight. Chief McCaughy, possibly a bit the worse for wear, climbed out of a taxi on the dock and gazed down at the *Aaron Ward*, or what was left of her. Mick had had a successful "survivor leave" in Quincy, Massachusetts, and was badly in need of something to help him survive further. As he ambled on board, the kid on gangway watch *saluted* him!

"Mr. McCaughey! Welcome aboard, Sir." The Chief bristled. Damn' fresh kid.

"Where do you get that Mister stuff? Knock off that crap!"

"No fooling, Sir. Your warrant came in. You're an officer now."

"Like hell I am an officer now. This war's over and I'm going to be a civilian now."

The gangway watch considered this. "Well, okay, Chief. There's a big AlNav came in tonight on the point system. The radiomen are making copies of it now. It tells how many points you need to get out."

"So, what else is new?"

"Oh, Mr. Dillon came back from leave. From Boston. Guess what? He shaved his beard."

"No! I'll be damned. Well, the Navy will never be the same again. Now I am getting out."

By two o'clock in the morning, Mick had read the AlNav, figured up his points, and decided he had more than enough. He went up to wardroom country, found Dave Rubel, the XO, and woke him up.

"Say, Mr. Rubel. I got my points! How do I get out of this outfit?"

Mr. Rubel looked at him bleakly. It had been a long war, and he was still tired. "Look, Mick. Could you just wait until eight o'clock in the morning?"

Mick considered this briefly. "Okay, Sir." He planned on being a civilian for a long time. He probably ought to prepare for it with a good night's rest.

In the last days of World War II, as Japan prepared to meet Allied surrender terms, headlines came thick and fast, fairly crowding one another off the front page. *Aaron Ward*'s hour of fame and glory was short. The Navy Department in Washington issued a press release on 24 August, telling of the ship's battle, and for a day or so her name popped up in headlines from coast to coast: AARON WARD SURVIVES SIX AIR SUICIDE ATTACKS . . . . CAME THOUGH DESPITE HER WOUNDS . . . . HOUR IN HELL OFF OKINAWA . . . . VESSEL SURVIVES SIX SUICIDE DIVES . . . . USS AARON WARD DOWN BUT FAR FROM OUT.

But on the same day the Chief of Naval Operations ordered a Board of Inspection and Survey to conduct an inspection of the ship and make recommendations for its disposition. *Aaron Ward* was not the only beat up wartime casualty in U. S. shipyards, and the Navy now had more new ships than it needed. To take the wrecks apart and repair them would cost more than to build new ships. "Tentative plans do not require their retention in the postwar Navy" said the CNO. That meant only one thing for the war-torn veterans, scrap 'em.

Weeks later, out in Elgin, Illinois, Harry Schroeder noticed a small news item saying that the famous fighting *Aaron Ward* was to be scrapped. That was the ship in which his son LaVerne had died. Except for the old stuffed cock pheasant in the parlor, they had nothing to remember LaVerne by. There was nothing from his ship; even the letters he had sent home were postmarked simply "U. S. Navy." Mr. Schroeder sat down, took his pen in hand, and wrote to the Navy Yard in New York. Since the ship was going to be scrapped, couldn't he have some piece of her—a gun, the bell, an anchor—as a memento of the ship on which their son had died?

The letter trudged around through the Navy Department, collecting endorsements, and in due time Mr. Schroeder received an answer. The Navy would consider letting him have a clock, or an anchor. The anchor was heavy, it explained; perhaps he would rather have the clock. Mr. Schroeder said he'd take the anchor. Eventually there came another letter, and another, and another. The gist of all this was that the anchor had to be declared Surplus Property before he could have it, and that he should write the

Shipyard in New York and say he wanted it. This he did; the next letter told him the starboard anchor of the USS *Aaron Ward* was his. The anchor weighed 4,000 pounds, and the going price for anchors was half a cent a pound. Please remit twenty dollars. Mr. Schroeder sent the money.

Friday, 28 September 1945. 12-16 Moored as before. 1400 Captain W. S. Keller, USN came aboard for the decommissioning of this vessel. 1425 Officers and men at quarters.

The loudspeakers hummed, clicked on for the last time.

"NOW HEAR THIS. ALL HANDS TO QUARTERS FOR DECOMMISSIONING CEREMONY."

The men—what were left of them, maybe 140 of the original crew, were ready.

The officers ranged themselves behind their Captain, Rubel, Lavrakas, Rainey, Clark, Rosengren, and Tiwald, while Captain Keller read the brief orders ordering the ship to be decommissioned. It seemed fitting that the gallant ship was going to spend her last day almost in sight of the Greenwood Cemetery in Brooklyn where the old warrior, Admiral Aaron Ward himself, had been buried 28 years earlier.

Now it was Sander's turn. Eleven months ago, to the very day, he had spoken the words that brought a ship to life. Now he was to say the words that took the life away from her, stripped her of her proud name, and reduced her to a hulk with a number.

"Haul down the colors." His voice broke. This was goodbye to what every officer in the Navy wanted for his command: a brave ship, brave men.

"Haul down the jack and commission pennant." Men watched the bright flags come down silently. They pretended not to hear the Skipper's voice break. Not until that moment had the full import of the end of the war, decommissioning, and demobilization become clear. Once they had been a crew, officers, and men; a team, ship and crew. But now the colors and jack and pennant were folded away and the *Aaron Ward* was no more.

Someone sniffed. A few men blinked their eyes. It was all over.

By tradition, when a ship is decommissioned, the commanding officer takes her commission pennant as his own. The colors of some of the Navy's great and famous ships hang in dusty splendor at Bancroft Hall at the Naval Academy, to inspire future generations of midshipmen. But *Aaron Ward* was only one destroyer among hundreds, no greater than any other ship on the picket line at Okinawa, no more famous than any other ship which helped Nimitz and Halsey and MacArthur make their victorious stand in Tokyo Bay. She was a brave ship, but only because she carried brave men. And Bill Sanders, Skipper of the *Aaron Ward,* knew how to handle brave men. Before the ceremony, the names of every officer and man on board had been typed on slips of paper, and mixed in a hat. Now the hat was brought forward, and two names were drawn, and handed to Sanders.

"Rogers, fireman first!"

"Here, Sir!"

"You get the union jack, son."

"Aye, Aye, Sir."

"Boles!"

"Here, Sir."

"The colors are yours, son. Take good care of them."

"Yes, Sir."

And that was it. They had been Captain and men, ship, and crew, for eleven months. Now, it was all over.

Boles had yet another duty to perform. This was nothing the Captain had asked him to do, it was nothing an officer could order him to do. This was a job which demanded more nerve than Navy Regulations required in a man. Later he took leave, and went down to Meigs, Georgia, to see Mr. and Mrs. Turner and tell them about their son's last night aboard the *Aaron Ward* at Okinawa. The Navy Department gave no medals for that sort of thing, but Boles earned one. As he talked to them, he could see and feel and smell again, the horror of the night, and hear Turner's voice, pleading:

"Tell my mother my body wasn't mangled."

Boles did the best he could. He lied like a Trojan.

In other towns, where planes and trains stopped, or where a man could drive another hundred miles for a friend, officers and men carried their respects to homes where they could only arouse fading memories.

Perhaps without understanding the need of a woman to speak with someone who had last seen her man alive, many crew members made such sad journeys. As painful as the visit could be for both concerned, it nevertheless served a purpose; it was a definite statement of fact, a simple declaration, by someone who was there and knew what had happened, of the last day, the last hour, sometimes the last minute of a loved one. The telegrams and letters, no matter how sincere, were only bits of paper.

But when a woman could talk with a man who had been there, feel his rough hands, hear his gruff voice, and see his sad shoulders go down the walk through her own tears, it was a little easier to accept the finality of death. So Norman Gross went to see Joe Zaloga's mother, Ray Biesmeyer went to see LaVerne Schroeder's folks, Wayne Fowers went to see Farrell Fletcher's mother. Bill Sanders, as he crossed the continent on duty during the next few years, stopped to see everyone he could. Only once was one of these sentimental journeys made in vain. As he drove through California, in 1948, Wayne Fowers detoured to see the parents of one of his *Aaron Ward* shipmates. The sorrow which had touched one home in 1945 had turned to bitterness; the dead boy's father refused to talk to or even see the visitor who had last seen his son in battle aboard the USS *Aaron Ward*.

It was all over now. With a few simple words a team had been broken up, a fighting organization had been scratched from the Navy's list of operational ships.

A brave ship had given her name back to the Navy's archives, and the brave men who gave her life were trudging off, their sea bags loaded down with dirty socks and bright memories. The ship was dead.

As the men drifted away, few of them looked back. One thing the Navy teaches a sailor is, never look back, never say "Goodbye." Just wave and say "So long."

"I'll be seeing ya."

"If you're ever in Chicago, look me up. I'm in the book." Or New York or San Francisco, or Washington, or a hundred other places. A crew comes, like the man Flammonde, from God knows where, and when the cruise is over the crew goes back where it came from. Some of these men were going back to places no one on the ship had ever heard of before, and no one might ever hear of again—the little towns that sent fighting Americans down to the sea when the need came, the little places that took them back home again when it was over, to run service stations, sell insurance, sing in the Methodist church almost as if nothing ever happened.

So they went back, to such places as Star City, Arkansas; Noel, Missouri; Holly, Michigan; to places such as Red Lodge, Montana; Bluecreek, Ohio; Gray, Maine; to Orient, Iowa; and CoOperative, Kentucky.

Back there a man could forget—almost—a distant green island named Okinawa. But there would come reminders—a sailor's white hat seen in a Greyhound bus station, a TV glimpse of destroyers lifting their bows to an ocean swell, a Purple Heart medal uncovered under the Sunday shirts in a dresser drawer—of the time they once stood at a battle station on the *Aaron Ward* and looked death right between the eyes. For a moment they would remember; hearing again the clamor of guns, seeing again the twisted wreckage, remembering again that once sudden death had brushed past so close they could still smell it the next morning.

In that moment the ship would live again.

But now, aboard the 345-foot-long hulk which once had been the USS *Aaron Ward*, "Rosy" Rosengren finished writing his log for the afternoon watch:

"The Commanding Officer gave the order to haul down the Flag, Jack, and Commissioning Pennant, Eleven months to the day, that order to hoist the colors was given, in fact almost to the hour, the colors were hauled down for the last time aboard a gallant ship. There remained aboard until the last the following Officers and Men, most of whom lived and fought OUR SHIP "The Ship that can't be licked."

Rosy listed the officers; Sanders, Rubel, Lavrakas, Rainey, himself, and Tiwald. Then came the names of the men; nearly a hundred of them ordered to the Armed Guard Center at Pier 92 for further assignment by Commander Service Force, Atlantic Fleet, to serve until they were eligible for discharge; another group of them directly to the Separation Center at Lido Beach, where they would become happy civilians again in forty-eight hours; a still smaller group to the Receiving Station for duty; the last five of them, Berry, Anastasio, Coward, James and St. Clair, going back to sea, to a sister ship of the *Aaron Ward*'s, DM 30—the "Shootin' Shea."

Rosy signed the log, and Sanders signed it. In one binder was contained the life of a ship, eleven months out of the lives of some 360 men, the names of those men who had given their lives for the ship. In a few days the men would be dispersed, never to meet as a crew again. In a few months the ship would be sold for scrap, and possible future reincarnation as Kaiser-Frazer bumpers or Norge washers. In a few years the only men who would remember *Aaron Ward* were the men who had sailed with her. There would be nothing else left but the log.

The log, several hundred sheets of fragile paper, outlasted the ship, and will outlast her crew. For many of the men it is the only monument they will ever have; a monument few eyes will ever see. Year after year, visitors trudge through the halls of the National Archives in Washington, D.C., to peer at the Constitution and the Declaration of Independence, without knowing that stacked above their heads for another twenty floors are all the written records of the nation. There are the naval log books—the records of the Navy's ships, some of them collecting dust since the days of John Paul

Jones, and in them are written the names of those who fought their ships against all enemies, whosoe'er they were. The names there are glorious—*Bon Homme Richard, Monitor, Oregon, Houston, Atlanta, Yorktown, Wahoo, Aaron Ward*. The silence there, in the dust, in the cool rooms where no one comes to read them, is thunderous.

On 4 April 1946, Captain William B. Sanders stood at proud attention in the office of the Commandant of the Eleventh Naval District in San Diego. Across the bright bay where destroyers and submarines clustered, he could see the pink walls and red tile roofs of the Training Center, where he had been an Apprentice Seaman twenty years before. On a desk lay two citations, two velvet lined boxes with medals in them. The Navy was about to honor Bill Sanders for what he had done on Radar Picket Station 10.

Vice Admiral Jesse B. Oldendorf, whose battleship fleet had virtually destroyed Japan's Southern Force in the slambang action of Suriago Strait in October of 1944, read the citations, pinned on the medals—the Bronze Star, the Navy Cross. It was difficult to listen to the Admiral's words; Sanders could not help seeing the planes looming out of the dusk off Okinawa, hearing the roar of the guns, the shouts of his men. They had all been in the battle with him, he wished they could have all been there for the ceremony. But there was only one Navy Cross; the crew won it for him, he would wear it for them.

One of the records Bill Sanders took with him when he left the *Aaron Ward* was a list of the home addresses of every member of the crew. In the next month he prepared a letter for each one of them. In it he quoted the citation for the Navy Cross, exactly as it had been signed by Secretary of the Navy John L. Sullivan. And then he added these words: "Although the above citation was presented to the Commanding Officer of the *Aaron Ward*, he feels that by their heroic conduct on the occasion of the action on 3 May 1945 during the Okinawan campaign, all the personnel of that vessel merit the honor. The ex-Commanding Officer, therefore, takes pleasure in commending you for your magnificent performance during that period, and in stating that you and your shipmates share equally in the award bestowed in the name of the President of the United States."

Aye, Aye, Sir. Wrobleski, Macukas, Dyhrkopp and me, we did it.

On 17 July 1946, the Chicago and Northwestern Railway agent in Elgin called Mr. Schroeder to say they had a flatcar down on the siding with a 4,000 pound anchor on it. The freight was thirty-five dollars and forty-three cents. Mr. Schroeder went into the station to settle up and got a receipt marked "Paid. Thanks! We hope to serve you again."

The *Aaron Ward*'s starboard anchor leaned against an elm tree on the Schroeder farm outside of Elgin for nearly a year. On Memorial Day of 1947, the Schroeders formally presented the anchor to the Naval Club of Elgin on behalf of their son, and as a war memorial to the thirty-nine men of the city who lost their lives in World War II.

A ship's anchor looks strangely out of place, resting on the sidewalk of an inland town a thousand miles from the sea, yet the citizens of Elgin have become used to it. Many of them no longer notice it. At odd times the anchor has had a visitor; an out-of-state car will roll down State Street, and stop opposite the anchor. A man will get out of the car, walk around the anchor, look up and down the busy little street, look at the anchor again, with unseeing eyes. At such times the grimy red brick buildings fade away, the fields around the town change from green to restless salty blue, and the thunder of long silent guns comes echoing back as planes again smash down out of the sky. Anyone who once fought on Radar Picket Station 10 needs only see the starboard anchor of the *Aaron Ward* to remember the ship, the picket line, the battle, the fire, the blood, and the broken bodies. For a moment the long gray ship fills State Street from end to end, her guns roaring defiance. Then the stranger drives off, taking his memories with him, and the ship is gone. There is only an old anchor, 4,000 pounds of cold metal resting silently on State Street.

Aaron Ward and her fighting men need no monument to keep their memory bright. The most heroic bronze or marble can never show the true meaning of bravery. The finest medals and most stirring citations can never delineate true devotion to duty. Sooner or later time and corrosion will cover them all with dust. Yet the name of *Aaron Ward* lives on, carrying honor the Navy could never bestow. The Navy can only take the names of dead men and give them to its ships. Robert and Linda Deacon took the name of a dead ship and gave it life.

In October, 1949, ninety-eight years after Admiral Aaron Ward was born in Philadelphia, the Deacon's first son was born in a small town in Iowa. Memories of Okinawa were still fresh for Bob Deacon then, although the USS *Aaron Ward* was gone. The Navy no longer needed the name, so they gave it to their son; Aaron Ward Deacon started out in life with a proud name. The men who died in fiery battle off Okinawa could ask no finer memorial than this boy who would be a son to all those who never lived to have one of their own.

Aaron Ward was a brave ship. The men who fought and died aboard her were brave men. Nothing more could be said; the finest words must be limited by definition. Perhaps the most moving tribute to the ship and her crew was never expressed in words at all, but in a simple show of emotion.

One Saturday morning in 1946, aboard the aircraft carrier *Princeton*, the PA system blared:

"NOW HEAR THIS! FRANK CECKOWSKI, ELECTRICIAN'S MATE THIRD, REPORT TO THE CAPTAIN'S OFFICE."

Ceckowski? What had Ceckowski done? On a big aircraft carrier, sailors weren't invited to the Captain's Office to discuss whether they liked beans for breakfast or not. Ordinary sailors went there so seldom they needed help in finding the place. Ceckowski's visit was short.

"Ski? The Captain's going to present you with a medal at inspection this morning. Be on the hangar deck at 1000. That's all."

A medal? Ski hadn't done anything. But he was on hand when hundreds of men in snowy whites lined up at quarters for inspection. The Captain strode up to his speaking stand, where a yeoman had laid the crisp, white papers and a velvet lined box. A Master-at-Arms sang out Ceckowski's name, and a pair of seamen stepped to his side and escorted him across the deck to face the Captain.

Then the Captain's voice boomed out through the huge hangar:

"The President of the United States takes pleasure in presenting the Bronze Star Medal to Francis Anthony Ceckowski, Electrician's Mate third class, United States Naval Reserve for service as set forth in the following citation: For heroic achievement while serving on board the USS *Aaron Ward* in action against enemy Japanese forces . . . ."

While the Captain read the next five lines, Ceckowski's mind was far away, on Radar Picket Station 10, where guns thundered and the planes came smashing down. Again he could see flames leaping in the dark, hear ammunition exploding, smell blood and burned flesh and feel his hands cringe away from the bare bones in bodies he dragged out of flaming wreckage. The names flashed in his memory—Jerry Smith, Turner, Zaloga, Tony Macukas, Schroeder, Rae Good. Gone. All gone.

Even the ship was gone. He had seen her come alive, he had gone with her into battle, he had helped bring her back in triumph, he had been with her to the last hour she lived. Now she was gone; even a part of his life was gone, eleven months he would always remember but could never live again. The days had disappeared, one by one, into a sea of memory, like white birds following a ship across some far horizon. Nothing could bring them back, neither the days, nor the ship, nor the men who were still out there. Ski had been out there with them. He was one of the lucky ones. Forty-two were not. He stood there, stiff and proud, his heart filled with sorrow for the brave men of the *Aaron Ward* who had earned medals but would never wear them.

Ski didn't need a medal. He already had, from Sanders, from the ship, from the crew, more than a man could ever pin on a jumper: respect, discipline, devotion, and pride in being a part of the Navy and its tradition. That was enough for any man . . . .

But the Captain was still reading: ". . . . His initiative and courageous devotion to duty," he concluded, "were in keeping with the highest traditions of the United States Naval Service." *Sir, it was all of us: Vowvalidis, Putrzynski, Niwinski, and me. We all did that.*

While the crew of the USS *Princeton* stood at attention, the Captain pinned the bright ribbon on Ceckowski's chest. The big hangar deck was silent, but perhaps, for a moment, in some distant Valhalla, drums rolled and bright spears dipped in salute. The Captain shook hands with him, and Ski looked down at his shining medal, but he could not see it. Suddenly tears had filled his eyes.

THE SECRETARY OF THE NAVY

Washington

The President of the United States takes
pleasure in presenting the PRESIDENTIAL UNIT CITATION *to the*

UNITED STATES SHIP AARON WARD

for service as set forth in the following CITATION:

"For extraordinary heroism in action as a Picket Ship on Radar
Picket Station during coordinated attack by approximately twenty-
five Japanese aircraft near Okinawa on May 3, 1945. Shooting down

two Kamikazes which approached in determined suicide dives, the U.S.S. AARON WARD was struck by a bomb from a third suicide plane as she fought to destroy this attacker before it crashed into her superstructure and sprayed the entire area with flaming gasoline. Instantly flooded in her after engineroom and fireroom, she battled against flames and exploding ammunition on deck and, maneuvering in a tight circle because of damage to her steering gear, countered another coordinated suicide attack and destroyed three Kamikazes in rapid succession. Still smoking heavily and maneuvering radically, she lost all power when her forward fireroom flooded under a seventh suicide plane which dropped a bomb close aboard and dived in flames into the main deck. Unable to recover from this blow before an eighth bomber crashed into her superstructure bulkhead only a few seconds later, she attempted to shoot down a ninth Kamikaze diving toward her at high speed and, despite the destruction of nearly all her gun mounts aft when this plane struck her, took under fire the tenth bomb-laden plane, which penetrated the dense smoke to crash on board with a devastating explosion. With fires raging uncontrolled, ammunition exploding and all engineering spaces except the forward engineroom flooded as she settled in the water and listed to port, she began a nightlong battle to remain afloat and, with the assistance of a towing vessel, finally reached port the following morning. By her superb fighting spirit and the courage and determination of her entire company, the AARON WARD upheld the finest traditions of the United States Naval Service."

For the President,
JAMES FORRESTAL
Secretary of the Navy.

THE FOLLOWING OFFICERS AND MEN
WERE ON BOARD THE AARON WARD ON MAY 3, 1945

Sanders, W. H. Jr., Commander, Commanding Officer
Neupert, K. F., Lt. Cmdr., Executive Officer
Rubel, D. M., Lt. Gunnery Officer
Young, D. A., Lt., Engineering Officer
Wallace, T. L., Lt., Navigator
Lavrakas, L., Lt., Assistant Gunnery Officer
Biesmeyer, R. J., Lt., First Lieutenant and Damage Control
Rainey, C. H., Lt., Assistant First Lieutenant
Cathcart, G. "F.," Lt. (jg), Assistant First Lieutenant
Clark, D. C., Lt. (jg), Assistant Engineering Officer
Halsted, H. C., Lt. (jg), C.I.C. Officer
Woodside, L. A., Lt. (jg), Communication and Radar Officer
Rosengren, J. S., Ens., Sound Officer
Kelley, P. W., Ens., Assistant Gunnery Officer
Paine, C. S., Ens., Assistant Engineering Officer
Dillon, S., Jr., Ens., Fighter Director Officer and Radio Officer
Ferguson, D. P., Ens., Assistant Gunnery Officer
Tiwald, J. P., Ens., Signal Officer
Barbieri, J. K., Lt., (jg), Medical Officer
*McKay, R. N., Lt., (jg), Supply Officer
Danford, D. A., Lt., Fighter Director
Koehl, F. W., Lt., (jg), Fighter Direction
Siler, G. E., Warr. Gun, Mine Control

ENLISTED MEN:

Abbott, E. S., GM2/c
Abercrombie, H. L., EM3/c
Adams, B. C., WT2/c
Adams, W. H., S1/c
Ahrens, C. W., S1/c
Aitchison, P., RDM3/c
Anastasio, J. G., MM1/c
*Anderson, J. B., F1/c
Andrade, A., Bkr2/c
Andrade, J. W., S1/c
Antell, R. O., MM2/c
*Armand, M. J., MN1/c
Aylworth, A. A., RDM3/c
Bahlmiller, L., S1/c
Bailey, P. I., S1/c
Barker, C. L., S2/c
Ballard, A. C., WT2/c
Bartlett, V. (N) S2/c
Batchelor, P., (N) Jr., S2/c
Beadel, Allen (N), RDM3/c (T
*Beattie, V. E., S2/c
Beckner, J. D., MM3/c (T)
Beckmann, J. A., FC2/c
Bell, D. C., RDM3/c (T)
Berkey, J. D., S1/c
Bernas, A. R., S2/c
Berry, L. "C", MM1/c
Birley, C. G., Jr., F1/c
Bissonnette, R. L., S1/c (RM)
Blunck, T. J., SOM3/c
Boles, "J" L., Jr., GM 2/c
Border, R. R. WT3/c
Bosney, J. (N), Jr., F2/c
Brewster, J. H., F1/c
Bridgewater, K. B., S1/c
Brown, J. R., MN1/c
*Bruna, F., SC2/c
Brusky, J. A., CRM
Burchett, C. W., S1/c
Burgess, D. J., S1/c

Burns, C. P., EM3/c
Buschbacher, R., GM1/c
*Cain, J. R., S2/c
Caldwell, E. H., Y2/c
*Carpenter, C. L., S1/c
Carpenter, R. P., EM1/c
*Carrick, J. R., S2/c
Carroll, L. W., WT1/c
Carson, R. L., S1/c
Casaro, P. A. S1/c
Castagnola, L., S2/c
Castanien, L. E., GM1/c
Ceckowski, F. A., EM3/c
Cezus, J. G., EM3/c
Chmiel, C. S., S2/c
Christofferson, T. R., Cox.
Clark, C. E., ST1/c
Clark, E., S1/c
Clingenpeel, L. C., S1/c
Collins, C. M., GM3/c
*Coltra, P., MM2/c
*Connell, C. M., S2/c
Conrad, "L" "B", S1/c
Cooper, E. E., WT2/c
Cornutt, J. H., SM2/c
*Couie, R. L., Cox.
Coward, G. L., MM2/c
Cozby, L. E., RDM3/c
Crider, C. W., PHM2/c
Curr, A. J., EM2/ (T)
Curtis, T. M., S1/c
*Dalton, J. S., S1/c
*Dart, G. L., SSME3/c (T)
Day, J. D., S1/c
Deacon, R. B., S1/c
Deckert, A. E., S2/c
Demyen, J. F., SM2/c (T)
De Reimer, V. P., MM3/c
Despin, G., FC2/c
Devlin, J. G., Cox.

268

*Dial, B. R., SOM3/c
Dial, E. L., GM2/c
Dolliver, H. R., S1/c
Dove, H., (N), F2/c
Dow, R. A., Cox. (T)
*Dulin, F. H., S1/c
Duriavig, R. J., F2/c
Dyhrkopp, E. V., F2/c
Elliott, S. O., S1/c
Elrick, W. W., RM3/c
Enderle, R. M., F2/c (T)
Erice, T. "A", CK2/c
Erin, T. F., S1/c
Eves, C. H., S2/c
Fields, J. F., S1/c
Fisher, M. R., S1/c
Fitzpatrick, J. W., S1/c
Fletcher, C. T., GM3/c
*Fletcher, F. R., S2/c
Flinn, F. T., QM3/c (T)
Floyd, H. A., S2/c
*Follett, R. R., MN2/c
Forrey, P. D., WT1/c
Foster, B. H., FC1/c
Fowers, W. G., Y3/c (T)
Frederick, G. J., RM3/c (T)
Frenchik, P. E., F2/c
Friese, R. C., F2/c
Gaines, E. (N), STM1/c
Gaworski, V. C., S1/c (GM)
Gervais, A. A., GM1/c
Giese, W. F., Jr., RM2/c (T)
Glenn, J. L., S2/c (FCO)
*Good, R. G., S1/c (FC)
Gorczyca, S. P., MM1/c
Graver, E. H., EM2/c
Greenoe, W. S., MM2/c
Gross, N. A., MN2/c
Guyer, W. M., MM2/c
Haberek, M. C., F1/c
Hall, E. G., GM3/c

Hammock, E. A., GM3/c
Hansell, G. H., CY
*Harris, R. J., S1/c
Haubrich, J. J., WT1/c
Hejhall, C. J., S1/c
*Hendrickson, J. M., S1/c
Hetrick, F. M., S1/c
Higgins, O. K., F1/c
Hitchcock, A. L., MN2/c
Hodge, W. S., F1/c
Holte, R. T., QM1/c
Hosking, L. R., RDM3/c
Howard, M. S., MM3/c
Huckabee, C. M., SC3/c
Husted, R. O., S1/c
James, W. W., SF1/c
Jaroszewski, E. H., SOM3/c
Jefferson, T. B., S1/c
Johnson, K. R., F1/c
Johnson, T. A., WT3/c
Johnson, T. B., SM3/c
Jones, D. F., BM1/c
Jones, L. J., S2/c
Kellejian, C. P., SM1/c
Kennedy, J. J., PHM3/c
Kinman, R. E., WT2/c
Kinney, W. P., SC3/c
Kock, L. E., S1/c
Kock, L .E., S1/c
Kohne, A. E., S1/c
Kreyer, R. C., S1/c
Kroll, C. H., FC1/c
LaFlure, C. R., S1/c
Larson, G. O., GM3/c
Laymon, D. J., MM3/c
*Lepon, R. A., F1/c
Little, K., MM3/c
*Long, L. J., GM3/c
Long, S. S., F1/c
Longlois, O. W., FC3/c
Lunetta, J. A., MOMM1/c

269

MacPherson, E. B., EM2/c
*Macukas, A. P., F1/c
*Mann, S. B., CMM
Marchello, E. M., S1/c
Marquoit, W. J., S1/c
*Marshall, "J" "J", S1/c
Marston, J. D. L., BKR3/c
Martin, J. W., RM3/c
Martin, O. A., MM3/c
Martinez, J., S1/c
Mattei, X. F., F1/c
McCarthy, D. J., F1/c
McCaughey, C. R., CMM
McClendon, W. M., S1/c
*McCoy, B., S2/c
McCoy, W., MM2/c
McCurry, H. W., RM2/c
McGee, W. E., S1/c
McKanna, W. R., SOM3/c
*McLaughlin, M. J., S1/c
McMahan, E. H., F1/c
Mecca, D. A., WT3/c
Merington, J. L., Cox.
Michael, R. D., QM3/c
Miller, M., WT2/c
Moe, G. V., F1/c
Mogensen, H. R., MN3/c
*Morgan, J. J., F2/c
Moxley, R. S., S1/c
Muirhead, B. M., MM2/c
Murphy, O. E., Y1/c
Neuman, R. T., RDM3/c
Newman, G. H., RDM3/c
*Niwinski, H. W., S1/c
Norlen, K. C., S1/c
Noss, K. L., S2/c
Oden, J. W., BM1/c
Offins, J. A., CMN
*Olmeda, A., S1/c
Quimette, J. L., GM1/c
Padgett, N. R., S1/c

Panaro, J. T., CWT
Parker, J. L., MM2/c
Parker, B. L. SK1/c
*Pepoon, R. S., F1/c
Personius, O. S., MM2/c
Peters, R. N., F1/c
Peterson, D. H., WT3/c
Peterson, R. A., MM1/c
Phillips, I. M., MM2/c
Phillips, W. I., RT1/c
Piatt, B., WT3/c
Posey, R. A., MM1/c
Potter, R. E., SOM3/c
Preston, H. A., S1/c
Putrzynski, A. V., GM2/c
Queior, J. W., FC3/c
Quick, F. D., S1/c
Quinn, E. M., FC3/c
Rader, W. H., S1/c
Ragan, R. H., CCS
Ransom, J. M., BM2/c
Rapalee, P. A., MM2/c
*Rawlins, J. B., MM3/c
Raymond. R. E., MM3/c
Reber, G. T., Cox.
Reed, L. R., S1/c
Reed, W. M., S2/c (RDM)
Reich, J. G., RDM2/c
Reichard, J. L., RT2/c
Richards, E. G., SK2/c
Ritter, W., S1/c
Rogers, D., F1/c
Rogers, J. M., S1/c
Rotter, H., F1/c
Roumford, R. R., FC2/c
Ruby, T. A., S1/c
Russell, H. E., S1/c
Salisbury, H. B., CMM
Sandow, J. B., CM2/c
Sanford, J. L., S1/c
Sawchuck, L. W., F1/c

Schaefer, W. W., M1/c
Schmitt, J. C., S1/c
Schofield, R. W., S1/c
*Schroeder, L. H., S2/c
*Schroeter, C., WT1/c
Schurman, B. P., RDM3/c
Scoggins, R. P., S1/c
Scott, S., STM1/c
Scott, W., STM1/c
Seggerman, C. R., S1/c
Shaw, R. J., SC3/c
Shea, C. B., GM2/c
Shelley, C. A., CBM
Shores, G. P., BM2/c
Showalter, C. J., S2/c
Simons, G. F., S2/c
*Smith, J. E., EM3/c
Smith, R. A., SK3/c
Smith, S. B., CWT
Snow, R. D., S1/c
Soli, W. T., S2/c
Spradlin, L. R., S2/c
*Spradling, P. C., S2/c
St. Clair, W. J., CEM
Stacy, B. E., S2/c
Stamm, R. P., S2/c
Stark, L. A., S2/c
Stefani, S., F1/c
*Steinhilber, C. W., S2/c
Stokke, R. E., S1/c
*Stole, G. J., F1/c
Stolz, A., S2/c
Storey, C. E., SOM1/c
Strine, E. S., F1/c
Stucke, M., S1/c
Swedlund, H. D., S1/c
Sweeney, J. P., S1/c
*Symes, R. S., S1/c
Tedford, O. F., CPHM
Thibodeau, D. A., RM3/c
Thomas, V., F1/c

Thorp, T. J., QM2/c
Thostenson, A. P., S1/c
Throneberry, J. R., S1/c
Tippet, P. E., SC1/c
Titus, R. F., S1/c
Toye, W., SSML3/c
Trites, D. E., GM3/c
Trotter, "J", D., S1/c
*Turner, J. S., GM3/c
Vandenberg, G. F., MM1/c
Van Paris, F., S1/c
Veiga, A. E., S2/c
Vermie, M. F., RDM3/c
Voorhees, H. M., S1/c
Vornbrock, J. T., SOM2/c
Vowvalidis, L., S2/c
*Wagner, E. L., S2/c
Walsh, J. J., F1/c
Weed, M. F., S1/c
Wenta, J. V., RT2/c
West, W. H., F1/c
Weyrauch, H. F., MM3/c
Whelan, T. J., GM1/c
Whipple, H. D., S2/c
Widing, A. C., S2/c
Wike, C. A., F1/c
Willand, C. J., Cox.
Williams, A., S1/c
Williams, V. A., S1/c
Wilson, R. E., S1/c
Wilson, R. M., F1/c
Wimer, H. D., MN2/c
Windle, D. G., S1/c
Wingrove, A. C., S1/c
Winston, R. D., CQM
Wise, I., STM1/c
Wiseman, J. W., EM2/c
Withrow, K. L., SK2/c
Wittenberg, E. M., RDM3/c
Woodford, H. E., S1/c
Woods, D. E., RDM3/c

Woodward, L. O., S1/c
Wright, W. F., RDM3/c
Wrobleski, E., S2/c
Young, I., STM1/c

Zagone, A. J., SM3/c
*Zaloga, J. E., MN2/c
Zeug, L. J., S2/c
Zulick, M., S1/c

*KILLED IN ACTION